W9-BTQ-067

interactive
SCIENCE

The shape and position of its eyespots help protect the spicebush swallowtail caterpillar from predators.

SAVVAS
LEARNING COMPANY

Authors

You are an author!

You are one of the authors of this book. You can write in this book! You can take notes in this book! You can draw in it too! This book will be yours to keep.

Fill in the information below to tell about yourself. Then write your autobiography. An autobiography tells about you and the kinds of things you like to do.

My Photo

Name ....

School ....

Town, State ....

Autobiography ....

....

Copyright © 2016 by Savvas Learning Company LLC. All Rights Reserved. Printed in the United States of America.

This publication is protected by copyright, and permission should be obtained from the publisher prior to any prohibited reproduction, storage in a retrieval system, or transmission in any form or by any means, electronic, mechanical, photocopying, recording, or otherwise. For information regarding permissions, request forms, and the appropriate contacts within the Savvas Learning Company Rights Management group, please send your query to the address below.

Savvas Learning Company LLC, 15 East Midland Avenue, Paramus, NJ 07652

Attributions of third party content appear on pages EM20–EM22, which constitute an extension of this copyright page.

Savvas™ and **Savvas Learning Company™** are the exclusive trademarks of Savvas Learning Company LLC in the U.S. and other countries.

Savvas Learning Company publishes through its famous imprints **Prentice Hall®** and **Scott Foresman®** which are exclusive registered trademarks owned by Savvas Learning Company LLC in the U.S. and/or other countries.

Interactive Science™ and **Savvas Realize™** are exclusive trademarks of Savvas Learning Company LLC in the U.S. and/or other countries.

Planet Diary® is a trademark, in the U.S. and/or other countries, of Pearson Education, Inc., or its affiliates.

Certain materials herein are adapted from *Understanding by Design, 2nd Edition,* by Grant Wiggins & Jay McTighe © 2005 ASCD. Used with permission.

UNDERSTANDING BY DESIGN® and UbD® are registered trademarks of Backward Design, LLC and used under license.

Unless otherwise indicated herein, any third party trademarks that may appear in this work are the property of their respective owners, and any references to third party trademarks, logos, or other trade dress are for demonstrative or descriptive purposes only. Such references are not intended to imply any sponsorship, endorsement, authorization, or promotion of Savvas Learning Company products by the owners of such marks, or any relationship between the owner and Savvas Learning Company LLC or its authors, licensees, or distributors.

ON THE COVER
The shape and position of its eyespots help protect the spicebush swallowtail caterpillar from predators.

LEARNING COMPANY

ISBN-13: 978-0-328-87139-1
ISBN-10: 0-328-87139-7
18 2022

Program Authors

DON BUCKLEY, M.Sc.
Director of Technology & Innovation,
The School at Columbia University, New York, New York
Don Buckley has transformed learning spaces, textbooks, and media resources so that they work for students and teachers. He has advanced degrees from leading European universities, is a former industrial chemist, published photographer, and former consultant to MOMA's Education Department. He also teaches a graduate course at Columbia Teacher's College in Educational Technology and directs the Technology and Innovation program at the school. He is passionate about travel, architecture, design, change, the future, and innovation.

ZIPPORAH MILLER, M.A.Ed.
Coordinator for K-12 Science Programs, Anne Arundel County Public Schools.
Mrs. Zipporah Miller served as a reviewer during the development of Next Generation Science Standards and provides national training to teachers, administrators, higher education staff and informal science stakeholders on the Next Generation Science Standards. Prior to her appointment in Anne Arundel, Mrs. Miller served as the Associate Executive Director for Professional Development Programs and Conferences at the National Science Teachers Association (NSTA).

MICHAEL J. PADILLA, Ph.D.
Eugene P. Moore School of Education, Clemson University, Clemson, South Carolina
A former middle school teacher and a leader in middle school science education, Dr. Michael Padilla has served as president of the National Science Teachers Association and reviewed the Next Generation Science Standards. He is a former professor of science education at Clemson University. As lead author of the *Science Explorer* series, Dr. Padilla has inspired the team in developing a program that promotes student inquiry and meets the needs of today's students.

KATHRYN THORNTON, Ph.D.
Professor, Mechanical & Aerospace Engineering, University of Virginia, Charlottesville, Virginia
Selected by NASA in May 1984, Dr. Kathryn Thornton is a veteran of four space flights. She has logged more than 975 hours in space, including more than 21 hours of extravehicular activity. As an author on the *Scott Foresman Science* series, Dr. Thornton's enthusiasm for science has inspired teachers around the globe.

MICHAEL E. WYSESSION, Ph.D.
Associate Professor of Earth and Planetary Science, Washington University, St. Louis, Missouri
An author on more than 50 scientific publications, Dr. Wysession was awarded the prestigious Packard Foundation Fellowship and Presidential Faculty Fellowship for his research in geophysics. Dr. Wysession is an expert on Earth's inner structure and has mapped various regions of Earth using seismic tomography. He is known internationally for his work in geoscience education and research, and was an author of the Next Generation Science Standards.

Instructional Design Author

GRANT WIGGINS, Ed.D.
President, Authentic Education, Hopewell, New Jersey
Dr. Wiggins is a co-author with Jay McTighe of *Understanding by Design, 2nd Edition* (ASCD 2005). His approach to instructional design provides teachers with a disciplined way of thinking about curriculum design, assessment, and instruction that moves teaching from covering content to ensuring understanding.
UNDERSTANDING BY DESIGN® and UbD™ are trademarks of ASCD, and are used under license.

Activities Author

KAREN L. OSTLUND, Ph.D.
Past President, National Science Teachers Association, Arlington, Virginia
Dr. Ostlund has over 40 years of experience teaching at the elementary, middle school, and university levels. She was Director of WINGS Online (Welcoming Interns and Novices with Guidance and Support) and the Director of the UTeach/Dell Center for New Teacher Success with the UTeach program in the College of Natural Sciences at the University of Texas at Austin. She also served as Director of the Center for Science Education at the University of Texas at Arlington, as President of the Council of Elementary Science International, and as a member of the Board of Directors of the National Science Teachers Association. As an author of Scott Foresman Science, Dr. Ostlund was instrumental in developing inquiry activities.

ELL Consultant

JIM CUMMINS, Ph.D.
Professor and Canada Research Chair, Curriculum, Teaching and Learning Department at the University of Toronto
Dr. Cummins's research focuses on literacy development in multilingual schools and the role technology plays in learning across the curriculum. *Interactive Science* incorporates research-based principles for integrating language with the teaching of academic content based on Dr. Cummins's work.

Reviewers

Program Consultants

William Brozo, Ph.D.
Professor of Literacy, Graduate School of Education, George Mason University, Fairfax, Virginia.
Dr. Brozo is the author of numerous articles and books on literacy development. He co-authors a column in The Reading Teacher and serves on the editorial review board of the Journal of Adolescent & Adult Literacy.

Kristi Zenchak, M.S.
Biology Instructor, Oakton Community College, Des Plaines, Illinois
Kristi Zenchak helps elementary teachers incorporate science, technology, engineering, and math activities into the classroom. STEM activities that produce viable solutions to real-world problems not only motivate students but also prepare students for future STEM careers. Ms. Zenchak helps elementary teachers understand the basic science concepts, and provides STEM activities that are easy to implement in the classroom.

Content Reviewers

Brad Armosky, M.S.
Texas Advanced Computing Center
University of Texas at Austin
Austin, Texas

Alexander Brands, Ph.D.
Department of Biological Sciences
Lehigh University
Bethlehem, Pennsylvania

Paul Beale, Ph.D.
Department of Physics
University of Colorado
Boulder, Colorado

Joy Branlund, Ph.D.
Department of Earth Science
Southwestern Illinois College
Granite City, Illinois

Constance Brown, Ph.D
Atmospheric Science Program
Geography Department
Indiana University
Bloomington, Indiana

Dana Dudle, Ph.D.
Biology Department
DePauw University
Greencastle, Indiana

Rick Duhrkopf, Ph. D.
Department of Biology
Baylor University
Waco, Texas

Mark Henriksen, Ph.D.
Physics Department
University of Maryland
Baltimore, Maryland

Andrew Hirsch, Ph.D.
Department of Physics
Purdue University
W. Lafayette, Indiana

Linda L. Cronin Jones, Ph.D.
School of Teaching & Learning
University of Florida
Gainesville, Florida

T. Griffith Jones, Ph.D.
College of Education
University of Florida
Gainesville, Florida

Candace Lutzow-Felling, Ph.D.
Director of Education
State Arboretum of Virginia & Blandy Experimental Farm
Boyce, Virginia

Cortney V. Martin, Ph.D.
Virginia Polytechnic Institute
Blacksburg, Virginia

Sadredin Moosavi, Ph.D.
University of Massachusetts Dartmouth
Fairhaven, Massachusetts

Klaus Newmann, Ph.D.
Department of Geological Sciences
Ball State University
Muncie, Indiana

Scott M. Rochette, Ph.D.
Department of the Earth Sciences
SUNY College at Brockport
Brockport, New York

Ursula Rosauer Smedly, M.S.
Alcade Science Center
New Mexico State University
Alcade, New Mexico

Frederick W. Taylor, Ph.D.
Jackson School of Geosciences
University of Texas at Austin
Austin, Texas

K-8 National Master Teacher Board

Karyn Rogers, Ph.D.
Department of Geological
Sciences
University of Missouri
Columbia, Missouri

Laurence Rosenhein, Ph.D.
Dept. of Chemistry and Physics
Indiana State University
Terre Haute, Indiana

Sara Seager, Ph.D.
Department of Planetary Science
and Physics
Massachusetts Institute of
Technology
Cambridge, Massachusetts

William H. Steinecker. Ph.D.
Research Scholar
Miami University
Oxford, Ohio

Paul R. Stoddard, Ph.D.
Department of Geology and
Environmental Geosciences
Northern Illinois University
DeKalb, Illinois

Janet Vaglia, Ph. D.
Department of Biology
DePauw University
Greencastle, Indiana

Ed Zalisko, Ph.D.
Professor of Biology
Blackburn College
Carlinville, Illinois

Tricia Burke
E. F. Young Elementary School
Chicago, IL

Lisa Catandella
Brentwood UFSD
Brentwood, NY

Karen Clements
Lynch Elementary School
Winchester, MA

Emily Compton
Park Forest Middle School
Baton Rouge, LA

Pansy Cowder
Lincoln Magnet School
Plant City, FL

Georgi Delgadillo
East Valley School District
Spokane, WA

Dr. Richard Fairman
McGregor School of Education
Antioch University Midwest
Yellow Springs, OH

Joe Fescatore
Green Elementary School
La Mesa, CA

Mimi Halferty
Gorzycki Middle School
Austin, TX

Christy Herring
Prairie Trace Elementary School
Carmel, IN

Treva Jeffries
Toledo Public Schools
Toledo, OH

James Kuhl
Central Square Middle School
Central Square, NY

Dr. Patsy Latin
Caddo Public School District
Shreveport, LA

Greg Londot
Hidden Hills Elementary School
Phoenix, AZ

Stan Melby
Sheridan Road Elementary
Fort Sill, OK

Bonnie Mizell
Howard Middle School
Orlando, FL

Dr. Joel Palmer
Mesquite ISD
Mesquite, TX

Leslie Pohley
Largo Middle School
Largo, FL

Susan Pritchard
Washington Middle School
La Habra, CA

Anne Rice
Woodland Middle School
Gurnee, IL

Adrienne Sawyer
Chesapeake Public Schools
Chesapeake, VA

Richard Towle
Noblesville Middle School
Noblesville, IN

Dr. Madhu Uppal
Schaumburg School District
Schaumburg, IL

Maria Valdez
Mark Twain Elementary School
Wheeling, IL

Viv Wayne
Montgomery County Public Schools
Rockville, MD

Forces and Motion

The speed of a roller coaster changes as it moves.

SavvasRealize.com

Go online for engaging videos, interactivities, and virtual labs.

Chapter 2

Energy and Its Forms

The siren on this fire truck produces sound energy by causing matter to vibrate.

SavvasRealize.com

Go online for engaging videos, interactivities, and virtual labs.

Plants

*Plants need food, air, water,
and space to live and grow.*

SavvasRealize.com

**Go online for engaging
videos, interactivities,
and virtual labs.**

Chapter 4

Living Things

A young antelope inherits characteristics from its parent.

SavvasRealize.com

Go online for engaging videos, interactivities, and virtual labs.

Ecosystems

Box turtles interact with other living and nonliving things in their ecosystems.

SavvasRealize.com

Go online for engaging videos, interactivities, and virtual labs.

Weather Patterns

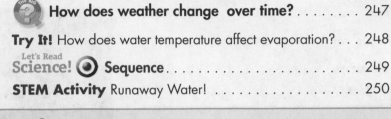

New Orleans, Louisiana, is
the third wettest city in the
United States.

SavvasRealize.com

**Go online for engaging
videos, interactivities,
and virtual labs.**

The Nature of Science

This scientist is recording her observations.

SavvasRealize.com

Go online for engaging videos, interactivities, and virtual labs.

Table of Contents

Technology and the Design Process

Engineers can look inside this digital audio player to learn about its design.

SavvasRealize.com

Go online for engaging videos, interactivities, and virtual labs.

"This is your book. You can write in it!"

interactive SCIENCE

Big Question

At the start of each chapter you will see two questions—
an **Engaging Question** and a **Big Question.**
Just like a scientist, you will predict an answer to the
Engaging Question. Each Big Question will help you
start thinking about the Big Ideas of science. Look for the
symbol throughout the chapter!

Why do kangaroos carry their young?

Living Things

Try It! How can shells be classified?

STEM Activity Bird Feather Cleaning

Lesson 1 How can you classify animals?

Lesson 2 How are offspring like their parents?

Lesson 3 What are the life cycles of some animals?

Investigate It! What do leaves have in common?

Chapter **4**

When a kangaroo is born, it is blind and has no
fur. It is about the size of a peanut. It climbs into
its mother's pouch to finish developing. The young
kangaroo stays there for months to eat, sleep,
and grow.

Predict What might happen if a baby kangaroo
left its mother's pouch too soon?

_____

How do living things grow and change?

Let's Read Science!

You will see a page like this toward the beginning of each chapter. It will show you how to use a reading skill that will help you understand what you read.

Let's Read Science!

Sequence
- **Sequence** is the order in which events take place.
- Clue words such as *first, next, then,* and *finally* can help you figure out the sequence of events.

Classify Animals

Scientists can classify animals according to their behaviors, such as how they act, and their physical characteristics, such as hair. Scientists may classify a slug such as the one below. Scientists may first identify whether or not the slug has a backbone. Next, they can find out what the slug eats. Finally, scientists can compare and contrast the slug to other animals.

Practice It!

Complete the graphic organizer to show the sequence of classifying animals.

First

Next

Finally

sea slug

PearsonRealize.com   155

Vocabulary Smart Cards

water cycle
precipitation
weather
climate
atmosphere
severe weather

climate — clima

water cycle — ciclo del agua

Play a Game!

Cut out the Vocabulary Smart Cards.

Work with a partner. Choose a Vocabulary Smart Card.

Say as many words as you can think of to describe the vocabulary word.

Have your partner guess the word.

Have your partner repeat with another Vocabulary Smart Card.

atmosphere — atmósfera

precipitation — precipitación

severe weather — tiempo severo

weather — tiempo atmosférico

279

Vocabulary Smart Cards

Go to the end of the chapter and cut out your own set of **Vocabulary Smart Cards.** Draw a picture to learn the word. Play a game with a classmate to practice using the word!

SavvasRealize.com

Go to **SavvasRealize.com** for a variety of digital activities.

"Engage with the page!"

interactive SCIENCE

Envision It!

At the beginning of each lesson, at the top of the page, you will see an **Envision It!** interactivity that gives you the opportunity to circle, draw, write, or respond to the Envision It! question.

Lesson 2

How are offspring like their parents?

Envision It!

Circle the two pictures that show behaviors an animal must learn.

Draw an X on the pictures that show behaviors an animal is born knowing how to do.

I will know that some characteristics and behaviors are inherited and some are learned or acquired.

Words to Know

inherit
instinct

MY PLANET DIARY DISCOVERY

Karl von Frisch

A honey bee scout flies out of the hive to look for food. It finds flowers full of sweet nectar. How can the scout communicate to the other bees where the food is? Beginning in the 1920s, Karl von Frisch studied bee behavior. He discovered that the scout bee performs a dance. The dance tells other bees where to find the food. The bees in the hive are born knowing what the dance means.

What do you think the bees will do after they see the scout's dance?

168

Both Alike and Different

Why do kittens look like cats and not like dogs? Why does a corn seed grow into a corn plant and not a tomato plant? Most young plants and animals grow to look like their parents. Some plants and animals look like their parents even when they are very young.

The young antelope in the picture shares many characteristics with its parent. For example, the young antelope has the same body shape as its parent. Its fur is about the same length too.

The young antelope is also different in some ways. For example, its horns are much smaller than its parent's horns. The young antelope's horns will grow larger as it gets older. But even then, its horns may not have the exact shape or size of its parent's horns.

1. **Compare and Contrast** Describe other ways in which the young antelope and its parent are alike and different.

PearsonRealize.com   169

MY PLANET DIARY

My Planet Diary will introduce you to amazing scientists, fun facts, and important discoveries in science. They will also help you to overcome common misconceptions about science concepts.

Read See DO!

After reading small chunks of information, stop to check your understanding. The visuals help teach about what you read. Answer questions, underline text, draw pictures, or label models.

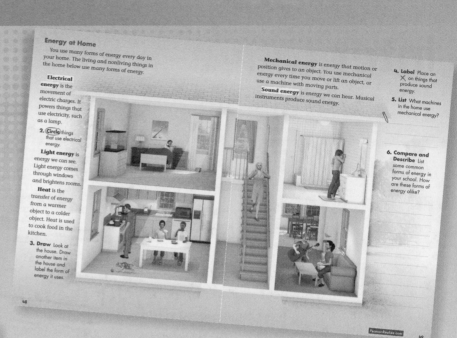

Do the math!

Scientists commonly use math as a tool to help them answer science questions. You can practice skills that you are learning in math class right in your *Interactive Science* Student Edition!

Got it?

At the end of each lesson you will have a chance to evaluate your own progress! At this point you can stop or go on to the next lesson.

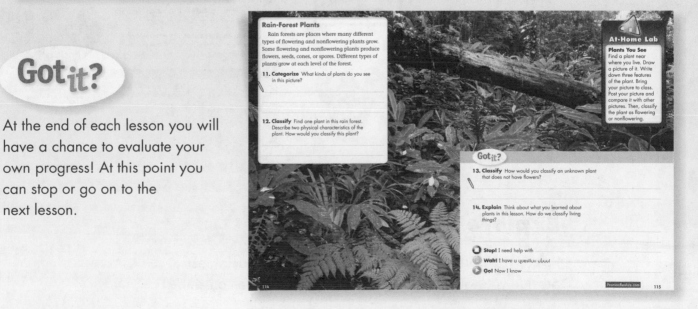

"Have fun! Be a scientist!"

interactive SCIENCE

Try It!

At the start of every chapter, you will have the chance to do a hands-on inquiry activity. The activity will provide you with experiences that will prepare you for the chapter lessons or may raise a new question in your mind.

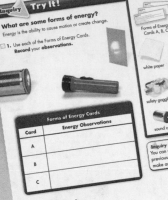

Inquiry Try It!

What are some forms of energy?
Energy is the ability to cause motion or create change.

☐ 1. Use each of the Forms of Energy Cards.
Record your **observations.**

Materials
Forms of Energy Cards A, B, C
wind-up toy
white paper
flashlight
safety goggles
color change ring
sound can

Forms of Energy Cards	
Card	**Energy Observations**
A	
B	
C	

Inquiry Skill
You can use observations and previous experience to help make an **inference.**

Explain Your Results
2. Infer Use your **observations** to tell how energy caused the changes you observed.

Station A _____
Station B _____
Station C _____

2

Lesson 2

How do plants use leaves to make food?

Envision It!

Tell how you think leaves help plants.

UNLOCK
I will know that leaves help plants live, grow, and make food.

Words to Know
photosynthesis
carbon dioxide
oxygen

Inquiry Explore It!

How does sunlight affect plant survival?

☐ 1. **Observe** a green leaf on a plant. Gently fold a piece of foil completely around the whole leaf. Be sure the foil cannot fall off.

☐ 2. Place the plant near a sunny window. Wait one week.

☐ 3. Take off the foil. Observe. Compare what you observed before and after the leaf was covered.

Materials

plant

foil

Be careful! Wash your hands when finished.

Explain Your Results
4. **Infer** What do you think happened to the leaf? Explain.

What Plants Need

Plants need food, air, water, and space to live and grow. Many plants live and grow in soil. The four main parts of a flowering plant are leaves, roots, stems, and flowers. In different kinds of plants, these parts may look alike. They may also look different.

Unlike animals, plants make their own food. Plants need energy from the sun to make food. Food is made in a plant's leaves, using the sun's energy. This food helps plants grow.

1. **Text Features** Look at the text features on this page. Identify one text feature and the clue it gives you.

Text feature	Clue
Heading	It tells me that I'll read about what plants need.

Bromeliad plants are like other plants. They use energy from the sun to make food.

116

117 PearsonRealize.com

Explore It!

Before you start reading the lesson, **Explore It!** activities provide you with an opportunity to first explore the content!

Design It!

The **Design It!** activity has you use the engineering design process to find solutions to problems. By finding a problem and then planning, drawing, and choosing materials, you will make, test, and evaluate a solution for a real world problem. Communicate your evidence through drawings and prototypes and identify ways to make your solution better.

Inquiry | Design It!

What parachute design works best?

A group of people on a small island need supplies dropped off. You cannot land a plane on the island. The supplies are fragile and must be dropped slowly so they do not break when they land. The area the supplies must be dropped off at is very small. You need to design a parachute to drop the supplies for the people that need them.

Identify the problem.

☐ 1. Identify the problems you need to solve with your **design**.

Possible Materials

chenille sticks · timer or stopwatch · meterstick · string · cups · rubber ball · rubber bands · masking tape · paper · plastic bag · aluminum foil · cloth (white) · wax paper

Do research.

☐ 2. Think about the problems you have identified. Research **design** solutions others have used. Brainstorm ideas with others. List three solutions others have used.

Investigate It!

At the end of every chapter, a Directed Inquiry activity gives you a chance to put together everything you've learned in the chapter. Using the activity card, apply design principles in the Guided version to Modify Your Investigation or the Open version to Develop Your Own Investigation. Whether you need a lot of support from your teacher or you're ready to explore on your own, there are fun hands-on activities that match your interests.

Inquiry | Investigate It!

How can you describe motion?

Materials: books, meterstick, ball, chutes, timer

Follow a Procedure

☐ 1. **Measure** 2 meters from a wall and place one end of the chute there.

☐ 2. Place 2 books under the other end of the chute.

☐ 3. Release the ball at the top of the chute. Start timing when the ball reaches the floor.

☐ 4. **Record** the time when the ball hits the wall.

☐ 5. Stop the timer when the ball comes back to the bottom of the chute. Record.

Ball Movement Results

Number of Books	From Bottom of Chute to Wall (Time A)	From Bottom of Chute to Wall and Back (Time B)	From Wall to Bottom of Chute (Time C = Time B – Time A)
2 books			
4 books			

Time (seconds)

☐ 6. Stack 4 books and repeat steps 2 to 5.

Analyze and Conclude

7. **Interpret Data** When did the ball move faster?

Inquiry Skill
Scientists **measure** carefully and record their measurements.

Guided Inquiry

Modify Your Investigation

Investigate the Question

How might a steeper chute affect the travel times of a ball?

The chute will be steeper if you stack more than 4 books. Decide how many books you will stack. Decide how to record the data you collect.

Predict what effect a steeper chute will have on the travel times of a ball.

Record your measurements.

Analyze and Conclude

Compare your prediction with your measurements. How did a steeper chute affect the travel times of a ball?

Share your results with others. Discuss any differences.

Open Inquiry

Design Your Own Investigation

Ask Your Own Question

Think of a question you could ask about the movement of an object.

Sample question Would a heavier ball travel as far as a lighter ball?

Use library and internet resources to investigate your idea before you begin.

Investigate Your Question

List what you will need. Write a plan with steps. You may wish to make a chart. Show your teacher your plan before you begin.

Analyze and Conclude

Tell what you learned. Draw a conclusion.

Compare your methods and results with others. How could you improve your plan?

Apply It!

These Open Inquiry activities give you a chance to plan and carry out investigations.

Inquiry | Apply It! Using Scientific Methods

How is motion affected by mass?

A force can cause an object to move. You will conduct an **experiment** to find out how the mass of an object affects the distance the object will move.

Materials: 2 metric rulers, 1/2 of a plastic cup and metal marble, 2 books, tape and 4 pennies, balance and gram cubes, calculator or computer (optional)

Ask a question.

What effect does the mass of a cup have on the distance a rolling marble will move the cup?

State a hypothesis.

1. Write a **hypothesis** by circling one choice and finishing the sentence.

If the mass of a cup is increased, then the distance the cup is moved by a rolling marble

(a) increases
(b) decreases
(c) remains the same

because

Inquiry Skill
A **hypothesis** is a statement that explains an observation. It can be tested by an experiment.

Identify and control variables.

2. In this experiment you will measure the distance the cup moves. You must change only one **variable**. Everything else must remain the same. What should stay the same? List two examples.

3. Tell the one change you will make.

Design your test.

☐ 4. Draw how you will set up your test.

☐ 5. List your steps in the order you will do them.

What is Savvas Realize?

Interactive Science is now part of Savvas' brand-new learning management system, Realize! With rich and engaging content, embedded assessment with instant data, and flexible classroom management tools, Realize gives you the power to raise interest and achievement for every student in your classroom.

Engaging Videos

Engage with science topics through videos! Start each chapter with an Untamed Science video.

Savvas Flipped Videos for Science give you another way to learn.

Interactivities and Virtual Labs

Practice science content with engaging online activities.

At **SavvasRealize.com** go online and conduct labs virtually! No goggles and no mess.

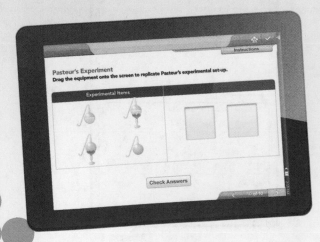

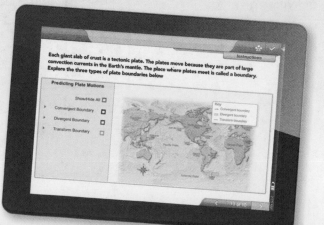

Connect to What You Know

Check what you know at the end of each lesson and chapter.

Get More Practice on skills and content, based on your performance.

Predict your exam readiness with benchmark assessments.

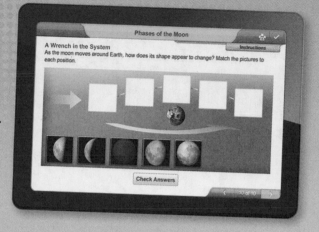

Savvas Realize offers powerful classroom management functionality, including:

Standards-aligned content — search by standard

Powerful Search tools — search by keyword, topic or standards

Customizable curriculum — reorder the table of contents, uploadfiles and media, add links and create custom lessons and assessments

Flexible class management tools — create classes, organize students, and create assignments targeted to students, groups of students, or the entire class.

Tracks student progress — instantly access student and class data that shows standards mastery on assessments, online activity and overall progress.

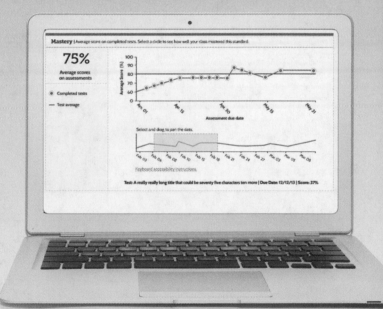

Track Your Learning Online.

SavvasRealize.com

STEM Quest

Where Have All the Organisms Gone?

Your Quest is to make solutions as an environmental engineer. New buildings are being built in a town. A pond will dry up. Tell your community about what to expect. Analyze possible solutions to the change.

Quest Kick-Off
Where have all the organisms gone?
Watch a video to learn about ecosystems. Learn about what you will do as an environmental change expert.

Quest Check-In 1
Food Chains
Watch an animation of a food chain. Make a model and label a food chain.

Quest Check-In 2
Characteristics of Organisms in Different Habitats
In this hands-on lab, you will observe the characteristics of living things. Look at living things on your school grounds.

Quest Check-In 3
Animal Groups
Learn about the benefits of living in a group. Research an animal that lives alone.

Quest Check-In 4
Environmental Changes
Watch a video on environmental change. Research the effects of natural and man-made changes to the environment.

Quest Findings
Reacting to Environmental Change
You will present a report about the pond that will dry up. Evaluate possible solutions.

SavvasRealize.com
Go online for all Quest digital interactivities and hands-on labs

Is the world in motion or are you?

Forces and Motion

The boy pedals hard down the path. The world around him becomes a blur. The trees seem to fly by.

Predict How do you know that it is the biker who is moving, and not the trees?

....

....

....

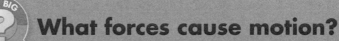

THE BIG ? What forces cause motion?

What can magnetic force move?

Magnetic force can make objects move.

☐ **1.** Place the objects in the circle.

☐ **2.** Bring the magnet close to the edges of the circle. **Observe** which objects move.

☐ **3. Record** List the objects that the magnet moved.

☐ **4.** List the objects that the magnet did not move outside the circle.

Materials

magnet

rubber band   metal marble

penny   paper clip   plastic paper clip

Inquiry Skill
You use what you observe to **infer.**

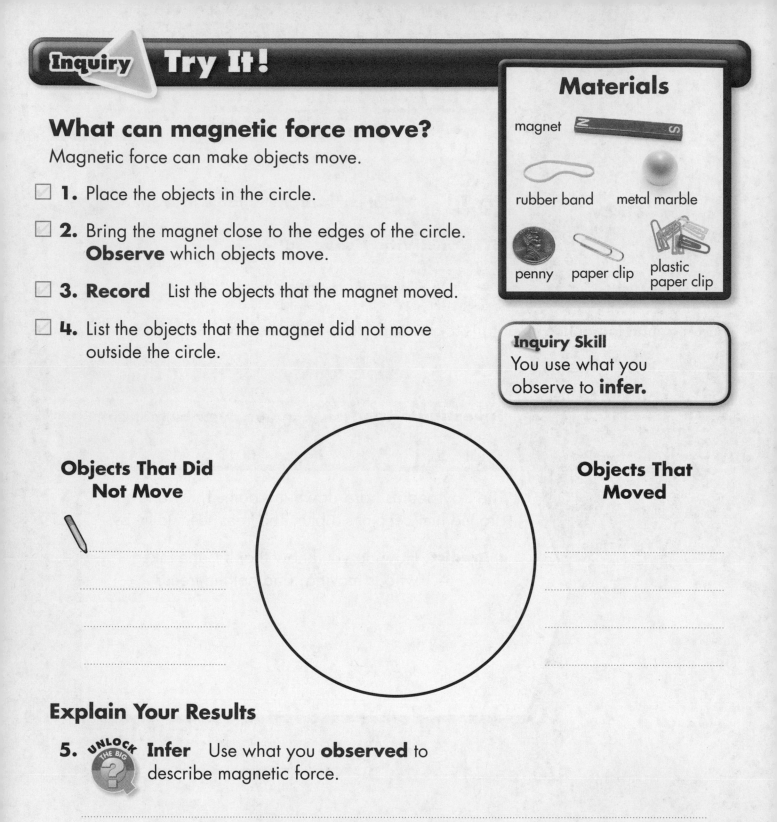

Objects That Did Not Move

....

....

....

....

Objects That Moved

....

....

....

Explain Your Results

5. **Infer** Use what you **observed** to describe magnetic force.

....

....

....

⊙ Draw Conclusions

- Learning to **draw conclusions** can help you evaluate what you read and observe.
- The conclusions that you draw should make sense and be supported by facts.

Walking Home

Jamal and Eric both walk home from school. They decide to do an experiment to see who gets home the quickest. They both leave school at the same time. Jamal walks faster than Eric. Eric lives farther away from school than Jamal. Jamal has fewer hills to climb.

Apply It!

Use the graphic organizer. List facts from the paragraph and draw a conclusion.

Fact

Fact

Fact

Conclusion

Heave Ho!

A pulley is a simple machine that uses a grooved wheel on an axle with a rope that runs over the wheel to move objects. Pulleys are used on cranes to lift heavy loads. They are also used to open and close blinds and to raise and lower flags and sails.

If you have pulled on a rope to raise a flag, you have used a single pulley. The pulley is not attached to the object being moved, in this case a flag. Instead, the pulley changes the direction of force being applied to the object. You pull down on the rope, and the flag goes up. Some pulleys are attached to the object to be moved. Attached, moveable pulleys multiply the amount of force applied to the object. Both kinds of pulleys can be combined to form a system of pulleys that will change the direction of force as well as reduce the amount of force needed.

You work for a local moving company and need an easier way to move things up and down stairs, so you design and build a pulley lifter with one or two wheels to help you.

Identify the Problem

☑ **1.** What problem will your pulley lifter help solve? In your response, include whether you want to change the direction of a force, increase the amount of

force, or both. _____

_____

_____

Do Research

Examine several pictures of pulley lifters.

☑ **2.** What functions do these pulley lifters provide?

_____

_____

☐ **3. Examine** the pictures again. What do you notice between a pulley lifter using one wheel and one using multiple wheels?

_____

_____

☐ **4.** What do you notice about the size of the pulley wheels?

_____

_____

Go to the materials station(s). Look at each material. Think about how it may or may not be useful for building your pulley lifter. Leave the materials where they are.

☐ **5.** What are your design constraints?

_____

_____

Develop Possible Solutions

☐ **6. Describe** two ways you could combine some of the materials to build a pulley lifter.

_____

_____

Choose One Solution

☐ **7.** Will your pulley lifter have one wheel or two? _____

☐ **8.** Why did you choose to build a pulley with this many wheels? _____

_____

_____

☑ **9. Draw** your design and describe your pulley and how you will build it.

_____

_____

☑ **10. List** the materials you will need. _____

_____

_____

Design and Construct a Prototype

Gather your materials plus a ruler, a wooden dowel (or broomstick), and the number of books you want your pulley to lift. Remember to get enough string to tie around the book like a package. **Build** your prototype.

☑ **11. Record** the design details of your prototype. Include the diameter (cm) of the wheel(s) on your pulley and the length (cm) of the string you will use. Also, use a spring scale to weigh the books you want to lift. **Record** their weight in grams (g).

_____

_____

Test the Prototype

Test your design. Set up your pulley lifter on the wooden dowel (or broomstick) between two chairs (or desks). Tie one end of the string around the book like a package. Run the loose end of the string around the wheel(s) of your pulley.

☐ **12.** What happens when you pull on the loose end? _____

_____

Communicate Results

Re-measure with a spring scale.

☐ **13.** Did your pulley lifter work like you expected? Explain. _____

_____

_____

☐ **14. Compare your data** with a classmate that made a pulley lifter with a different number of wheels. How do your results compare?

_____

_____

Evaluate and Redesign

☐ **15.** What changes could you make to your design to make it work better?

_____

_____

☐ **16. Record** the new design details, then make your changes.

_____

_____

☐ **17.** How well did your revised prototype work? Explain. _____

_____

_____

Lesson 1

What is motion?

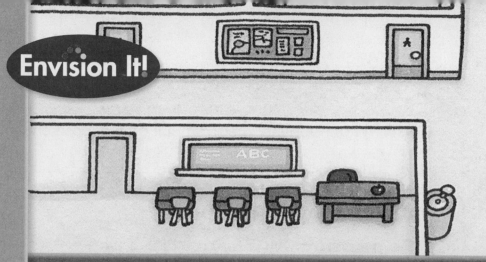

Draw a path from the classroom to the cafeteria.
Tell how to walk the path.

MY PLANET DIARY   VOICES FROM History

Isaac Newton (1642–1727)

When you learn how forces affect motion, you have Isaac Newton to thank. Even in his own day, Newton was considered one of history's greatest scientists. He had a deep curiosity about the natural world. He looked for clear and logical ways to explain everything he noticed. He put together ideas from all different areas of science in very creative ways. Among the results were his famous laws of motion. These laws, including his definition of force, caused people to think about science in a new way. Newton once said, "If I have ever made any valuable discoveries, it has been owing more to patient attention than to any other talent."

Isaac Newton stated the scientific laws of motion in his book Principia Mathematica.

How do you think patient attention could help you make scientific discoveries?

Patent attention help to stay foused the science discovering

According to Newton's third law of motion, these balls exert a force on each other when they collide.

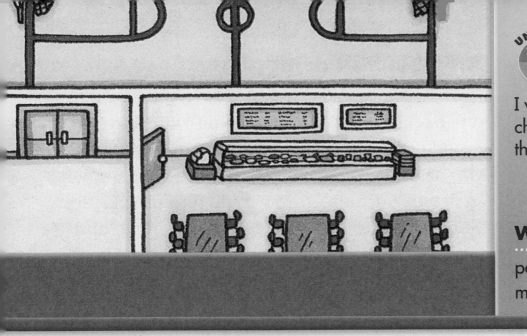

Words to Know

position   speed
motion

When Objects Move

Look at the picture of the students playing. How would you describe the position of the girl? **Position** is an object's location, or where something is. You might say the girl's position is on the ladder or beside the slide.

Now look at the boy sliding down the slide. The boy is in motion. **Motion** is a change in the position of an object. Motion describes the boy's movement from the top of the slide toward the bottom.

1. **Describe** Observe a classmate walking from one side of the room to the other. Describe the classmate's new position.

_____ in new
position when
_____ the door

2. ◎ **Draw Conclusions** After reading the paragraphs, what can you conclude about the boy's position?

_____ the boy
_____ the picture side

At-Home Lab

Observe and Describe Motion

On a sunny day, find an object with a shadow. Use pictures and position words to describe the shadow at three different times during the day. Then write a sentence that analyzes the change in the shadow's position over time.

4. [CHALLENGE] Sometimes a car near your car will move with the same speed and in the same direction as your car. What happens to your position compared to that car?

An Object's Position

The position of an object often depends on how a person looks at it. Suppose you wanted to tell a friend about the boat in the picture. How would you describe its position? You could use numbers to describe distances. You could also use position words, such as *in front of, behind, left, right,* and *beside.* The words you use might change if you were riding in the boat.

You could also draw a map. A map models the position of objects in relation to each other.

3. Illustrate Draw a map to show the position of the boat and cars in the picture after a few seconds.

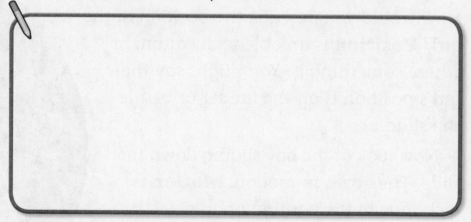

Positions of Moving Objects

Objects on a map are fixed in place. How do you describe the position of moving objects? The cars and the boat in the picture are in motion. The way you describe their position may change depending on the position and motion of other objects.

5. Analyze How would the position of the boat seem to change as the white car moves along the road?

6. Describe If you were riding in the white car, the red car would appear to move toward you. How would you describe the position of the red car once you passed it?

the car is in front

7. Analyze Write a caption that tells about the yellow car's position.

the yellow car is in front is on left side of blakcar

You could say that the position of the boat is to the right of the bridge. You could also use distance to tell about position. The boat is 20 meters from the right side of the bridge.

How Fast Objects Move

How can you describe how fast objects move? You can tell their speed. **Speed** is the rate at which, or how fast, an object changes its position. A jet plane's speed is about 900 kilometers per hour. Your speed on a bike might be about 15 kilometers per hour. The jet plane changes position faster than your bike, so its speed is greater.

Constant Speed

If the motion of an object has a regular pattern, you may be able to predict future motion. Sometimes moving objects move at a constant speed. A plane that flies steadily at 900 kilometers per hour is moving at a constant speed. The plane does not change how fast it moves. If the plane does not change its speed, then the future motion of the plane can be predicted. You can predict the speed of the plane.

8. ◉ **Main Idea and Details Underline** the main idea of the first paragraph.

Do the math!

Find an Object's Speed

You can find the speed of an object if you know the distance it moved and how much time it took to move that distance. To find speed, divide distance by time.

distance ÷ time = speed

The table shows distances and times for three runners. Distances are in meters (m) and times are in seconds (s).

Runner	Distance	Time
Sheela	100 m	25 s
Jack	40 m	8 s
Kara	200 m	50 s

1 Write number sentences to show each runner's speed in meters per second $\left(\frac{m}{s}\right)$.

A. Sheela's speed

.... m ÷ .... s = ... $\frac{m}{s}$

B. Jack's speed

.... m ÷ .... s = ... $\frac{m}{s}$

C. Kara's speed

.... m ÷ .... s = ... $\frac{m}{s}$

2 Who ran fastest?

....

Variable Speed

The fun of a roller coaster comes from slowly climbing up and quickly moving down the track. The roller coaster moves at a variable speed. It changes speed as it moves. When a roller coaster moves along its track, its riders can predict when it will go faster and slower. They can predict this by looking at the track and deciding if the roller coaster will climb up or move down the track.

9. **Exemplify** Give two examples of objects that move at a variable speed.

racecar
runing don
hills bus

10. **Exemplify** Describe three examples of motion you might see on a playground.

11. **Analyze** How does the motion and position of each roller skate change as a person skates down a sidewalk?

⏹ **Stop!** I need help with

⏸ **Wait!** I have a question about

▶ **Go!** Now I know

How does force affect motion?

Envision It!

Tell which way you predict the leash will move.

Explore It!

How does mass affect motion?

☐ **1.** Compare the mass of the two balls.

☐ **2.** Place the table tennis ball at the bottom of the ramp. Roll the rubber ball down the ramp. **Record** the distance the table tennis ball rolls.

....

3. Predict What will happen if the balls switch places?

....

....

....

☐ **4.** Test your prediction.

Explain Your Results

5. Draw a Conclusion How did mass affect motion?

....

....

....

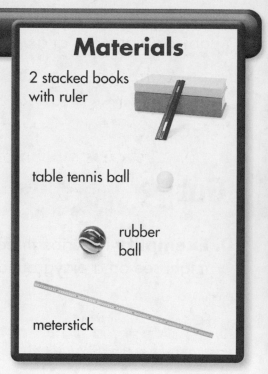

Materials

2 stacked books with ruler

table tennis ball

rubber ball

meterstick

Words to Know

force   magnetism
friction

Causes of Motion

Crack! A baseball player hits the ball. The bat pushes against the ball. The bat has all the power of the player's swing. A force causes the motion, speed, and direction of the ball to change. A **force** is a push or a pull.

Most of the forces you use are contact forces. When you hit a baseball with a bat, the bat's force changes the speed and direction of the ball. If the bat does not make contact with the ball, these changes cannot occur.

A bat needs contact to apply force.

1. ◉ **Draw Conclusions** Complete the graphic organizer. List facts that support the conclusion.

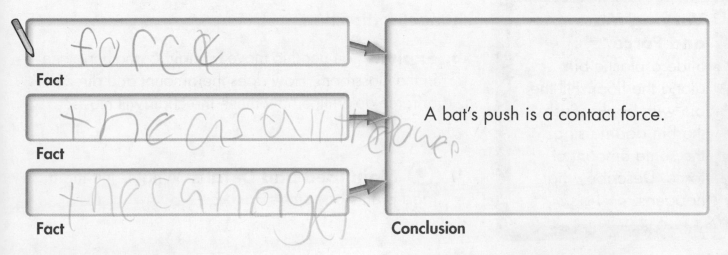

Fact	*force*
Fact	*the ball the power*
Fact	*the change*

Conclusion: A bat's push is a contact force.

2. Classify (Circle) the picture where the girl is pushing more mass. Put an ✗ on the picture where she must use more force to change the motion.

Effects of Mass and Friction

A force can change an object's position or the direction of its motion. A push by the girl can cause the shopping cart to start moving. If she then pushes to the right, the moving cart will change direction to the right.

How much an object changes its direction and speed depends on how much force is used. A large force will cause a greater change in motion than a smaller force. The cart will go faster if the girl pushes harder.

How an object moves also depends on its mass. When the girl starts shopping, her cart is empty. She does not need much force to push it. As the girl shops, she stops and puts objects in the cart. Each time she does, the cart's mass gets larger. The girl must then use more force to push the cart or change its direction.

3. Explain You need to move a chair to another place in the classroom. How does the amount and direction of force determine how much the chair will move?

4. ◎ **Main Idea and Details** What is the main idea of this page?

Lightning Lab

Varying Mass and Force
Slide a plastic bin along the floor. Fill the bin with books. Push the bin again using the same amount of force. Describe what happens.

While the girl's grocery cart moves down the aisle, its wheels rub against the floor. This causes friction. **Friction** is a contact force that opposes the motion of an object. Friction can cause a moving object to slow down or to stop.

The amount of friction between two objects depends on their surfaces. Pushing a grocery cart over smooth tiles in a store is pretty easy. You need more force to push a cart across the asphalt parking lot. The smooth tile produces less friction on the wheels than the asphalt does.

5. List Write two places in the picture where friction is acting.

6. [CHALLENGE] Why do bowling alley owners keep the surface of the lanes smooth and polished?

Motion and Combined Forces

As a kite flies through the air, it dips and it dives. What forces act on the kite? The force of the wind pushes it up. Weight is one of the forces pulling it down. The boy also pulls down on the string. Each push or pull has its own amount of force. Each force also acts in its own direction. An object's motion depends on all the forces that act together. The amount of force can be called the strength of the force.

Balanced Forces

Sometimes a kite hangs in the air. It is almost motionless. This is because the forces acting on the kite balance each other. Forces that work together and make no change in motion are called balanced forces.

You can see balanced forces all around you. Think of two strong football players pushing against each other. If they each push with the same force but in opposite directions, neither player moves.

7. **Illustrate** Draw and label arrows on the picture to show the forces acting on the kite.

8. **Explain** Each player is applying force. The two players do not move. What is happening?

....

....

....

9. **Illustrate** Draw arrows to show the balanced forces.

Unbalanced Forces

If the forces acting on an object are not balanced, the motion of the object will change. Unbalanced forces can cause an object at rest to move. They can also change the speed or direction of a moving object.

You might compare the forces acting on an object to a game of tug-of-war. In tug-of-war, two teams pull a rope in opposite directions. If the forces are equal, the rope does not move. To win, one team must pull with greater force than the other team. One team must unbalance the forces acting on the rope. The rope will then move in the direction of the greater pull.

10. Apply Complete the sentence.

.......Forces....... forces cause the rope in tug-of-war to move in a certain direction.

11. Infer Look at the picture below. Which way do you think the rope is moving? Why?

....

....

....

....

....

More force

Less force

Magnetism

A noncontact force can push or pull an object without touching it. **Magnetism** is a noncontact force that pulls on, or attracts, metal objects containing iron. Steel is a metal that has iron in it. Magnets do not attract wood, plastic, paper, or other objects that do not contain iron.

If you place some steel paper clips near a magnet, the magnet will pull the paper clips toward it until they come in contact with the magnet. A very strong magnet might pull a steel paper clip from a distance that is halfway across your desk. A very weak magnet might not pull the paper clip unless the paper clip was a much smaller distance away from the magnet.

This crane is using a large magnet to pick up objects.

12. Infer Look at the picture. How do you know that the objects being lifted are made of metal containing iron?

....

....

....

Magnets work because they have a magnetic field around them. The field is strongest near the magnet's poles. Each magnet has a north pole and a south pole. The north pole of one magnet will attract the south pole of another magnet. The north pole and south pole have opposite orientation. When two north poles or two south poles are near each other, they have the same orientation. Poles that have the same orientation will push away from each other.

The magnetic field's force pulls the paper clips toward the magnet.

13. Infer Why is magnetism a noncontact force?

....

....

....

Got it?

14. Explain What happens if you hit a baseball hard? softly? Why?

....

....

15. UNLOCK THE BIG ? How can the force of magnetism cause objects to move?

....

....

....

⏹ **Stop!** I need help with ....

⏸ **Wait!** I have a question about ....

▶ **Go!** Now I know ....

What is gravity?

Envision It!

Why do you think the skydivers fall back to Earth?

Inquiry Explore It!

How does gravity pull an object?

☐ **1.** Place a ball in the smaller cup.
Raise the free end of the meterstick about 80 cm.

☐ **2.** Release the stick. Gently push it down.

☐ **3. Observe** and **record** where the ball lands.

Explain Your Results

4. Communicate Describe the path of the ball.

....

....

....

5. Interpret Data Explain your results using what you know about gravity.

....

....

....

....

....

Materials

meterstick with cups

rubber ball

goggles

folding meterstick

Law of Gravity

There are different forces acting on people all of the time. A force is any push or pull. One kind of force is a noncontact force. A noncontact force is a push or pull that affects an object without touching it. **Gravity** is a noncontact force that pulls objects toward one another. The law of gravity states that all objects are pulled toward one another by gravity. Skydivers and water from this fountain are pulled toward Earth by gravity. Without gravity, they would float away. Gravity pulls you and everything else on Earth toward Earth's center.

1. **Compare** Tell how tossing a coin is like water flowing from this fountain.

SavvasRealize.com

Gravity and Weight

The pull of gravity on an object gives an object its weight. An object's weight depends on where it is. When the pull of gravity is weaker, the object's weight is less. For example, the moon has less gravity than Earth. So, you weigh less on the moon. The pull of gravity is also less the farther you are from Earth's center. So, you weigh less on a mountaintop than in a valley.

An object's weight also depends on the amount of matter in an object. Objects with more matter have more mass. So, the pull of gravity is greater on an object with more mass. For example, the pull of gravity is greater on an elephant than on an apple. Even if the pull of gravity changes, the object's mass stays the same. Your mass on Earth and on the moon is the same, but your weight is different.

2. **Apply** Compare the pull of gravity on the dog to the pull of gravity on the frisbee.

the dog would have gravty becaus the dog weighs more

Do the math!

Multiplication

You learned that the mass of any matter is the same everywhere. The weight of an object depends on the pull of gravity.

Example

The pull of gravity on Earth is 6 times as strong as the pull of gravity on the moon. If a cat weighs 3 pounds on the moon, how much would the same cat weigh on Earth?

3 pounds × 6 = 18 pounds

The cat weighs 3 pounds on the moon but 18 pounds on Earth.

1 **Solve** The pull of gravity on Earth is 3 times as strong as the pull of gravity on Mars. If a bike weighed 9 pounds on Mars, how much would that bike weigh on Earth? Show your work.

9 X 3 = 27 pounds

2 **Solve** If a dog weighed 9 pounds on the moon, how much would the same dog weigh on Earth? Show your work.

9 X 6 = 54 pounds

24

Gravity is a force that can be overcome. For example, when you toss a ball in the air, the ball overcomes gravity for a few moments. Then it falls back to Earth. If your push is stronger than the pull of gravity, the ball will go up. Gravity pulls the ball back down. It is easier to overcome gravity with a light object than with a heavy object.

Lightning Lab

Overcoming Gravity
Get a light object and a heavy object. Hold them up. Describe what resists the force of gravity. Drop them at the same time. Describe how they fell.

3. Determine How does gravity affect juggling?

gravtry tries to bring whatev youre juggling kedaown

Got it?

4. Determine What makes it easier to carry an object down stairs than up stairs?

5. Predict How would throwing a ball on the moon be different than throwing a ball on Earth?

Stop! I need help with

Wait! I have a question about

Go! Now I know

How can you describe motion?

Follow a Procedure

☐ **1. Measure** 2 meters from a wall and place one end of the chute there.

☐ **2.** Place 2 books under the other end of the chute.

☐ **3.** Release the ball at the top of the chute. Start timing when the ball reaches the floor.

☐ **4. Record** the time when the ball hits the wall.

Materials

books

meterstick

chutes

ball

timer

Inquiry Skill
Scientists **measure** carefully and record their measurements.

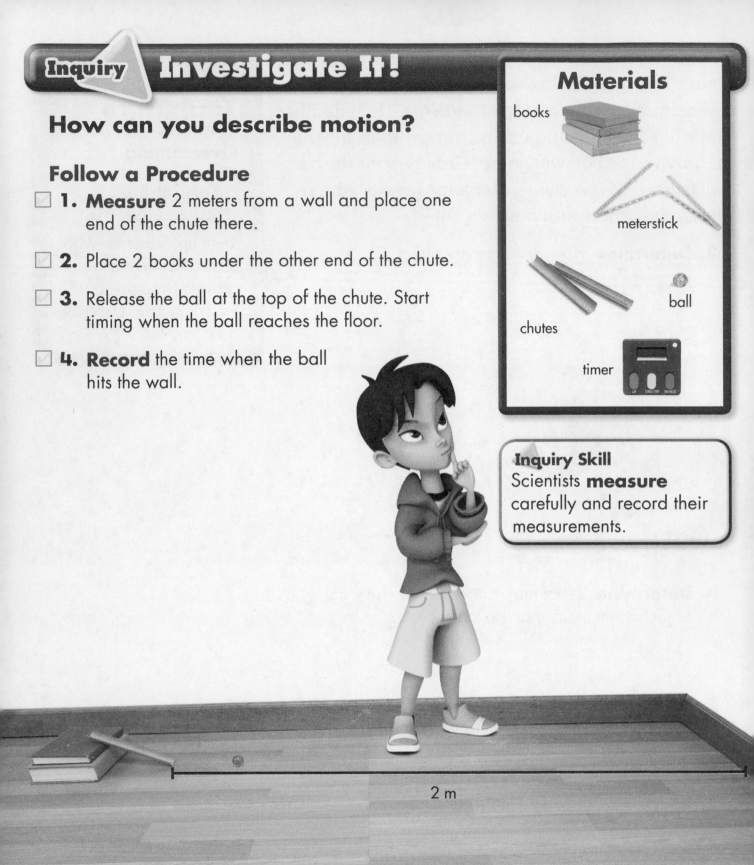

2 m

5. Stop the timer when the ball comes back to the bottom of the chute. Record.

Ball Movement Results			
Time (seconds)			
Number of Books	From Bottom of Chute to Wall (Time A)	From Bottom of Chute to Wall and Back (Time B)	From Wall to Bottom of Chute (Time C = Time B – Time A)
2 books			
4 books			

6. Stack 4 books and repeat steps 2 to 5.

Analyze and Conclude

7. Interpret Data When did the ball move faster?

....

....

....

8. **UNLOCK THE BIG ?** What effect did the wall have on the motion of the ball?

....

....

....

....

The Wright Brothers

Orville and Wilbur Wright were born in Dayton, Ohio. In 1892, they opened a bicycle shop together. They built and sold their own bicycles. However, the brothers soon turned their attention to flying machines!

The Wright brothers studied the motion of aircraft. They examined the forces that keep a craft in the air or pull it down. They examined the forces that move the craft forward or slow its motion.

Orville and Wilbur tested their ideas on gliders. Success came in 1902. They built a glider that a pilot could control in the air.

Their next step was to design and build an engine-powered aircraft. They needed a gasoline engine that did not weigh too much. Yet it had to provide enough force to move the craft in the air. In 1903, Orville and Wilbur made the first controlled flight in an aircraft with an engine.

 REVIEW THE BIG ? How might building bicycles have helped the brothers build airplanes?

....

....

....

....

Vocabulary Smart Cards

position
motion
speed
force
friction
magnetism
gravity

Play a Game!

Cut out the Vocabulary Smart Cards.

Work with a partner. Choose a Vocabulary Smart Card.

Write a sentence using the vocabulary word. Draw a blank where the vocabulary word should be.

Have your partner fill in the blank with the correct vocabulary word.

29 ✂

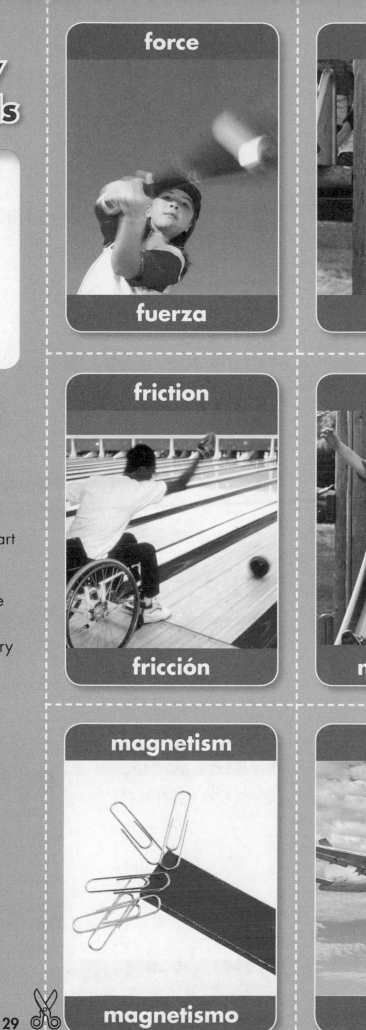

force
fuerza

position
posición

friction
fricción

motion
movimiento

magnetism
magnetismo

speed
rapidez

the location of an object	a push or a pull
Use a dictionary. Write as many synonyms for this word as you can.	Write a sentence using this word.
....	....
....	....
....	....
....	....
ubicación de un objeto	empujón o jalón

magnetism

force · magnet

non-contact · magnetic

iron

Make a Word Magnet!

Choose a vocabulary word and write it in the Word Magnet. Write words that are related to it on the lines.

a change in the position of an object	a contact force that opposes the motion of an object
Write a sentence using this word.	Make a drawing that shows what this word means.
....	
....	
....	
cambio en la posición de un objeto	fuerza de contacto que se opone al movimiento de un objeto

the rate at which an object changes position	a non-contact force that pulls objects containing iron
Write the definition as a formula.	Draw an example of this word.
....	
....	
....	
tasa a la cual un objeto cambia de posición	fuerza sin contacto que atrae objetos que contienen hierro

gravity

gravedad

a noncontact force that pulls objects toward one another

Draw an example.

fuerza sin contacto que hace que los objetos se atraigan entre sí

Chapter 1
Study Guide

 What forces cause motion?

Physical Science

Lesson 1

What is motion?

- Motion is a change in position.
- Position is the location of an object, or its place.
- Speed is the rate at which an object changes its position.
- If the motion of an object has a regular pattern, you may be able to predict future motion.

Lesson 2

How does force affect motion?

- A force is a push or a pull.
- The amount of force used affects an object's motions.
- Mass, friction, and magnetism affect an object's motion.

Lesson 3

What is gravity?

- Gravity is a noncontact force that pulls objects toward one another.
- The pull of gravity on an object gives the object its weight.

SavvasRealize.com

Lesson 1

What is motion?

1. **Vocabulary** Which word means the same as *position*? Circle the correct answer.
   A. motion
   B. location
   C. direction
   D. speed

Do the
math!

2. **Calculate** The caterpillar crossed this leaf in 5 seconds. Use the formula for speed to find out exactly how fast the caterpillar traveled.

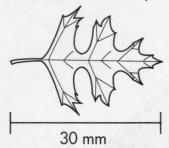

30 mm

distance ÷ time = speed

caterpillar's speed =

 _____ mm ÷ _____ s = _____ mm/s

3. **Explain** How do you know when an object is in motion?

....

....

....

Lesson 2

How does force affect motion?

4. **Predict** What would happen if more force were applied to a moving cart? The force acts in the same direction in which the cart is moving.

....

....

....

5. **Write About It** Describe friction and give an example of it.

....

....

....

....

....

....

6. ◉ **Draw Conclusions** A volleyball is headed toward you. You hit the ball back in the direction from which it came. What can you conclude about force?

....

....

....

Lesson 3

What is gravity?

7. Infer Why would a crayon roll down a ramp but need force to move up a ramp?

....

....

....

....

8. Analyze Without gravity, what would happen if you threw a ball straight up in the air?

....

....

....

....

9. Justify How could you show that gravity affects an apple?

....

....

....

....

10. 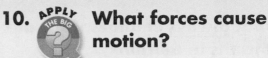 **What forces cause motion?**

....

Describe what happens when you open a door. Use the terms *force*, *motion*, and *position*.

....

....

....

....

....

....

....

....

....

....

....

....

....

....

....

Read each question and choose the best answer.

1 **What <u>always</u> changes when an object is in motion?**

   A its direction
   B its speed
   C its mass
   D its position

2 **Look closely at the bicycles. What force would cause the wheels to slow down?**

   A gravity
   B position
   C magnetism
   D friction

3 **Which will make a bowling ball roll faster?**

   A Increase the distance it rolls.
   B Apply a greater force.
   C Increase the ball's weight.
   D Increase the ball's mass.

4 **Jake and Maria are playing catch. Jake misses catching the ball. What causes the ball to fall to Earth?**

   A friction
   B speed
   C gravity
   D mass

5 **Which of the following would <u>not</u> affect the motion of an object?**

   A a change in mass
   B balanced forces
   C a greater force
   D more friction

6 **Would a person's weight on one planet be different from the same person's weight on another planet? Explain.**

....

....

....

STEM

Roller Coasters

Roller coasters can be fun! If you have been on a roller coaster, did you move right or left? Did you move up or down? What forces did you feel? Engineers use science, technology, and math to design roller coasters. Roller coasters test the limits of technology! Engineers test different materials for strength before building a roller coaster. Steel is very strong. Steel allows engineers to build taller hills and tighter loops. Engineers use math to calculate how fast the cars will travel. Roller coasters use science, technology, engineering, and math to make the ride more fun!

During a roller coaster ride, energy is constantly changing. Potential energy is greatest at the top of hills. It is the least at the bottom of hills.

Illustrate Roller coasters use both potential and kinetic energy. Potential energy is stored energy. Kinetic energy is energy of motion. In this image, circle where the roller coaster has the most kinetic energy. Draw an X where the roller coaster has the most potential energy.

How can energy keep you running?

Energy and Its Forms

Chapter 2

Try It!   How can energy of motion change?

STEM Activity   Sun, Light, Energy

Investigate It!   How does heat cause motion?

Physical Science

Apply It!   How does energy affect the distance a toy car travels?

When was the last time you took a long run? Running on sand takes a lot of energy. It takes more energy to run on sand than to run on a paved surface.

Predict   How does this runner use energy?

....

....

THE BIG ?   How can energy change?

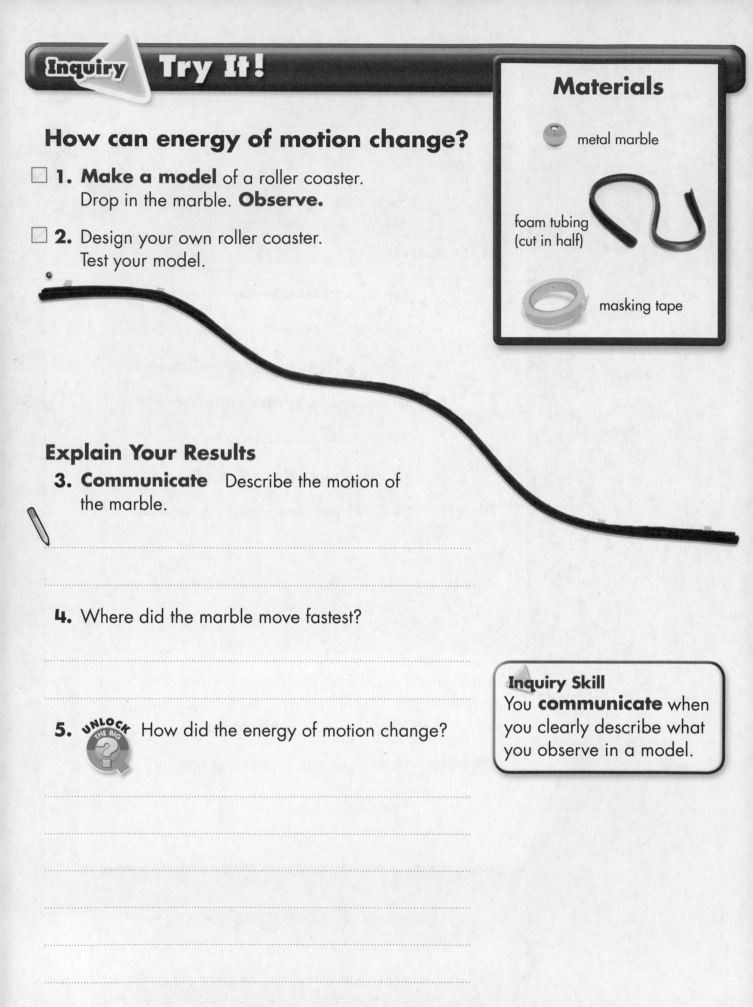

Materials

metal marble

foam tubing
(cut in half)

masking tape

How can energy of motion change?

☐ **1. Make a model** of a roller coaster.
   Drop in the marble. **Observe.**

☐ **2.** Design your own roller coaster.
   Test your model.

Explain Your Results

3. Communicate   Describe the motion of
   the marble.

....

....

4. Where did the marble move fastest?

....

....

5. **UNLOCK THE BIG ?**   How did the energy of motion change?

Inquiry Skill
You **communicate** when
you clearly describe what
you observe in a model.

....

....

....

....

....

◉ Cause and Effect

- A **cause** makes something happen.
- An **effect** is what happens.
- Science writers often use clue words and phrases such as *makes, if,* and *as a result* to signal cause and effect.

Boiling Water

If enough energy is added to liquid water, it boils. It becomes the invisible gas called water vapor. At a temperature of 100°C (212°F), liquid water boils. Energy added at the bottom of a container makes water at the bottom change into a gas. The gas forms bubbles that are lighter than the water around them. As a result, the bubbles of gas float to the water's surface. These bubbles break open and release hot water vapor into the air.

Practice It!

Complete the graphic organizer. Use it to identify a cause and effect in the above paragraph.

Cause

Effect

Sun, Light, Energy

Solar energy is a renewable source of energy. Solar panels collect solar energy. These panels work best when they receive strong and direct light. That is why they are often placed in the middle of fields or on rooftops. In these places nothing can come between the panel and the sun.

For a science fair project, you decided to design a way to direct more sunlight onto a model solar panel, and then analyze how well your method worked.

Identify the Problem

☑ **1.** What is your task? _____
_____

Do Research

Examine a mirror, a salad bowl, and a piece of cardboard. Turn off the overhead lights in the classroom. Shine a flashlight at each material and observe how the light reflects. **Write** your observations.

☑ **2.** Mirror: _____
_____

☑ **3.** Salad bowl: _____
_____

☑ **4.** Cardboard: _____
_____

☑ **5.** Which material reflected light the most precisely? _____

Go to the materials station(s). Pick up each material one at a time. Think about how it may or may not be useful in your design. Leave the materials where they are.

☑ **6.** What are your design constraints? _____
_____

Develop Possible Solutions

☐ **7. List** two different ways you could combine some of the materials to build a solar collector and direct more sunlight onto your model solar panel.

_____

_____

_____

_____

Choose One Solution

☐ **8. Describe** your solar collector and how you will build it. _____

_____

_____

_____

_____

☐ **9. List** the materials that you will need. _____

_____

_____

_____

☐ **10. Draw** a diagram of your solar collector.

Design and Construct a Prototype

Gather your materials plus a thermometer to use when you test your prototype. **Build** your solar collector.

☐ **11. Record** the design details of your prototype.

_____

_____

_____

Test the Prototype

Test your solar collector. First, place your model panel in the sunlight. Record the temperature of the panel after 10 minutes. Then, put your collector in place. Again record the temperature on the surface of your model panel after 10 minutes.

12. What was your starting temperature? _____

13. What is the temperature of the surface of your model panel after 10 minutes in your solar collector? _____

Communicate Results

14. Did your solar collector work? Explain. _____

_____

_____

_____

Evaluate and Redesign

15. Describe how you would change your design to make your solar collector more efficient. _____

_____

_____

_____

What are some forms of energy?

Circle any place you see energy in this picture.

my planet Diary

by Maddie
Wesley Chapel,
Florida

I use a lot of energy because it makes my life easier. However, I try to be responsible and use less energy.

I also turn off the lights when I leave a room. Sometimes I want the lights on. Instead, I open the blinds, so I do not waste energy.

by Jordyn
Daytona Beach,
Florida

Hi, Maddie. My family and I are also committed to using less energy. I turn off my fan and my radio before I go to school.

I save more energy at school. Whenever our class leaves the room, we turn off the lights. It would save a lot of energy if every class in the school did that!

Let's Blog!

If you could blog back to Maddie and Jordyn, what would you blog about saving energy?

....

....

....

....

....

....

....

UNLOCK THE BIG ?

I will know energy takes many forms, causes motion, and creates change.

Words to Know

energy   potential
electrical   energy
  energy   kinetic
sound energy   energy

Energy

The ability to do work or to cause change is called **energy.** Work is done when a force moves an object. The sun is the main source of energy at Earth's surface. Energy from the sun causes many effects. Energy from the sun makes Earth a place where we can live. Light from the sun helps plants grow. Energy from the sun causes winds to blow and water to move through the water cycle.

Energy from the sun causes lettuce to grow.

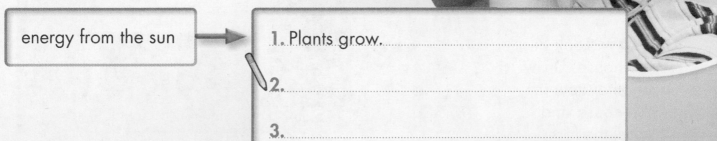

1. ⊙ **Cause and Effect** Complete the graphic organizer below. Write three effects of the sun's energy.

Cause

energy from the sun

Effects

1. Plants grow.
2. ....
3. ....

Energy at Home

You use many forms of energy every day in your home. The living and nonliving things in the home below use many forms of energy.

Electrical energy is the movement of electric charges. It powers things that use electricity, such as a lamp.

2. (Circle) things that use electrical energy.

Light energy is energy we can see. Light energy comes through windows and brightens rooms.

Heat is the transfer of energy from a warmer object to a colder object. Heat is used to cook food in the kitchen.

3. **Draw** Look at the house. Draw another item in the house and label the form of energy it uses.

Mechanical energy is energy that motion or position gives to an object. You use mechanical energy every time you move or lift an object, or use a machine with moving parts.

Sound energy is energy we can hear. Musical instruments produce sound energy.

4. **Label** Place an ✗ on things that produce sound energy.

5. **List** What machines in the home use mechanical energy?

....

....

....

6. **Compare and Describe** List some common forms of energy in your school. How are these forms of energy alike?

....

....

....

....

....

....

....

....

....

Stored Energy

Energy can be stored. As you stand ready to jump, run, or snowboard, your body has stored energy. Stored energy makes movement possible. Stored energy is **potential energy.** Potential energy changes into another kind of energy if you use it to do work or cause a change.

A raised object has potential energy due to gravity. For example, the snowboarder at the top of the hill in the photo below has potential energy because of his high position. Potential energy is also gained from stretching or compressing objects. For example, you can stretch or compress a spring to store potential energy.

The stored energy in food, fuels, and batteries is chemical energy. Stored chemical energy can change into a form that can do work. For example, the stored energy in food is released to help you move. It can also keep your body warm.

7. **List** Look again at the illustration on the previous pages. List two examples of potential energy in the home.

8. **Describe** How do you use the stored chemical energy in batteries?

At-Home Lab

Make Motion
Get a bowl and a table-tennis ball. Put the ball in the bowl. Move the bowl around. Tell how the ball moves. Tell where the ball has the most potential energy. Tell where it has the least potential energy.

Energy of Motion

Potential energy can change to **kinetic energy,** or the energy of motion. A car moves when the chemical energy stored in gasoline changes to kinetic energy. Potential energy changes to kinetic energy when you release a stretched spring. The potential energy the snowboarder has at the top of the hill in the photo at right changes to kinetic energy as he moves down the hill. He moves down the hill because gravity pulls him.

Energy can be used to lift objects. When a snowboarder carries a snowboard to the top of a hill, he and the snowboard gain potential energy. They now have the potential to slide to the bottom of the hill. At the bottom of the hill the snowboarder may have enough kinetic energy to lift him and his snowboard to the top of the next hill.

The snowboarder's potential energy due to gravity changes to kinetic energy.

9. **Underline** the words that tell about kinetic energy.

Got it?

10. **Explain** Write one way each type of energy is used in everyday life.

Electrical ....

Mechanical ....

Sound ....

11. **Give an Example** How can energy be used to move or lift objects?

....

....

⬛ **Stop!** I need help with ....

⏸ **Wait!** I have a question about ....

▶ **Go!** Now I know ....

How does energy change form?

Envision It!

Tell how you think energy changes form as this electric train travels.

Inquiry ## Explore It!

What can produce potential energy?

☐ **1.** Tape one end of a 60 cm string to the edge of a table. Hang five washers from the other end.

☐ **2.** Pull the washers sideways about 30 cm. Let them go. **Describe** their motion.

....

....

Materials

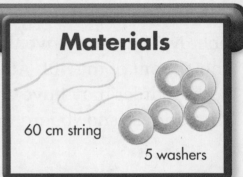

60 cm string

5 washers

Explain Your Results

3. Infer   When do the washers have the most potential energy? Why?

....

4. Infer   When do the washers have the least potential energy? Why?

....

5. Hypothesize   The washers lose potential energy and get it back with each swing. How do you think they get it back?

....

Changing Forms of Energy

There are different forms of energy. Energy can change from one form to another. People change energy into forms they can easily use. For example, a music player changes electrical energy into sound energy.

Your body changes energy into forms that are useful for you. For example, your body stores potential energy from food as chemical energy. The chemical energy stored in your body changes to kinetic energy as you move objects or lift them.

1. Circle five forms of energy in the paragraphs above.

2. **Predict** Into what form of energy does this robot dog change electrical energy?

SavvasRealize.com

53

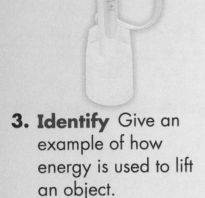

Using Energy

Sometimes people use machines to change forms of energy. You use kinetic energy to turn on a light switch, a common machine. When the light switch is turned on, electrical energy changes to light energy. A cable car, another machine, changes potential energy to kinetic energy.

An electric toothbrush is another machine. It has an electric cord that plugs into an outlet. Electrical energy is stored as chemical energy in the battery of the toothbrush. The chemical energy changes back to electrical energy when the toothbrush is turned on. The electrical energy then changes to kinetic energy as the toothbrush moves.

Energy does not change completely from one form to another. Energy does not go away, either. Some energy always produces heat. After you turn on a light bulb, it becomes warm. This is because some of the energy produces heat.

3. Identify Give an example of how energy is used to lift an object.

....

....

....

4. Hypothesize How do you think the cable car gains potential energy?

....

....

Go Green

Reduce Energy Usage

Gasoline contains a form of stored energy. It is made from oil. There is a limited supply of oil on Earth. Think of some ways people use gasoline. Tell three ways people could use less gasoline.

cable car

POWELL AND MARKET

3

How Energy Travels

Energy can travel from one place to another. Suppose a moving object strikes another object. Some kinetic energy passes to the second object. Have you ever gone bowling? When the bowling ball hits the group of pins, the ball slows down and the pins begin moving. Before hitting the pins, the bowling ball has all of the kinetic energy. The pins have no kinetic energy. When the ball hits the pins, some kinetic energy transfers to the pins. Heat is also produced, which causes some energy to be lost. The total amount of energy does not change.

5. Underline one cause and (circle) one effect in the paragraph.

Do the math!

Model and Apply Division

In bowling, you roll a ball about 18 meters down the lane to hit the pins. If a bowling ball is thrown at 6 meters per second, how long does it take to hit the pins?

Rule: Time = Distance ÷ Speed

You can use repeated subtraction to find how many groups of 6 are in 18.

18 – 6 = 12
12 – 6 = 6
6 – 6 = 0

You can subtract 6 three times. There are three groups of 6 in 18.

The ball takes 3 seconds to hit the pins.

1 Solve If you throw the bowling ball at 3 meters per second, about how long will it take for the ball to hit the pins?

....

2 Hypothesize When a bowling ball hits the pins, energy transfers from the ball to the pins. If you roll the ball too slowly, what might happen when it reaches the pins?

....

....

....

Waves

Energy can travel as waves. For example, light and sound travel as waves. A **wave** is a disturbance that carries energy from one point to another point. Waves of energy can look like the wave of moving rope below. The rope goes from one side of the dotted line to the other. Energy causes this effect as it travels from one end of the rope to the other.

6. ⊙ **Main Idea and Details** Read the paragraph. Write the main idea.

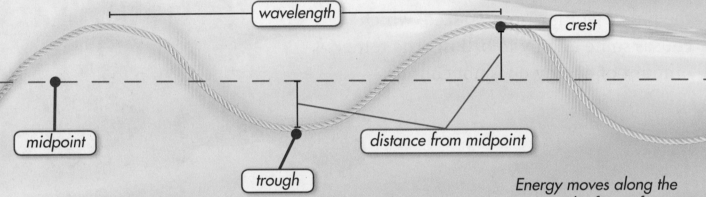

Energy moves along the rope in the form of waves.

The shape of a wave can tell about how much energy it carries. The wavelength and the distance from the midpoint to the crest or trough can indicate about how much energy a wave carries.

The bottom of a wave is called a trough. The top of a wave is called a crest. Waves with greater distance from the midpoint to a crest or trough have more energy than waves with less distance.

Wavelength is the distance between one crest and the next crest or one trough and the next trough. Waves with shorter wavelengths have more energy than waves with longer wavelengths.

7. Produce Draw a wave that carries less energy than the rope above.

Waves in water can be small, like the ripples in the bucket below. Waves caused by hurricanes can be huge! The size of a wave depends on how much energy it carries. The energy a wave carries can change. Look at the bucket. First, the energy from the falling drop disturbs the water surface. Then, as the waves move away from the source, they carry less energy.

8. **Compare** Some toys get their energy from batteries, and some from a windup key. What are some advantages of each method?

....

9. **UNLOCK THE BIG ?** Think about what you learned in this lesson. How can energy change?

....

....

⏹ **Stop!** I need help with ....

⏸ **Wait!** I have a question about ....

▶ **Go!** Now I know ....

How do light and matter interact?

Envision It!

Tell where you think light is coming from in these sea jellies.

Inquiry **Explore It!**

What happens when light is reflected in many directions?

☐ **1.** Shine the flashlight through the water. **Observe** the water from all directions. **Record** what you see.

....

....

☐ **2.** Add $\frac{1}{3}$ spoonful of milk. Stir. Repeat step 1. Does the color of the water look the same from all directions?

....

....

Explain Your Results

3. Compare your **observations** before and after the milk was added.

....

....

Materials

flashlight

milk

spoon

clear plastic cup with water

I will know how objects reflect, refract, and absorb light. I will know how light forms shadows.

Words to Know

light energy   refract
reflect   absorb

Path of Light

You can see objects because of light energy. **Light energy** is energy we can see. Light travels outward from its source in all directions. Light travels in straight lines until it strikes an object or travels from one medium to another. For example, light from a light bulb can brighten a whole room. The light from the spotlights below does not travel in all directions. The sides of the spotlight direct the light to travel in one direction. Light can pass through some of the objects it strikes. For example, light can pass through a window or a glass of water. These objects do not block all light that passes through them.

1. **List** Write three objects that do not block all light.

....

....

....

How Light Changes

The path of light can change in different ways. Light can be reflected, refracted, or absorbed.

Reflect

You can see an object because light **reflects**, or bounces off the object. Some objects reflect light better than others. Flat, smooth surfaces reflect light evenly. A mirror or a smooth lake reflects light evenly. Other objects do not reflect light evenly. A rough lake does not reflect light evenly.

Refract

What happens to light in an ice cube? The ice cube **refracts**, or bends, light. Refracted light changes direction. The ice cube below refracts light that reflects off the strawberry. The refracted light forms images of the strawberry.

Light refracts when it passes through different materials at different speeds. Light passing through air slows down when it enters water. This causes the straw in the glass at left to look broken.

2. Explain Why can you see the reflection of the insect?

refraction

3. Draw an ✗ where you see the strawberry reflected or refracted inside the ice cube.

Absorb

Have you ever wondered why you see colors? You see colors because of what happens to light when it hits different materials.

Light is made up of different colors. An object **absorbs**, or takes in, some of the light that hits it. The object reflects the rest. Most objects reflect light. Different objects absorb and reflect different colors of light. For example, red flowers reflect the color red. Red flowers absorb other colors of light. The reflected color red is what your eyes see. White light is made up of all colors of light. If an object looks white, it reflects all colors of light. If an object looks black, it absorbs all colors of light.

4. CHALLENGE Will you be cooler on a hot day in a light-colored shirt or a dark-colored shirt? Explain.

Light and Objects

Some materials refract light.
Water and air are two
materials that refract light.

5. **State** How does each
   water droplet change the
   image of the flower?

....

....

Objects such as these hot-air
balloons absorb some colors
of light and reflect other
colors.

6. **Explain** Why do you see
   the color blue on a hot-air
   balloon?

....

....

The rocks and lake reflect
light. The rocks do not have
a smooth surface. They
reflect light from the sky in
many directions. This is why
you do not see an image of
the sky on the rocks.

7. **Draw** Finish drawing the
   reflection on the water on
   the next page.

refract

absorb

reflect

Shadows

During a sunny day, you might use an umbrella to shade yourself from the hot sun. The shade the umbrella creates is a shadow.

Light travels outward from its source in all directions until it strikes an object. When light is blocked by an object, a shadow is formed. A shadow is a dark area made when an object blocks light between a light source and a surface. You can see shadows on surfaces. The length of the shadow depends on the angle of the light. For example, the length and direction of shadows caused by sunlight change during the day.

8. **Analyze** Why do these tables and chairs make shadows in the sunlight?

....

....

....

....

At-Home Lab

Make Shadows
Stand in a place with bright sunlight. Make a shape with your hand. Look at the shadow it makes. Make the shadow look sharper. Make the shadow look fuzzier.

7:00 A.M.	12:00 P.M.	5:00 P.M.

The morning shadow of the bicycle is long. The morning shadow stretches west when the sun is in the eastern sky.

At noon, the sun appears to have moved higher in the sky. The shadow becomes shorter.

In the afternoon, the sun appears to have moved across the sky. The shadow becomes longer. The afternoon shadow stretches east when the sun is in the western sky.

9. Describe Tell how the length and direction of the bicycle shadows above change during the day.

Got it?

10. Contrast How are reflection and refraction different?

....

....

11. Demonstrate How might you demonstrate that light can travel in a straight line?

....

....

....

⬛ **Stop!** I need help with ....

⏸ **Wait!** I have a question about ....

▶ **Go!** Now I know ....

What are heat and light energy?

Tell how you think light affects this picture.

my planeT DiaRY

//// MISCONCEPTION ////

"Close the door. You're letting the heat escape!"

Have you ever heard someone say this? In fact, it's true that heat moves from place to place. On a cold day, heat will transfer from the warm air inside a house to the cooler air outside. But closing a door won't completely stop this from happening. On a cold day, heat inside a house is constantly moving to the air outside.

Look at the picture and read the caption. Where are the warmest parts of the house?

....

....

....

This photo was taken with a camera that detects heat. Red and yellow areas show where temperatures are warm.

I will know how heat and light energy affect matter and can be produced.

Words to Know

thermal energy

Thermal Energy and Heat

Matter is made of very small moving particles. Each particle of matter moves because it has energy. The energy of moving particles is called **thermal energy.** Thermal energy is the kinetic energy and potential energy of particles in matter. Energy from the sun makes the particles in objects move faster. The object becomes warmer. That is why sunlight feels warm on your skin. When the sun's energy no longer reaches the matter, its particles slow down and the matter cools. That is why you feel cooler when you are in the shade.

Heat is the transfer of energy from one place to another. Heat can take the form of thermal energy traveling from warmer objects to cooler objects. When you place a metal spoon into a pot of cooking food, heat travels from the warmer pot through the cooler spoon. In a short time, the top of the spoon will feel warm.

1. **Predict** What would happen to the hot spoon if it was placed in a pot of cool water?

....

....

....

....

When the warm pot and the spoon reach the same temperature, the flow of energy stops.

SavvasRealize.com

Heat and Light

When energy changes form, one result is heat. For example, heat is produced when you rub two objects together. You can investigate heat by rubbing your hands together. Your hands warm up because kinetic energy is changed to heat.

Energy heats your home. Some people heat their homes with natural gas. Some people use electricity. Other people use solar panels that collect energy from the sun.

When energy changes form, some energy is always given off in the form of heat. Think about light. Energy changes form when light is produced. This means that sources of light are also sources of heat.

Burning is a chemical change that can produce light and heat. For example, candles, campfires, and matches give off light that helps heat the space around them as they burn.

2. **Infer** Why might people rub their hands together when they are cold?

....

....

3. **Analyze** List three things you use that produce both light and heat.

....

....

....

....

Electricity can also be a source of light and heat. Electricity makes the wire in a light bulb get so hot that it gives off light. Bulbs in heat lamps can be used to keep food warm.

Lightning Lab

Heat and Colors
Find a sunny place. Get a sheet of white paper. Get a sheet of black paper. Tell if the sheets of paper feel warm. Place them in the sunlight. Wait five minutes. Feel the sheets. Tell how the sheets of paper feel.

Got it?

4. **Infer** What happens when two liquids of different temperatures are mixed? Explain.

....

....

5. **Understand** What are two ways heat can be produced?

....

....

⬛ **Stop!** I need help with ....

⏸ **Wait!** I have a question about ....

▶ **Go!** Now I know ....

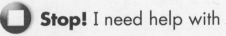

What is sound energy?

Write words to describe the sound you think this party blower makes.

Inquiry **Explore It!**

What can affect the sound made by a rubber band?

☐ **1.** Stretch a thick rubber band and a thin rubber band around a box.

☐ **2. Observe** Pluck each band. How does each sound? **Record.**

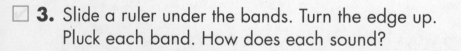

☐ **3.** Slide a ruler under the bands. Turn the edge up. Pluck each band. How does each sound?

Explain Your Results

4. Draw Conclusions How does a rubber band's thickness affect its sound?

Materials

safety goggles

thick rubber band

plastic tub (or shoebox)

thin rubber band

ruler

 Be careful! Wear safety goggles. Be careful not to snap the rubber bands.

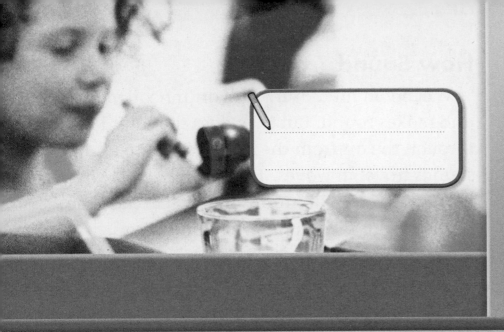

Sound

At a party, you hear loud music and noisemakers. In a field, you hear crickets chirp quietly. You hear many different sounds every day. Some sounds are loud, and others are soft. You hear high sounds and low sounds. Yet all sounds are made in the same way. Sound happens when matter vibrates. *Vibrate* means to move quickly back and forth.

Any matter that vibrates can make sound. You can even make sound with a ruler. Hold one end of a ruler tightly against a table. Press the other end down so the ruler bends, then let it go. The ruler vibrates and makes sound.

1. ◉ **Cause and Effect** Complete the graphic organizer to show an effect.

Cause

The ruler vibrates.

→

Effect

.

2. **Circle** the areas in the diagram where air particles are squeezed together.

3. CHALLENGE Suppose you build a chain of dominoes and knock over the first one. As each domino falls, it knocks over the one next to it. In what way is this a good model for the way sound energy moves through air?

....

....

....

....

How Sound Travels

When you hit a drum, the drumhead vibrates and makes sound. But how does the sound move through the air from the drum to your ear? All sounds travel in waves. These waves form when matter vibrates. Vibrations in matter cause the particles that make up air to vibrate too.

Think about the vibrating drumhead. As the drumhead vibrates, it causes the air particles around it to move. The moving particles form waves. In some areas, the air particles are squeezed together. In other areas, the particles spread apart. This pattern repeats as the drumhead continues to vibrate.

As a sound wave travels, the air particles that make up the wave do not move along with it. They vibrate in place and bump into each other. When they bump, energy transfers from one particle to the next. In this way, the sound energy moves through the air from particle to particle until it reaches your ear.

Volume

Sound waves can have different properties. Because of this, the sounds we hear have different properties.

Think about the siren on a fire truck. The first thing you might notice about a siren is its **volume,** or how loud or soft a sound is. Volume is a property of sound. Volume is related to how much energy a sound has.

A siren sounds very loud if you are standing near the siren.

When you whisper, you make a soft sound. The sound waves you create have little energy. When you shout, you use more energy to make a sound. The sound waves you create have more energy. The sound is louder.

Volume also depends on how far away a listener is from the source of the sound. Suppose you are near a siren when it goes off. The sound would not have to travel far to get to your ears. But if you are far away, the siren would not seem as loud. The sound waves do not lose energy as they travel away from the siren. But the energy spreads out in all directions over a larger area.

4. **Illustrate** Draw a picture to show how sound spreads out as it moves away from a roaring lion.

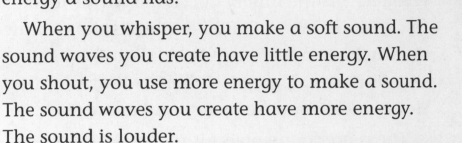

Lightning Lab

Change Vibrations, Change Sounds

Rest your fingers on your throat near your voice box. Talk loudly and then whisper. Describe what you feel each time. Tell what changes when you make softer or louder sounds.

Pitch

How is the song of a bird different from the roar of a lion? It certainly is softer than the lion's roar. It is different in another way too.

A bird makes a higher sound than a lion. **Pitch** is how high or low a sound is. The bird makes a high-pitched sound. The lion makes a low-pitched sound.

A sound's pitch depends on its frequency. Frequency is the number of sound waves made in a certain amount of time. Objects that vibrate quickly have a high frequency. High-frequency sounds have a high pitch. Objects that vibrate slowly have a low frequency and a low pitch.

The material an object is made of affects its pitch. The size and shape of an object also affect pitch. For example, a small drum will usually have a higher pitch than a big drum.

This songbird can make sounds of many different pitches. Its voice sounds musical.

5. **Compare** A mouse and a lion make different sounds. Use the words *high* and *low* to compare their pitch.

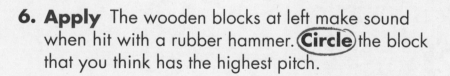

....

....

....

6. **Apply** The wooden blocks at left make sound when hit with a rubber hammer. (Circle) the block that you think has the highest pitch.

Pitch in Stringed Instruments

Guitars, violins, cellos, and harps are kinds of stringed instruments. Stringed instruments make sound when you pluck their strings or rub a bow across their strings. Each string's pitch depends on the string's properties. A thin string vibrates faster than a thick string, so a thin string has higher pitch. In the same way, a short or tight string vibrates faster than a long or loose string. So the string that is shorter or tighter makes a sound with a higher pitch.

Each string of a guitar has a different pitch.

7. **Infer** When you stretch a rubber band and pluck it, it vibrates and makes a sound. How could you change the pitch of the vibrating rubber band?

....

....

Got it?

8. **Compare** Use the words *loud* and *soft* to compare the sounds of a bicycle and a large truck.

....

....

9. **Predict** A guitar has thick strings and thin strings. Would you expect the thick strings to sound higher or lower than the thin strings? Explain why.

....

....

⏹ **Stop!** I need help with ....

⏸ **Wait!** I have a question about ....

▶ **Go!** Now I know ....

Lesson 6

What is electrical energy?

Circle two examples of electrical energy in this picture.

Inquiry ▸ Explore It!

How can you control electrical energy?

Be careful! Wear safety goggles.

Materials

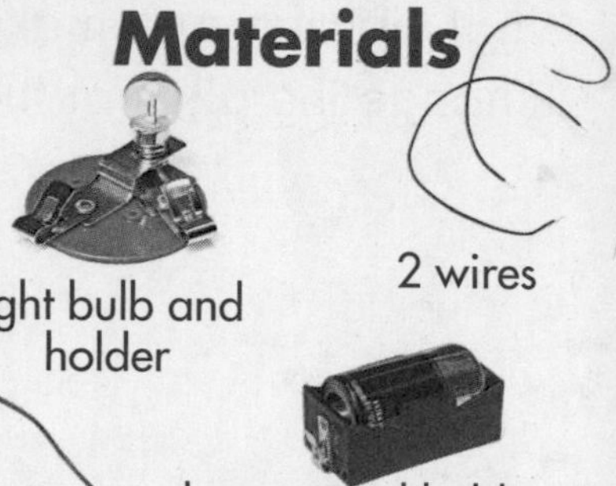

light bulb and holder

2 wires

battery and holder

☐ **1.** Connect the wires.
   Observe and **record** what happens.

....

☐ **2.** Turn the light on and off.

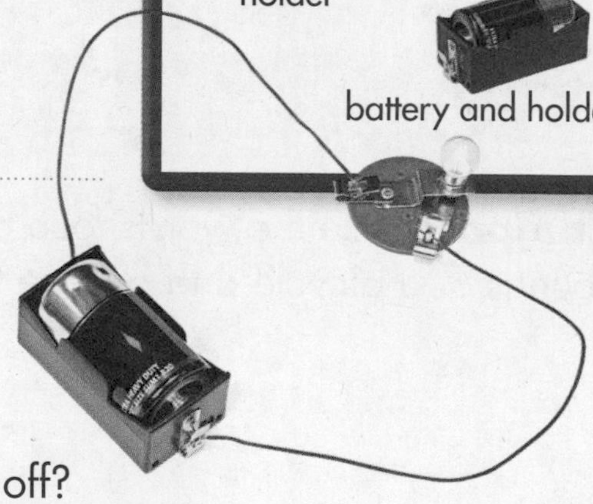

Explain Your Results

3. Communicate How did you turn the light off?

....

....

4. Infer How does a light switch work?

....

....

....

UNLOCK THE BIG

I will know how electricity moves through circuits. I will know some materials that conduct electricity.

Words to Know

closed circuit
open circuit

Electric Charges

All matter is made up of small particles that have electric charges. An electric charge is a property of some particles that causes them to attract or repel each other, even if the particles are not touching. Particles of matter have both positive (+) and negative (-) electric charges. When particles have an equal number of positive and negative charges, the matter has no overall charge. Matter with more negative charges than positive charges has a negative charge. Matter with more positive charges than negative charges has a positive charge.

Put two objects with the same charge near each other. They push away from each other. Two objects with opposite charges attract each other. If you rub the girl's hair with the balloon, the balloon picks up negative charges from the hair. The girl's hair then has an overall positive charge. The balloon has a negative charge. The balloon and the hair have opposite charges, so they attract each other.

1. **Label** Write the symbols + and – on the girl's hair and the balloon to show their electric charges.

SavvasRealize.com

77

Electric Currents and Circuits

The movement of electric charge from one place to another is electric current. Lightning is an uncontrolled electric current. Lightning can travel in any direction. To be useful, an electric current must travel in a controlled path through wires and other materials. This way, electric current can provide the energy needed to turn on lights or make a CD player work.

The path that a controlled electric current flows through is an electric circuit. The path must be unbroken for electric current to flow through it. Every circuit needs a source of energy, such as a battery or an outlet that you can plug a cord into. The diagram below shows a circuit made from a battery, wires, and a light bulb.

2. **Demonstrate** Draw arrows to show the direction electric current flows in the diagram below.

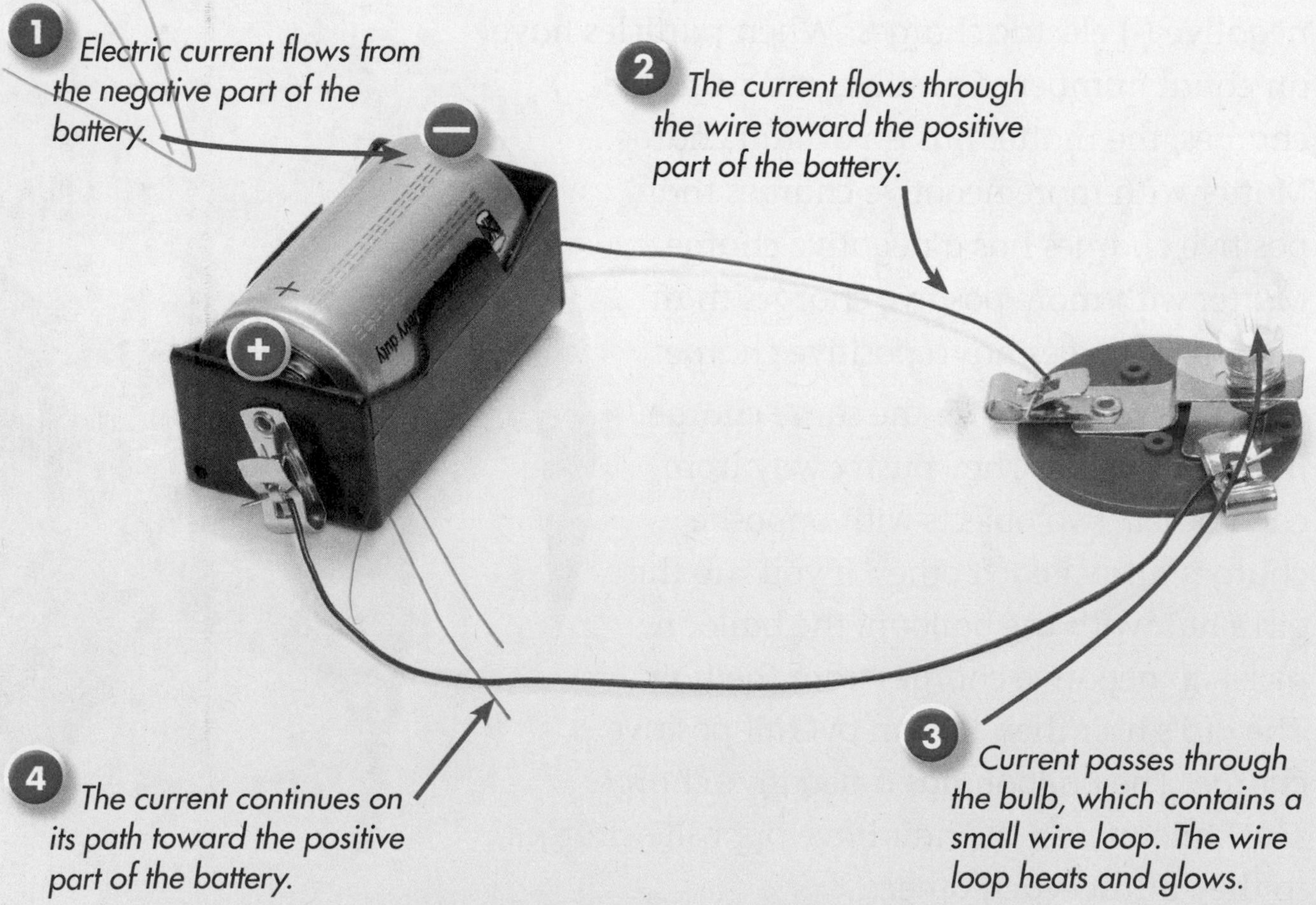

1 Electric current flows from the negative part of the battery.

2 The current flows through the wire toward the positive part of the battery.

4 The current continues on its path toward the positive part of the battery.

3 Current passes through the bulb, which contains a small wire loop. The wire loop heats and glows.

Closed Circuits and Open Circuits

A circuit with no gaps or breaks is called a **closed circuit.** Electric current will continue to flow through a closed circuit until it is broken. A circuit with a broken path is called an **open circuit.** Current will not flow through an open circuit.

You can create a break in a circuit by disconnecting a wire from a battery or light bulb. Most circuits have a device called a switch. A switch allows you to open and close the circuit without disconnecting a wire. When you lift the lever on the switch, the circuit is open. The light turns off. When you lower the lever, the circuit is closed. The light turns on.

an open switch

3. **Explain** What happens to the movement of electric current when you open a switch?

The switch in this circuit is closed. Current flows through the circuit and lights the bulb.

4. **Illustrate** Draw an open circuit. Draw an arrow to show where there is a break in the circuit.

Go Green

Electricity Budget
List five ways you use electricity in your home. Draw or write the ways. Tell how to use less electricity for each way.

Conductors and Insulators

Why are wires used to build electric circuits? Wires are usually made of metal with a covering of plastic or rubber. Electric charge moves easily through metals such as copper, gold, silver, and aluminum. The metal part of wire carries electric current throughout a circuit.

A material through which electric charge moves easily is called a conductor. Metals are not the only conductors. For example, the mineral graphite is a conductor. Graphite is the material you write with in a pencil. Most of the water around us is also a strong conductor.

Some materials stop the movement of electric charge. These materials are called insulators. Rubber and plastic are kinds of insulators. Glass and wood are also insulators.

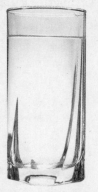

Pure water is a weak conductor. When chemicals such as salt are added to water, it becomes a strong conductor. Most water around us is a strong conductor.

6. Infer Where would you find water that is a strong conductor?

ocean

7. Compare Tell why metals, such as copper and silver, are good conductors.

5. Conclude Why do electric wires have a covering of plastic or rubber?

sof plople toch it then get shoc

Inside the plastic covering of a cord are metal wires.

80

Classify Conductors

You can use a circuit like the one below to investigate whether an object is a conductor. You touch the bare ends of the wires to the object. Does the bulb light up? If so, electric charge is moving through the object.

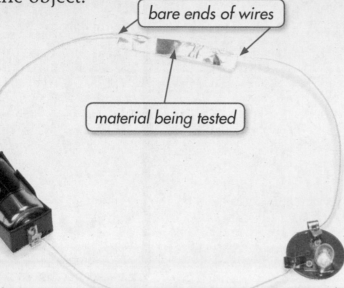

bare ends of wires

material being tested

8. Classify Suppose you tested a penny, a rubber eraser, and a paper clip. Which objects do you think are conductors? Why?

....

....

....

....

....

Got it?

9. Infer Workers who fix electrical equipment often use tools with parts made of plastic, rubber, or other insulators. Why does this make sense?

....

10. Explain When you turn on the switch on your classroom wall, the overhead lights go on. Explain why this happens. Use the term *closed circuit* or *open circuit*.

....

....

◐ **Stop!** I need help with ....

⏸ **Wait!** I have a question about ....

▶ **Go!** Now I know ....

How does heat cause motion?

Follow a Procedure

☐ **1.** Cut out the spiral.

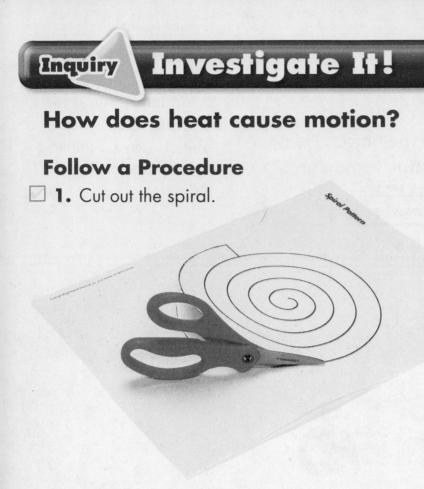

Materials

Spiral Pattern

scissors

tape

string

lamp

☐ **2.** Tape one end of the string to the middle of the spiral.

☐ **3.** **Predict** what will happen if you hold the spiral over the lamp before the bulb is turned on. **Record.**

☐ **4.** Predict what will happen if the bulb is turned on. Record.

Inquiry Skill
A **prediction** can be based on what you already know or what you observe.

Motion of Spiral		
	Predictions	**Observations**
Lamp off		
Lamp on		

5. Test your predictions.
Record your **observations.**

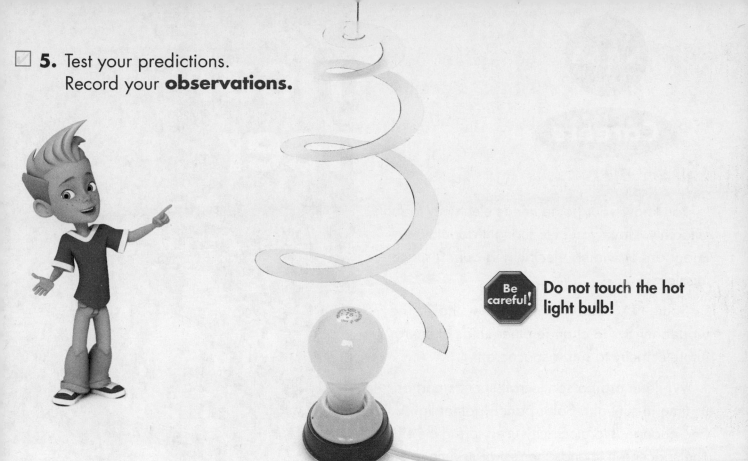

Be careful! Do not touch the hot light bulb!

Analyze and Conclude

6. Compare your **predictions** and **observations.**

....

....

....

7. Infer What caused the spiral to move?

....

....

8. UNLOCK THE BIG ? What forms of energy did you observe in your investigation?

....

....

....

Electrical Engineer

You know your home needs electricity to run smoothly. Have you ever thought about how important providing electricity is during space missions?

Some NASA electrical engineers have. They work on ways to change other kinds of energy into electricity to run a spacecraft.

While in orbit a spacecraft spends part of its time in sunlight. Solar panels gather light and change it to electricity used to run the ship. The spacecraft spends the rest of its time in the shadow of Earth, where there is no sunlight. How does it get electricity then?

Electrical engineers design generators that make electricity. One kind uses a heavy wheel called a flywheel. While in sunlight, motors make this wheel spin quickly. The kinetic energy from spinning is used to generate electricity while the spacecraft is in the dark.

UNLOCK THE BIG ? How could the work of electrical engineers change how you make electricity at your home?

....

....

....

....

The International Space Station has a complex electrical system. It functions because of the work of electrical engineers.

Vocabulary Smart Cards

energy
electrical energy
sound energy
potential energy
kinetic energy
wave
light energy
reflect
refract
absorb
thermal energy
volume
pitch
closed circuit
open circuit

Play a Game!

Choose a Vocabulary Smart Card.

Write a sentence using the vocabulary word. Draw a blank where the vocabulary word should be.

Have a partner fill in the blank with the correct vocabulary word.

Have your partner repeat with another card.

potential energy

energía potencial

kinetic energy

energía cinética

wave

onda

energy

energía

electrical energy

energía eléctrica

sound energy

energía sonora

the ability to do work or to cause change	stored energy
Write three other forms of this word.	Write two examples.
....	....
....	....
	....
	....
capacidad de hacer trabajo o causar cambios	energía almacenada

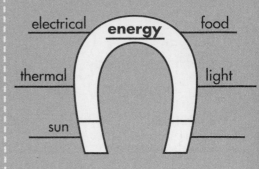

electrical   **energy**   food

thermal   light

sun

Make a Word Magnet!

Choose a vocabulary word and write it in the Word Magnet. Write the words that are related to it on the lines.

the movement of electric charges	energy of motion
Draw an example.	Write a sentence using this term.
	....
	....
	....
	....
el movimiento de cargas eléctricas	energía de movimiento

energy we can hear	a disturbance that carries energy from one point to another point
Draw an example.	Write another meaning of this word.
	....
	....
	....
energía que podemos oír	perturbación que lleva energía de un punto a otro

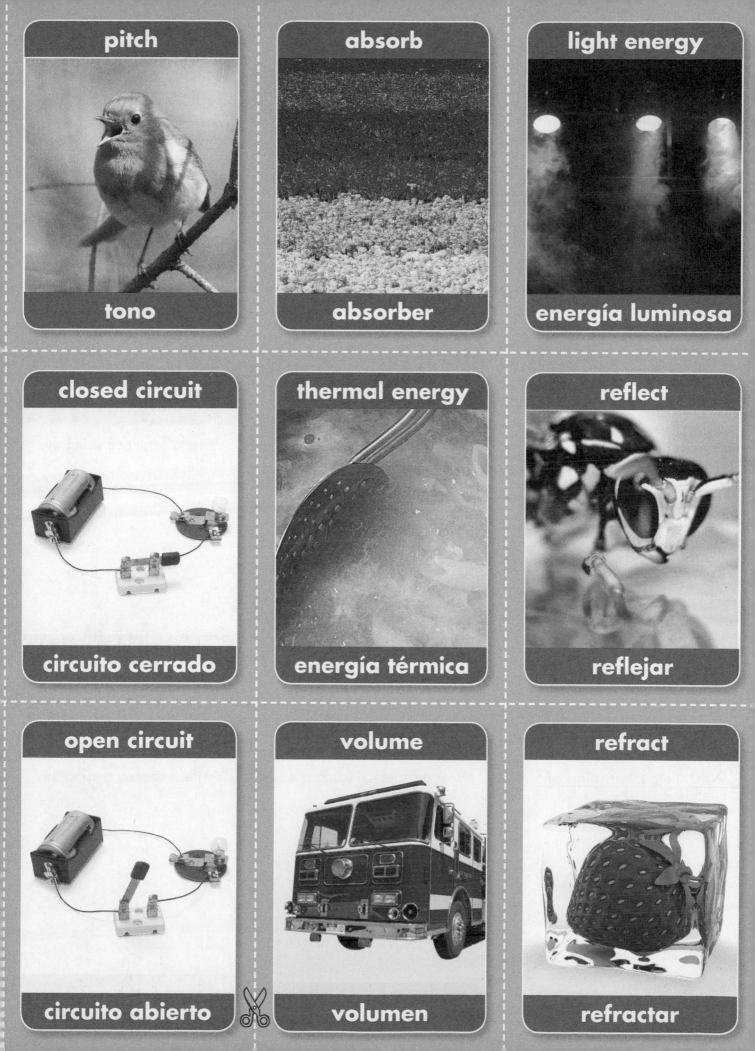

pitch	absorb	light energy
tono	absorber	energía luminosa

closed circuit	thermal energy	reflect
circuito cerrado	energía térmica	reflejar

open circuit	volume	refract
circuito abierto	volumen	refractar

energy we can see

Write two examples.

....

....

....

....

energía que podemos ver

to take in

Write a sentence using this word.

....

....

....

....

....

retener

how high or low a sound is

Write an example of a sound with a high pitch.

....

....

....

....

cuán agudo o grave es un sonido

to bounce off

Write a sentence using the noun form of this word.

....

....

....

....

hacer rebotar algo

the kinetic energy and potential energy of particles in matter

Write a sentence using this term.

....

....

....

energía cinética y energía potencial de las partículas que forman la materia

a circuit with no gaps or breaks

Write a sentence using this term.

....

....

....

....

circuito que no tiene rupturas ni interrupciones

to bend

Write three other forms of this word.

....

....

....

....

desviar o inclinar

how loud or soft a sound is

Write a sentence using this word.

....

....

....

....

cuán fuerte o suave es un sonido

a circuit with a broken path

Write a sentence using this term.

....

....

....

....

circuito que tiene una ruptura en su ruta

Lesson 1

What are some forms of energy?
- Energy is the ability to do work and cause change.
- Energy makes things move, change, or grow.
- People use many forms of energy every day.

Lesson 2

How does energy change form?
- Energy can change from one form to another.
- Energy of motion can be transferred.
- Some energy travels as waves.

Lesson 3

How do light and matter interact?
- Objects can reflect light evenly or unevenly.
- Some objects refract light.
- Some objects absorb some of the colors of light that hit them.

Lesson 4

What are heat and light energy?
- Things that give off light also give off heat.
- Heat affects the temperature of matter.
- Heat is produced when objects rub against each other.

Lesson 5

What is sound energy?
- Sound happens when matter vibrates.
- A sound's energy determines how loud or soft the volume is.
- A sound's pitch is how high or low the sound is.

Lesson 6

What is electrical energy?
- An electric charge can attract or repel.
- Electric current is the movement of an electric charge.
- An electric circuit is a path for electric current.

Lesson 1

What are some forms of energy?

1. **Determine** (Circle) the image that best shows kinetic energy.

2. **Analyze** What is one way that stored energy can change to become energy of motion?

....

....

....

....

....

Lesson 2

How does energy change form?

3. ⊙ **Cause and Effect** When you turn on an electric toothbrush, chemical energy in the battery changes to electrical energy. List two additional energy changes that happen as a result.

....

....

....

....

Lesson 3

How do light and matter interact?

4. **Vocabulary** A blue book _____ blue light that strikes it.
   A. colors
   B. absorbs
   C. reflects
   D. shadows

5. **Describe** Why do shadows form behind some objects?

....

....

....

Lesson 4

What are heat and light energy?

6. **Communicate** How are the sun, a campfire, and a street lamp alike?

7. **Describe** How could you use two objects to produce heat?

Lesson 5

What is sound energy?

8. **Predict** A bell vibrates quickly when you ring it. Will the bell have a high pitch or a low pitch? Explain.

Lesson 6

What is electrical energy?

9. **Write About It** Explain the movement of electricity through a closed electric circuit made of a battery, wire, and a bulb.

10. **APPLY THE BIG ?** **How can energy change?**

Think about a trip to the grocery store. What forms of energy can you experience? Explain how this energy can change form.

Read each question and choose the best answer.

1 A car moves when the stored energy in gasoline changes to kinetic energy. What is this stored energy called?

A gravity

B chemical energy

C thermal energy

D light energy

2 Which word describes the pitch of a guitar string vibrating slowly?

A loud

B low

C high

D soft

3 What is an electric circuit?

A movement of electric energy

B an outlet you plug a cord into

C the path that electric current flows through

D a machine used to change sunlight into electricity

4 Jack's mom lit some candles for the dinner table. Which form of energy does the fire from a candle release?

A mechanical

B sound

C light

D chemical

5 A banana is the color yellow because _____.

A it absorbs the color yellow

B it refracts the color yellow

C it reflects all colors except yellow

D it absorbs all colors except yellow

6 How is the path of light hitting a mirror different from the path of light going through a water droplet?

....

....

....

SavvasRealize.com

Electrical Energy Conservation

Go Green!

We use electrical energy every day. We use electrical energy to light our homes and run appliances, such as televisions and refrigerators. Most electrical energy comes from nonrenewable sources. After a nonrenewable source of energy is used up, it cannot be replaced. Most electricity in the United States is made from the burning of coal. Coal is a nonrenewable source of energy.

Scientists are developing different sources of energy to use instead of nonrenewable sources. For example, scientists are working to develop solar energy and wind energy. Meanwhile, we can reduce the amount of energy we use by following the tips on this page.

Use a thermostat with a timer.

Use compact fluorescent light bulbs.

Turn off lights when leaving a room.

Suggest Write two more ways you can conserve electrical energy in your home.

Materials

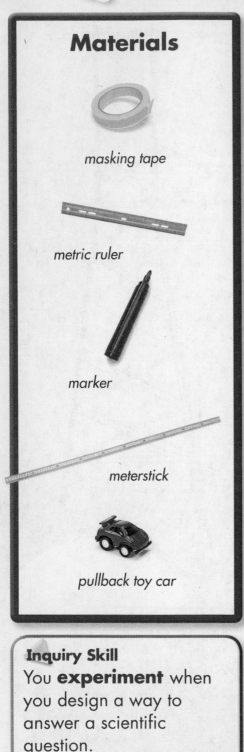

masking tape

metric ruler

marker

meterstick

pullback toy car

Inquiry Skill
You **experiment** when you design a way to answer a scientific question.

How does energy affect the distance a toy car travels?

Potential energy is stored energy. The more you pull back a toy car, the more potential energy it has.

Ask a question.

How does a car's potential energy affect the distance it travels?

State a hypothesis.

1. Write a **hypothesis** by circling one choice and finishing the sentence.
   If a car's potential energy increases, then the distance it travels will
   (a) *increase*
   (b) *decrease*
   (c) *stay the same*
   because

....

....

....

Identify and control variables.

2. When you **experiment,** you need to change just one **variable.** Everything else must remain the same. What should stay the same? List two examples.

....

....

3. Tell the one change you will make.

....

....

Design your test.

☐ **4.** Draw how you will set up your test.

☐ **5.** List your steps in the order you will do them.

Do your test.

☐ **6.** Follow the steps you wrote.

☐ **7.** Make sure to **measure** carefully. **Record** your results in the table.

☐ **8.** Scientists repeat their tests to improve their accuracy. Repeat your test if time allows.

First see how far the car travels. Then decide if you will measure with a metric ruler or a meterstick.

Work Like a Scientist

Scientists work with other scientists. They compare their methods and results. Talk with your classmates. Compare your methods and results.

Collect and record your data.

☐ **9.** Fill in the chart.

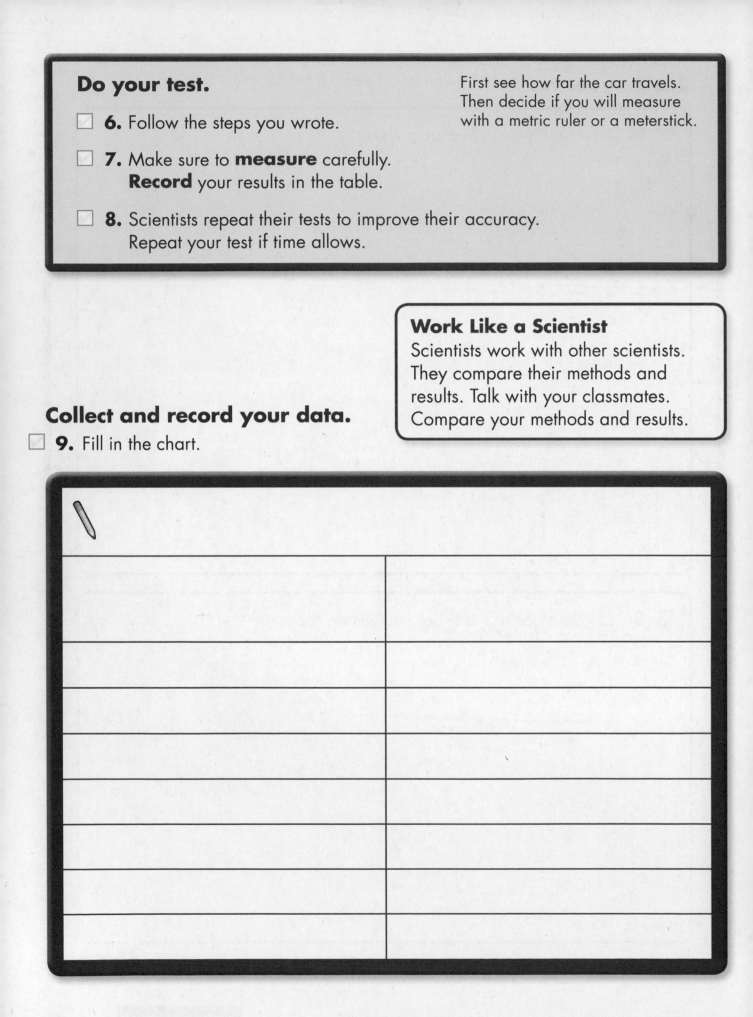

Interpret your data.

☐ **10.** Use your data to make a bar graph.

☐ **11.** Look at your graph closely. Did the distance you pulled the car back affect the distance it traveled? Identify the evidence you used to answer the question.

....

....

State your conclusion.

12. Communicate your conclusion. How does increasing the toy car's potential energy affect the distance it travels? Compare your **hypothesis** with your results. Compare your results with others.

Technology Tools
Your teacher may wish you to use a computer (with the right software) or a graphing calculator to help collect, organize, analyze, and present your data. These tools can help you make tables, charts, and graphs.

....

....

....

....

Performance-Based Assessment

Use Light Energy

Use a shallow pan filled with water and a piece of clear plastic wrap to show how the energy from sunlight can change matter. Set the pan in a place that receives direct sunlight. Cover the pan with the clear plastic wrap. Write a prediction of how the energy of the sun will affect the liquid water.

After an hour, observe the pan. Write a description of what you see.

- Do your observations support your prediction?
- What would happen if you removed the clear plastic wrap from the pan?

Toy Power

Choose a wind-up toy. Observe the toy as it works. Look for ways the toy transfers energy from one part to another.

- How does your wind-up affect the distance the toy travels?
- How might some kinetic energy be transferred from one part to another

Science and Engineering Practices

1. Ask a question or define a problem.
2. Develop and use models.
3. Plan and carry out investigations.
4. Analyze and interpret data.
5. Use math and computational thinking.
6. Construct explanations or design solutions.
7. Engage in argument from evidence.
8. Obtain, evaluate, and communicate information.

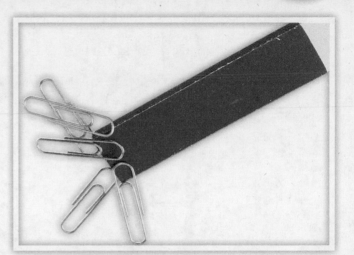

Solve a Problem

Have you ever used a magnet to hang a picture on your refrigerator? Magnets have many uses in everyday life. They can be used to make a door latch. Work in a small group to design a door latch. Your design should use magnets to keep a door shut. Draw your design. Then build and test it.

- How well did your design work?
- What improvements might make your design work better?

Plan an Investigation

Work with a partner to investigate balanced and unbalanced forces on an object. Remember that balanced forces work together and make no change in motion. Unbalanced forces cause an object at rest to move. Identify the object you will use in your investigation. Ask a question about the force you will test. Use the following questions as a guide.

- What happens when you push the object?
- Push on one side of the object, while your partner pushes on the other side of the object. Make sure the force with which you are pushing is the same strength. What happens when you both push on opposite sides of the object?
- State a conclusion based on your observations.

How can trees live in Blue Cypress Lake?

Plants

 Try It! How do plants change?

 STEM Activity Watch It Grow!

Investigate It! How does water move through celery?

This lake is in southeastern Florida. Cypress trees can live and grow in slow-moving water.

 Predict How can cypress trees live and grow in water?

....

....

....

THE BIG ? How do plants grow and change?

How do plants change?

Materials

plastic bag

pinto beans

tape

wet paper towels

☐ **1.** Put a wet paper towel in a plastic resealable bag. Add three pinto beans between the towel and the bag.

☐ **2.** Seal the bag shut. Tape it to a window.

☐ **3. Collect Data** Draw and **record** your **observations** every other day.

Data Table	
Day	**Observations**

☐ **4.** Choose a **variable** to change when the seeds grow roots. For example, change the direction of the bag, the amount of light the bag receives, or the temperature inside the bag.

☐ **5. Predict** how your plants will change.

....

....

Inquiry Skill
As you observe the growing plants, you **collect data** to show how they change.

Explain Your Results

6. Communicate Explain how your plants reacted to the change.

....

....

⊙ Text Features

Text features, such as headings, highlighting, pictures, and captions, give you clues about what you will read.

A **heading** tells what the content that follows is about.

A **picture** shows something you will read about.

A **caption** tells specific information about a picture.

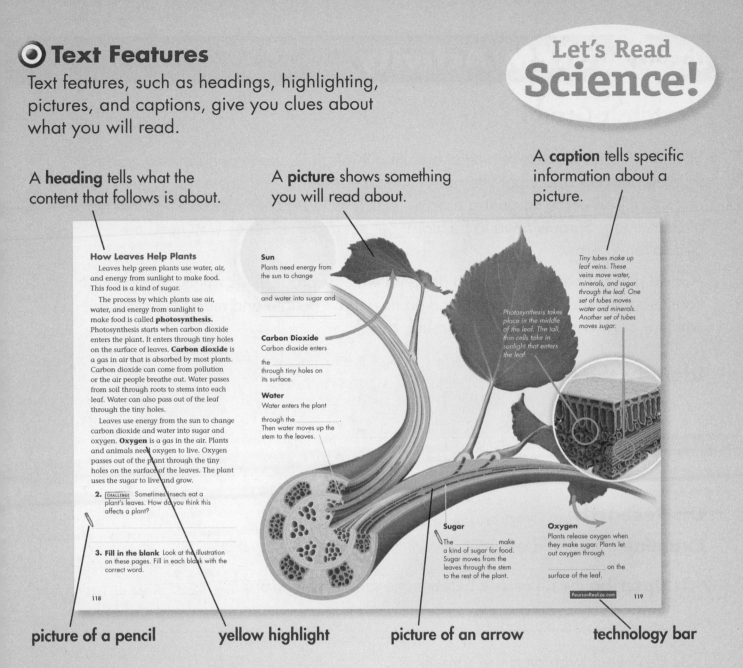

picture of a pencil   yellow highlight   picture of an arrow   technology bar

Practice It!

Read the text features in the chart below. Find the text features in the textbook pages shown above. Write a clue that each one gives you about the content.

Text feature	Clue
yellow highlight	
picture of a pencil	
technology bar	

Watch It Grow!

Sprouting is the process of a seed breaking through its seed coat and beginning to grow. Sprouts are full of vitamins, minerals, proteins, and enzymes. Water is an important part of the sprouting process, which includes continual soaking, rinsing, and draining. Sprouts need to be moist, but not drowned. They also need air circulation to grow.

A local nursery has asked you to design a way to sprout seeds without using soil. Your seed sprouter will be evaluated on how large (length and mass) the sprouts within it grow during a five-day period.

Identify the Problem

☐ **1.** What is your task? _____

_____

Do Research

Examine a seed and a sprout.

☐ **2. Describe** the difference between the seed and the sprout. _____

_____

☐ **3.** How would you describe sprouting? _____

_____

Before you sprout your seeds, you need to soak them. Gather five seeds and a paper cup. Place the seeds in the cup and half-fill the cup with water. Soak them for at least two hours.

☐ **4. Record** your observations of the soaked seeds. _____

_____

Go to the materials station(s). Pick up each material one at a time. Think about how it may or may not be useful in your design. Leave the materials where they are.

☐ **5.** What are your design constraints? _____

_____

Develop Possible Solutions

☐ **6. List** two different ways you could combine some of the materials to solve the problem. _____

_____

_____

Choose One Solution

☐ **7. Describe** your seed sprouter and how you will build it. _____

_____

_____

_____

Your seeds will need to be watered, rinsed, and drained every day.

☐ **8. Describe** your daily procedure for tending to your seeds. _____

_____

_____

☐ **9. List** the materials that you will need. _____

_____

Design and Construct a Prototype

Gather your materials plus your soaked seeds. Take the appropriate measurements of your materials. Build your seed sprouter and place your seeds in it. When your sprouter is completed, including having treated the seeds with water, record the mass of your sprouter and seeds in the table below in the row labeled "Day 0."

☐ **10. Record** the design plans for your prototype. ✎ _____

_____

_____

_____

Test the Prototype

Test your seed sprouter. Place it someplace warm, but not in direct sunlight. Follow your daily procedure for five days. Each day, write your observations, the mass of the sprouter after your daily procedure, and the average length of your sprouts in a table like the one started below.

☐ **11.**

Day	Observations	Mass after daily procedure (g)	Average length of sprouts (cm)
0			
1			
2			
3			
4			
5			

Communicate Results

Present your sprouter, your procedure, and your table to your class. Prepare your presentation by answering the following questions.

☐**12.** What are the most notable observations from your table? _____

_____

_____

☐**13.** What did you notice about the weight of your sprouter before and after your daily procedure and throughout the week? _____

_____

_____

☐**14.** How long are your ending sprouts? _____

Evaluate and Redesign

☐**15. Explain** how you would change your sprouter or your procedure to make it more effective. If you would not change anything, explain why. _____

_____

_____

_____

_____

How can you classify plants?

Tell which characteristics you think can help you classify each plant.

MY PLANET DIARY

Science Stats

Statistics are pieces of information that can help us answer questions. Statistics can help us determine the oldest known living plant. In 2004, scientists in Sweden discovered tree roots that are about 9,550 years old. The tree they found is called a Norway spruce. It is only 4 meters tall. The part of the tree we see is not very old. The roots of the tree are old. Each time the tree above ground dies, a new tree starts growing from the roots.

Which trees have lived above ground the longest? The oldest trees above ground are most likely bristlecone pine trees. One bristlecone pine tree in California is almost 5,000 years old.

bristlecone pine tree

What is the oldest part of the oldest tree in the world? roost

Underline the statistic that tells about the age of the Norway spruce.

I will know how to classify plants into major groups based on the physical characteristics of the plants.

Words to Know

flowering plant
spore

Classify Plants

At grocery stores, people sort food into groups. This helps shoppers find the right foods. Scientists classify living things, such as plants, in a similar way. Scientists classify plants by sorting them into groups. This helps us identify plants.

You can classify plants into groups by color, size, and shape. You can classify plants by how they reproduce, or produce offspring. You can also classify plants by their flowers or seeds.

1. ◉ **Text Features** Look at the text features on this page. Identify one text feature and the clue it gives you.

Text feature	Clue
Heading	It tells me I will be learning how plants are classified.

2. **Classify** These water lilies have large leaves that float on water. What is another way you can classify these water lilies?

by color
scop size

Flowering Plants

One way to classify plants is by whether a plant produces flowers. An orange tree and a cactus do not look alike, but they are both flowering plants. **Flowering plants** are plants with seeds that grow flowers. Orange trees grow flowers with seeds. These seeds can grow into new plants.

There are different groups of flowering plants. Each group has different kinds of roots, stems, leaves, and flowers. For example, dogwood trees have a stiff, woody stem. This stem helps dogwoods grow tall. Iris plants do not have a woody stem. Iris plants grow closer to the ground.

Leaves fall off dogwood trees in the fall. The leaves grow back in the spring. Trees that lose and grow leaves in this way are called *deciduous* trees.

3. Circle the words that tell about flowering plants.

4. ◎ **Text Features** Why does the word *deciduous* look different from other words on this page?

....

....

Dogwood trees can grow taller than 6 meters. Dogwoods produce flowers. These flowers make seeds. The seeds can grow into new dogwoods.

Groups of Flowering Plants

One kind of flowering plant is the magnolia tree. It produces colorful flowers. Some magnolias are deciduous. Others keep their leaves all winter. Magnolia trees have a strong, woody stem. This stem helps magnolias grow tall. They range in height from shorter than 3 meters to taller than 20 meters.

Iris plants grow a long, thin stem and leaves. This stem allows iris plants to bend when winds blow against them. Iris plants lose both stem and leaves in the fall. The roots live through the winter. The stem and leaves grow back from the roots in the spring. During the spring, iris plants produce colorful flowers.

Rosebushes are another kind of flowering plant. They grow as small shrubs or long vines. Rose stems are strong and have sharp prickles. These stems allow rosebushes to grow large. The prickles protect the plant. Most rose flowers are colorful.

5. ◉ **Compare and Contrast** Look at the flowering plants on this page. How are they alike and different?

....

....

6. **Evaluate** What is an advantage of a thin stem?

....

Nonflowering Plants

Some kinds of plants do not grow flowers to make seeds. *Coniferous* trees grow cones instead of flowers to make seeds. Seeds grow inside each cone. The seeds fall out of the cones and down to the ground. These seeds can make new plants.

The leaves of most coniferous trees look like needles or brushes. Most coniferous trees do not lose all their leaves in the fall. Pine and spruce trees are types of coniferous trees.

7. **Word Structure** The word *coniferous* is made up of the base word *conifer,* which means "cone-bearing," and the suffix *-ous,* which means "full of." Why do you think trees that grow cones are called coniferous trees?

....

....

....

8. **Hypothesize** Write why you think these cones have scales all around them.

....

....

....

....

cone

Spores

Ferns and mosses are two kinds of nonflowering plants that do not make seeds. They reproduce by making spores. A **spore** is a small cell that grows into a new plant. Mosses produce spores at the end of their stalks. Ferns produce spores on the undersides of their leaves.

Mosses and ferns reproduce by making spores.

spore

fern

moss

9. Distinguish How are spores and seeds different from cones?

....

....

....

....

10. Classify Look at the three plants to the right. How would you classify each plant?

....

....

....

....

Rain-Forest Plants

Rain forests are places where many different types of flowering and nonflowering plants grow. Some flowering and nonflowering plants produce flowers, seeds, cones, or spores. Different types of plants grow at each level of the forest.

11. Categorize What kinds of plants do you see in this picture?

....

....

....

12. Classify Find one plant in this rain forest. Describe two physical characteristics of the plant. How would you classify this plant?

....

....

At-Home Lab

Plants You See
Find a plant near where you live. Draw a picture of it. Write down three features of the plant. Bring your picture to class. Post your picture and compare it with other pictures. Then, classify the plant as flowering or nonflowering.

Got it?

13. Classify How would you classify an unknown plant that does not have flowers?

....

....

14. Explain Think about what you learned about plants in this lesson. How do we classify living things?

....

....

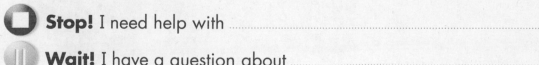

⬛ **Stop!** I need help with ....

⏸ **Wait!** I have a question about ....

▶ **Go!** Now I know ....

Lesson 2

How do plants use leaves to make food?

Envision It!

Tell how you think leaves help plants.

Inquiry **Explore It!**

How does sunlight affect plant survival?

Materials

plant

foil

☐ 1. **Observe** a green leaf on a plant.
Gently fold a piece of foil completely around the whole leaf.
Be sure the foil cannot fall off.

☐ 2. Place the plant near a sunny window.
Wait one week.

☐ 3. Take off the foil. Observe. Compare what you observed before and after the leaf was covered.

Be careful! Wash your hands when finished.

....

....

Explain Your Results

4. **Infer** What do you think happened to the leaf? Explain.

....

....

116

UNLOCK THE BIG ?

I will know that leaves help plants live, grow, and make food.

Words to Know

photosynthesis
carbon dioxide
oxygen

What Plants Need

Plants need food, air, water, and space to live and grow. Many plants live and grow in soil. The four main parts of a flowering plant are leaves, roots, stems, and flowers. In different kinds of plants, these parts may look alike. They may also look different.

Unlike animals, plants make their own food. Plants need energy from the sun to make food. Food is made in a plant's leaves, using the sun's energy. This food helps plants grow.

1. ◉ **Text Features** Look at the text features on this page. Identify one text feature and the clue it gives you.

Bromeliad plants are like other plants. They use energy from the sun to make food.

Text feature	Clue
Heading	It tells me that I'll read about what plants need.

How Leaves Help Plants

Leaves help green plants use water, air, and energy from sunlight to make food. This food is a kind of sugar.

The process by which plants use air, water, and energy from sunlight to make food is called **photosynthesis.** Photosynthesis starts when carbon dioxide enters the plant. It enters through tiny holes on the surface of leaves. **Carbon dioxide** is a gas in air that is absorbed by most plants. Carbon dioxide can come from pollution or the air people breathe out. Water passes from soil through roots to stems into each leaf. Water can also pass out of the leaf through the tiny holes.

Leaves use energy from the sun to change carbon dioxide and water into sugar and oxygen. **Oxygen** is a gas in the air. Plants and animals need oxygen to live. Oxygen passes out of the plant through the tiny holes on the surface of the leaves. The plant uses the sugar to live and grow.

2. CHALLENGE Sometimes insects eat a plant's leaves. How do you think this affects a plant?

3. **Fill in the blank** Look at the illustration on these pages. Fill in each blank with the correct word.

Sun

Plants need energy from the sun to change

air

and water into sugar and

food

.

Carbon Dioxide

Carbon dioxide enters the leaves through tiny holes on its surface.

Water

Water enters the plant through the root . Then water moves up the stem to the leaves.

Tiny tubes make up leaf veins. These veins move water, minerals, and sugar through the leaf. One set of tubes moves water and minerals. Another set of tubes moves sugar.

Photosynthesis takes place in the middle of the leaf. The tall, thin cells take in sunlight that enters the leaf.

Sugar

The _____Lesve_____ make a kind of sugar for food. Sugar moves from the leaves through the stem to the rest of the plant.

Oxygen

Plants release oxygen when they make sugar. Plants let out oxygen through _____Thv_____ on the surface of the leaf.

Other Ways Leaves Help Plants

Leaves help plants in other ways. Leaves can help plants control the amount of water in the plant. If plants have too much water, leaves let some water out through the tiny holes on their surface. A plant can also stop water loss by closing these holes. Plants in dry environments may have wax- or fuzz-coated leaves. This coating helps keep in water. The stonecrop succulent has waxy-coated leaves to keep in water.

Plant leaves can also protect the plant from being eaten. Leaves can be poisonous, sharp, or tough to chew. Sharp leaves may have spines. Hungry animals may not eat a cactus plant with sharp leaves.

4. **Identify** List two ways a leaf can help a plant.

....

....

....

At-Home Lab

Leaves and Air
Place a clear sandwich bag over leaves on a tree branch. Observe the bag for two days. Tell what you see. Explain your observations.

stonecrop succulent

5. Draw Think about a plant in your neighborhood. Draw a leaf from this plant. Describe to a partner how you think the leaf helps the plant.

Poison ivy is a woody vine. It is found in forests across North America. Poison ivy causes an itchy rash, blistering, and burning of the skin.

 Got it?

6. List five things plants need to make food.

....

....

7. Think about what you learned about plant leaves in this lesson. How do plants grow and change?

....

....

⬛ **Stop!** I need help with ....

⏸ **Wait!** I have a question about ....

▶ **Go!** Now I know ....

Lesson 3

How do plants use roots and stems to grow?

Envision It!

Circle, in different colors, the roots, stems, and leaves of these mangrove trees.

Inquiry **Explore It!**

Which way will roots grow?

☐ **1.** Fold and place the towels in the cup. Wet the towels.

☐ **2.** Place the seeds in different directions.

☐ **3. Observe** the seeds every day for one week. Watch the way the roots grow.

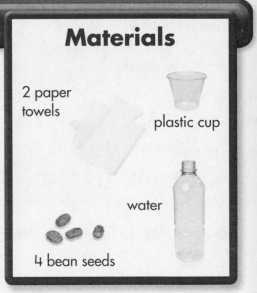

Materials

2 paper towels

plastic cup

water

4 bean seeds

Explain Your Results

4. Infer Write what you learned about the way roots grow.

....

....

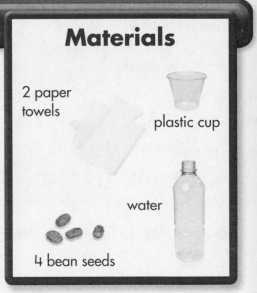

I will know how roots and stems take in, transport, and store water and nutrients the plant needs to grow.

Word to Know

nutrient

How Roots Help Plants

Look at all the roots of the fir tree in the picture. Plants need roots and stems to take in and move materials a plant needs to live and grow.

The root system of a plant is often below the ground. You usually cannot see it. Roots keep the plant stable in the ground. Roots store food made by the plant's leaves. Roots also take in water and materials called minerals from the soil. The plant gets nutrients from the water and minerals. A **nutrient** is any material needed by living things for energy, growth, and repair. Plants need nutrients to live and grow.

1. **Determine** Look at the picture of the fir tree roots. What would happen if the plant's roots did not store food?

   ....

   ....

2. **Underline** three ways that roots help plants.

Fir tree roots take in nutrients from the soil.

Types of Roots

Have you ever eaten a carrot? Many plants have one large root called a *taproot*. Carrots and dandelions are examples of taproots. Taproots grow deep into the soil toward Earth's center due to gravity. Taproots take in water and nutrients from the soil. The roots also store food made by the plant.

In some plants, such as grass and pine trees, roots spread out in many directions. This type of root is called a *fibrous root*. Like taproots, fibrous roots store food, take in water and nutrients, and grow toward Earth's center due to gravity. Fibrous roots of the same plant are all about the same size. Some may grow longer than taproots. Fibrous roots also grow close to the surface to take in water after it rains.

root hair

3. **Fill in the blank** Look at the illustration of the root. Fill in each blank with the correct word.

_____ enters the root through the root hairs. All roots have root hairs. The more root hairs a plant has, the more water the plant can take in. Roots with many root hairs grow far into the soil to

reach water and _____.

4. CHALLENGE Which type of roots could help a plant more in a dry area—a fibrous root or a taproot?

5. **Analyze** What is the role of the pumpkin's stem?

....

....

....

....

....

....

pumpkin stem

How Stems Help Plants

Stems support the leaves, flowers, and fruits of plants. Stems often grow up toward the light, their main source of energy. Most plant stems have tiny tubes that move water and minerals from the roots to the leaves. Other tubes move food from the leaves to the stems and roots.

Some stems are thin and grow along the surface of the ground. For example, the stem of a pumpkin can grow roots and a new plant. Other stems, called vines, grow parts that wrap around objects that support the plant. Ivy is a vine that grows on the ground or on buildings.

Lightning Lab

Look at Plant Roots
Work with an adult. Cut a carrot in half. Look at the cross section. List what structures you see. Try this with another root. On the same paper, list the structures of the other root.

Types of Stems

Plant stems come in many different shapes, sizes, and colors. Some stems grow below ground. Other stems such as this cactus stem grow above ground. Notice how thick cactus stems can grow. Cactus stems swell up to store water. As the cactus uses stored water due to heat, the stems shrink. Cactus stems are thick and waxy. This keeps them from losing water. Cactus stems help them survive in a desert.

6. ◉ **Text Features** Which text features on this page help you understand different types of stems?

....

....

....

More water makes stems swell outward.

Water from roots is stored in this area.

The spines growing out of this cactus stem are a special kind of leaf.

Water from roots moves up these tubes.

Parts of some stems grow below ground. Have you eaten a potato? You eat the part of the stem that stored food below ground. Stems that grow below ground can make new stems from buds, such as the potato's "eyes." These buds grow up out of the ground and become new plants.

7. **Compare** Look at the cactus stem and potato. How do these stems help each plant?

....

....

....

....

Got it?

8. **Hypothesize** How could a plant grow in soil without many minerals?

....

....

9. **UNLOCK THE BIG ?** Why are roots and stems important to the growth of a plant?

....

....

⬛ **Stop!** I need help with ....

⏸ **Wait!** I have a question about ....

▶ **Go!** Now I know ....

Lesson 4

How do plants use flowers or cones to reproduce?

Envision It!

Circle what is helping these plants make new plants.

Inquiry **Explore It!**

What is inside a seed?

☐ **1.** Split your seed in half.

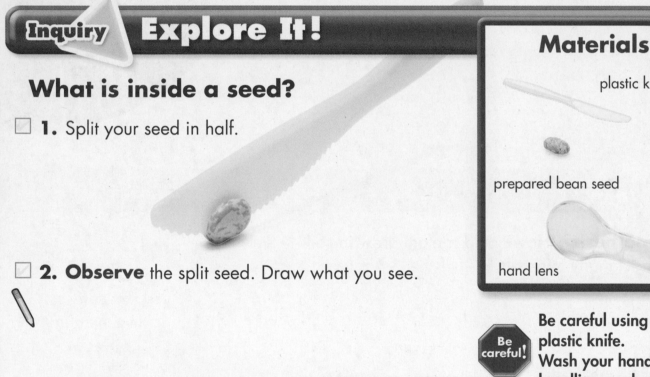

☐ **2. Observe** the split seed. Draw what you see.

Materials

plastic knife

prepared bean seed

hand lens

Be careful! Be careful using the plastic knife. Wash your hands after handling seeds.

Explain Your Results

3. Infer Where do you think a tiny young plant gets the food it needs to grow?

....

....

Reproduction

Most plants make seeds that grow into new plants. Some plants grow stems or roots that grow into new plants. Plants can reproduce both ways. When plants **reproduce,** they make more of the same kind. For example, maple trees produce seeds. These seeds can grow into new maple trees.

Each seed carries information from the parent plants. The seed uses this information and food stored from the parent plant in the seed to grow into a new plant. The new plant will be like its parents. After seeds are produced, they may scatter or move away from the parent plant. This gives the new plant more room to grow.

1. **Predict** What may happen if seeds do not scatter?

2. **Determine** Each seed in the picture below has a tiny parachute. How do you think these parachutes help the seeds scatter?

seed with parachute

Parts of a Flower

Flowering plants grow flowers that make seeds. Flowers have different parts. One part makes pollen. Another part, the petals, attracts bees and other animals to the flower. Animals or wind can **pollinate,** or carry pollen to, another flower. Pollination happens when animals or wind move pollen to the part of the flower that makes seeds. After pollination, seeds form near the center of the flower. Another part, fruit, often grows around the seed to protect it. A peach is an example of a fruit.

3. ⊙ **Text Features** Tell what these captions helped you learn about plant reproduction.

4. Summarize What is the function of one part of a flower?

Pollen sticks to the bodies of bees as bees look for food. Bees can carry this pollen to the part of another flower that makes seeds.

A flower's colorful petals attract insects and other animals that pollinate the flower.

The tip of this part of the flower makes pollen.

Pollen from this part of the plant helps form seeds.

seed

seed coat

developing plant leaf

seed leaf

seed germinating

How Seeds Grow

Seeds have different shapes, sizes, and colors. All seeds have the same parts. Every seed has material inside it that can grow into a new plant. The seed is covered by a seed coat. The seed coat protects this material. Many seeds have one seed leaf or two seed leaves. As the tiny plant grows, it uses food from the seed.

Seeds need air, the right amount of water, and the right temperature to **germinate,** or begin to grow. With the right conditions, the young plant, or seedling, germinates. The seedling uses food stored in the seed to grow.

As the seedling grows, it grows out of the soil. Leaves grow from the stem. The leaves use sunlight to make sugar. The plant uses the sugar for food. The seedling can grow into an adult plant that has flowers. The flowers are pollinated and new seeds form. If these new seeds germinate, they can grow into new plants. Then the cycle begins again.

5. [CHALLENGE] Look at the illustration of the seed. Why do you think the seed coat is important?

....

....

....

Go Green

Food and Energy
Energy and resources are needed to grow food. The food must be moved from the farm to the store. This also uses energy. Think of ways you can avoid wasting food. Make a list. Share your list with your classmates.

How Cones Help Plants

Cones are made by conifer plants. Conifer plants grow cones instead of flowers to make seeds. Conifers make two types of cones. One cone is a small pollen cone. The other cone is a large seed cone. Wind blows pollen from small pollen cones to large seed cones. When pollen sticks to the large seed cones, seeds begin to grow inside. A seed grows under each scale of the seed cone. When the seeds are fully developed, they float to the ground. If conditions are right, each seed can grow into a new plant.

First, wind blows pollen from these small cones to larger cones on other trees.

Next, seeds begin to grow inside the cones.

6. Describe What happens after the seed in a cone is fully developed?

....

....

7. State Write a caption for the photo below.

....

....

....

....

Elapsed Time

If you plant a green bean seed, when can you eat green beans? You can eat them when fruit ripens. Different plants have different lengths of time from seed to fruit. Use the table and calendars to answer the questions.

1 Solve If you plant cucumber seeds on May 21, when can you eat cucumbers?

2 Solve If you eat ripe tomatoes on July 29, when were the seeds planted?

Days from Seed to Fruit	
green bean seeds	58 days
cucumber seeds	55 days
tomato seeds	59 days

Got it?

8. Analyze What role do flowers play in plant reproduction?

....

....

9. Think about what you learned in this lesson. How do plants grow and change?

....

....

⬜ **Stop!** I need help with ....

⏸ **Wait!** I have a question about ....

▶ **Go!** Now I know ....

Lesson 5

What are the life cycles of some plants?

Write the numbers 1, 2, 3, or 4 to show the sequence in the life of this tomato plant.

MY PLANET DIARY

FunFact

The titan arum is a plant that produces a very large flower. The titan arum begins life as a seed. Each year the plant develops a single large leaf. The leaf produces food for the plant. After the leaf dies, the plant remains inactive for a few months. Then a new leaf forms.

When the titan arum is mature, or fully grown, it produces a flower. The flower is typically 1.5 meters tall. That's probably taller than you are! The biggest flowers can grow over 3 meters tall. The flower gives off a foul smell. This smell attracts insects.

Why do you think the titan arum needs to attract insects?

The titan arum grows on the island of Sumatra, in Indonesia. Here, the flower has opened.

....

Plant Life Cycles

Living things change during their lives. Most living things begin their lives small and then grow larger. They may develop certain features as they change into adults. They reproduce to make more living things of the same kind. Eventually, living things die. The stages through which a living thing passes during its life are called a **life cycle.**

Most plants go through similar stages during their life cycles. But plant life cycles can differ in important ways. For example, plants reproduce in different ways. Most plants make seeds that can grow into new plants. Some plants reproduce by making spores instead of seeds. Plants that reproduce in different ways have different life cycles.

1. ⊙ **Text Features** ⟨Circle⟩ three text features on this page.

Every acorn contains a seed. The seed can grow into a new oak tree. Most oak trees grow for at least 20 years before making seeds.

Life Cycle of a Flowering Plant

A pumpkin plant is a kind of flowering plant. The life cycle of a pumpkin plant has several stages, as shown in the diagram.

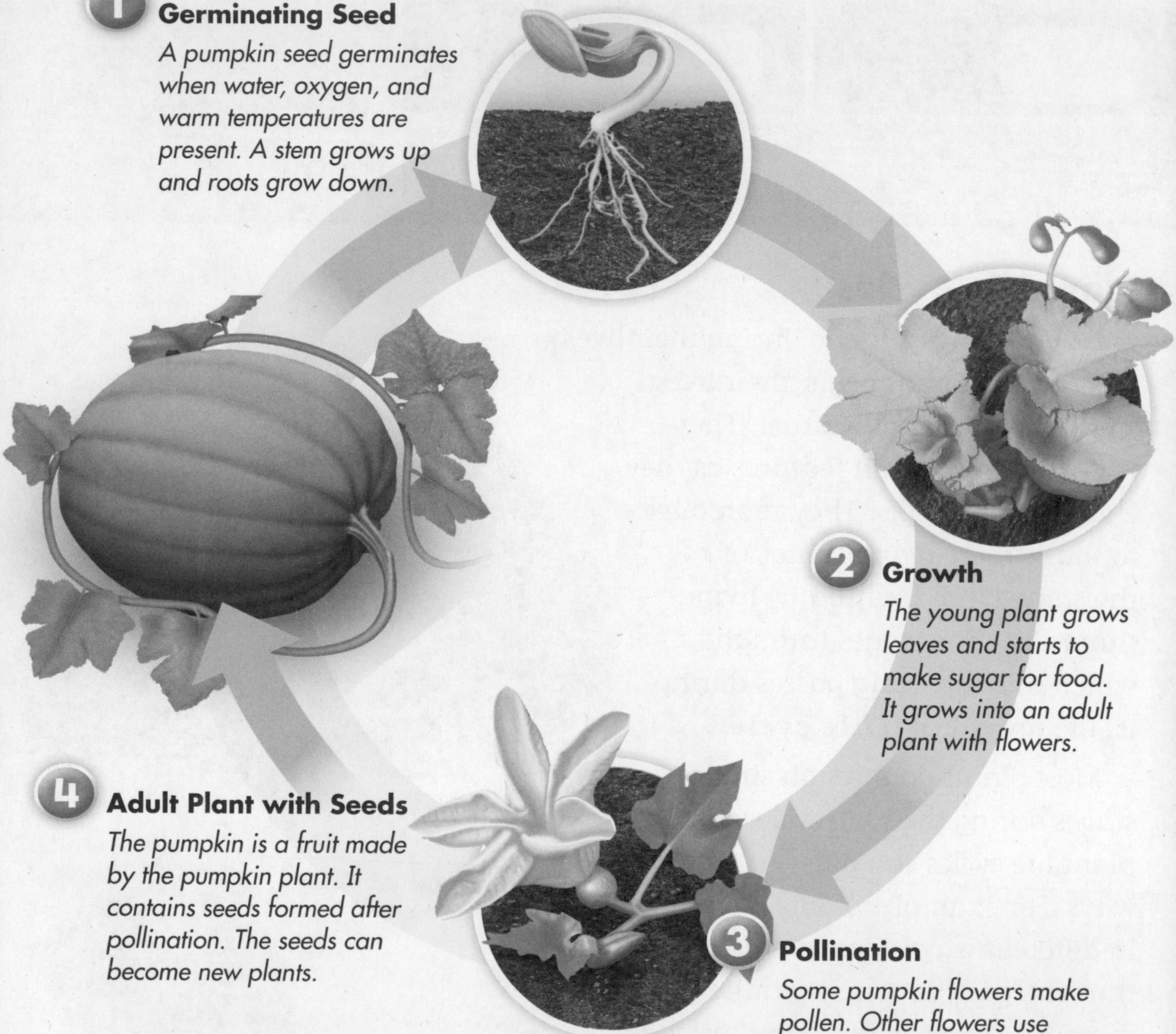

1 **Germinating Seed**

A pumpkin seed germinates when water, oxygen, and warm temperatures are present. A stem grows up and roots grow down.

2 **Growth**

The young plant grows leaves and starts to make sugar for food. It grows into an adult plant with flowers.

3 **Pollination**

Some pumpkin flowers make pollen. Other flowers use that pollen to make seeds. Pollination happens when pollen moves from one pumpkin flower to another.

4 **Adult Plant with Seeds**

The pumpkin is a fruit made by the pumpkin plant. It contains seeds formed after pollination. The seeds can become new plants.

2. Infer In stage 3, what likely moves pollen from one flower to another?

....

....

Life Cycle of a Conifer Plant

Pine trees are conifers. Conifer plants grow cones instead of flowers to make seeds.

1 **Germinating Seed**

To germinate, a pine tree seed needs water, oxygen, and warm temperatures. A seedling grows from the germinated seed.

4 **Adult Plant with Seeds**

Seeds develop in the seed cones. The seeds fall to the ground when the cones open. The seeds can become new plants.

2 *Over many years, the pine seedling grows into a tall adult tree. The tree makes small pollen cones and larger seed cones.*

3 *Small pollen cones make pollen. Wind carries the pollen to the large cones, where seeds are made.*

3. ⊙ **Text Features** Compare the two life cycles shown on these pages. Then, in the blank spaces, write titles for stage 2 and stage 3 in the life cycle of the pine tree.

Draw a Life Cycle
Work with an adult. Put potting soil in a flowerpot. Plant two bean seeds. Put the pot in a sunny place and keep the soil moist. As the bean plant grows, draw each stage of its life cycle. Make a poster using your drawings.

4. **Draw** In the box, draw a simple life cycle for a Kalanchoe plant.

Other Plant Life Cycles

Some plants have two kinds of life cycles. They make seeds that can grow into new plants. But they can also reproduce another way. The stem of a strawberry plant can bend over and touch the soil. New roots form on the stem. They grow into the soil and a new strawberry plant forms. Dandelion plants use their roots to reproduce. Their roots send stems up out of the soil. The stems grow into new dandelion plants.

Some plants use leaves to reproduce. The Kalanchoe plant shown below reproduces this way. Tiny new plants grow from the edges of the adult's leaves. The tiny plants fall off and send roots into the soil.

Ferns and mosses make spores instead of seeds. A spore can start to grow when it falls to the ground. This forms a new fern or moss plant.

This Kalanchoe plant is forming tiny new plants along its leaf edges.

Life Cycle Length

Some plants live for only a short time. For example, many desert plants grow, flower, and make seeds over a period of a few weeks. Their seeds germinate only when rain falls. Other plants have a one-year or two-year life cycle. For example, farmers have to plant new green bean seeds every spring.

Many trees can live longer than humans do. The chart to the right shows the average length of the life cycles of some of these trees.

Type of Tree	Average Length of Life Cycle
American elm	175 to 200 years
Bristlecone pine	3,000 years
Douglas fir	300 years
Redwood	500 years

5. ⊙ **Sequence** Look at the chart. List the tree names in order from the shortest life cycle to the longest.

....

....

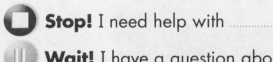

6. **Compare** How are the life cycles of flowering plants and conifer plants alike?

....

....

7. **UNLOCK THE BIG ?** Think about what you learned about plant life cycles in this lesson. How do plants grow and change?

....

....

⬜ **Stop!** I need help with ....

⏸ **Wait!** I have a question about ....

▶ **Go!** Now I know ....

How does water move through celery?

Follow a Procedure

☐ **1.** Cut a thin slice from the end of a celery stalk. **Observe** it with a hand lens or microscope. In the chart, draw what you see.

☐ **2.** Put the stalk into the water with blue food coloring. Wait 24 hours.

☐ **3.** Cut 2 cm off the stalk's end. Then cut a thin slice from the new end. Observe it with a hand lens or microscope. Draw what you see.

☐ **4.** Observe the whole stalk. Draw what you see.

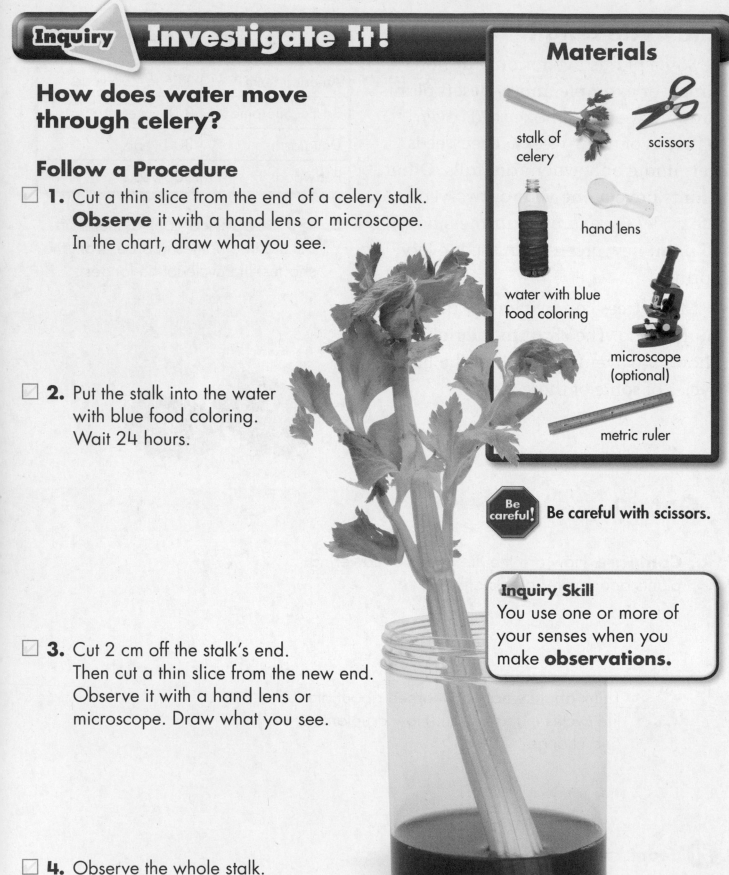

Materials

stalk of celery

scissors

water with blue food coloring

hand lens

microscope (optional)

metric ruler

Be careful! Be careful with scissors.

Inquiry Skill
You use one or more of your senses when you make **observations.**

Observations of Celery		
Slice Before Dye	**Slice After Dye**	**Whole Stalk After Dye**

Analyze and Conclude

5. Compare the slices. How are they different?

....

....

....

6. Infer During this **investigation,** what happened to the celery stalk in the blue water?

....

....

....

7. UNLOCK THE BIG ? Which parts of plants move water to the leaves?

....

....

....

Botanical Illustrator

Do you like to draw? If so, perhaps you would like to be a botanical illustrator. A botanical illustrator draws or paints plants to show what they look like. To draw plants well, you have to be a good observer of nature. This way you can show the details that make plants different. When you draw, you must show the right size and shape of each plant part.

To be a botanical illustrator, you need a degree from a college or art school. Most of your classes would be in art. Some of your classes might also be in biology. You could work for a museum or botanical garden. You might draw illustrations to be used in science books or nature–reserve brochures.

Heeyoung Kim is a botanical illustrator who paints wildflowers. She researches each flower before painting it. Heeyoung Kim wants people to see the beauty of flowers.

REVIEW THE BIG ?

Illustrate What did you learn in this chapter that can help you draw detailed images of how a plant grows and changes?

Vocabulary Smart Cards

flowering plant
spore
photosynthesis
carbon dioxide
oxygen
nutrient
reproduce
pollinate
germinate
life cycle

Play a Game!

Cut out the Vocabulary Smart Cards.

Work with a partner. Spread out the Vocabulary Smart Cards on a table. Use the word in a sentence. Refer to the definition if you are not familiar with the word.

Have your partner repeat with another Vocabulary Smart Card.

143

carbon dioxide

dióxido de carbono

flowering plant

angiosperma

oxygen

oxígeno

spore

espora

nutrient

nutriente

photosynthesis

fotosíntesis

a plant with seeds that grows flowers

Draw an example.

planta con semillas que produce flores

a gas in air that is absorbed by most plants

Write a sentence using this term.

....

....

....

gas en el aire que la mayoría de las plantas absorben

a small cell that grows into a new plant

Write a sentence using this word.

....

....

....

célula pequeña que se convierte en una planta nueva

a gas in the air that plants and animals need

Write a sentence using this word.

....

....

....

gas en el aire que las plantas y los animales necesitan para vivir

the process by which plants use air, water, and energy from sunlight to make food

Draw a picture.

proceso por el cual las plantas usan el aire, el agua y la energía del sol para producir alimento

any material needed by living things for energy, growth, and repair

Write two words related to this word.

....

....

....

cualquier sustancia que los seres vivos necesitan para obtener energía, crecer y reponerse

Interactive Vocabulary

Make a Word Frame!

Choose a vocabulary word and write it in the center of the frame. Write or draw details about the vocabulary word in the spaces around it.

needs right amount of water

germinate

seed growing into a plant

144

life cycle

ciclo de vida

reproduce

reproducir

pollinate

polinizar

germinate

germinar

to make more of the same kind

Write the noun form of the word.

....

....

....

hacer más de una misma cosa

---

the stages through which a living thing passes during its life

Write a sentence using this word.

....

....

....

estados por los que pasa un ser vivo durante su vida

....

....

....

....

---

to carry pollen to

Draw an example.

llevar polen de un lugar a otro

....

....

....

....

....

....

....

....

....

....

---

to begin to grow

Draw an example.

empezar a crecer

....

....

....

....

....

....

....

....

....

....

Lesson 1

How can you classify plants?

- Plants can be classified according to their characteristics, such as flowering and nonflowering.
- Some plants make seeds and some plants make spores.

Lesson 2

How do plants use leaves to make food?

- Leaves use air, water, and energy from the sun to make food for plants. This process is called photosynthesis.
- Leaves can help control the amount of water in a plant.

Lesson 3

How do plants use roots and stems to grow?

- Roots hold the plant in the ground and store food.
- Stems support and protect plants.

Lesson 4

How do plants use flowers or cones to reproduce?

- Many plants make seeds using flowers or cones.
- A seed has material inside it that can grow into a new plant.
- If conditions are right, a seed can germinate into a seedling.

Lesson 5

What are the life cycles of some plants?

- The stages through which a living thing passes during its life are called a life cycle.
- Plants that reproduce in different ways have different life cycles.

SavvasRealize.com

Lesson 1

How can you classify plants?

1. ⊙ **Compare and Contrast** What do cones and flowers have in common?

_____

_____

2. **Suggest** Name one kind of plant that grows very tall and does not produce flowers.

_____

Lesson 2

How do plants use leaves to make food?

3. ⊙ **Text Features** What do captions for pictures in a lesson tell you?

_____

4. **Decide** What is one thing a plant must do before it can make sugar and oxygen?

_____

_____

Lesson 3

How do plants use roots and stems to grow?

5. **Explain** How does the stem of a plant respond to light?

_____

_____

6. **Analyze** Describe one way stems help a plant.

_____

_____

_____

7. ⊙ **Compare and Contrast** How are roots and stems alike and different?

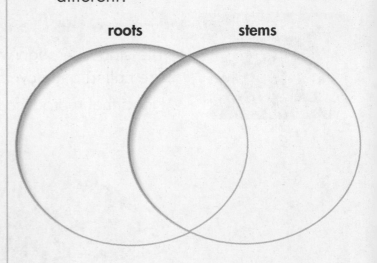

Lesson 4

How do plants use flowers or cones to reproduce?

8. Vocabulary When a plant _____, roots grow and a seedling begins to grow.

    A. reproduces

    B. scatters

    C. germinates

    D. blows

9. Infer Bees help pollinate apple trees. How might a disease that kills bees affect the number of apples on the trees? Explain.

....

....

....

....

Lesson 5

What are the life cycles of some plants?

10. Identify In the life cycle of a conifer, what stage must happen before the plant can make seeds?

....

11. Determine Do all plants begin their life cycle as a seed? Explain.

....

....

....

12. **How do plants grow and change?**

....

Use the terms *carbon dioxide*, *oxygen*, and *nutrient* to describe how plants grow and change.

....

....

....

....

....

....

Benchmark Practice

Life Science

Read each question and choose the best answer.

1 How would you classify a pine tree?

A spore
B flowering plant
C nonflowering plant
D fern

2 A new plant that has just grown out of the soil is a _____.

A germinate
B system
C seedling
D seed leaf

3 What might happen to a plant if the tiny holes on the surfaces of the leaves were covered?

A More roots would grow.
B Leaves would use more carbon dioxide.
C Leaves would produce more oxygen.
D Leaves would not produce much oxygen and sugar.

4 A cactus stores the <u>most</u> water in its _____.

A roots
B leaves
C stem
D flowers

5 Leaves turn carbon dioxide and water into what two things?

A sugar and oxygen
B seedlings and sugar
C oxygen and stems
D nutrients and sugar

6 How are roots and leaves important to a plant?

....

....

....

....

SavvasRealize.com

International Space Station

What if astronauts run out of food during long space missions? They grow more on the ship! NASA researchers have tested ways to grow wheat aboard the International Space Station (ISS). They also test the ability of plants to clean the air and water that astronauts use.

Scientists use a greenhouse on the ISS to test plant growth in space.

Growing plants in space is tricky, however. When seeds germinate on Earth, roots grow down and stems grow up. In space, there is no up or down. As a plant researcher you might be asked to solve problems like this one.

Plant researchers at Kennedy Space Center help prepare experiments to go to the International Space Station. They also study the findings of the astronauts at the space station. You can visit plant researchers at Kennedy Space Center to learn more.

Infer What other problems need to be solved so that plants can grow in space?

....

....

....

Why do kangaroos carry their young?

Living Things

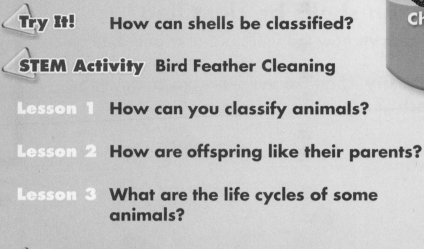

Try It! How can shells be classified?

STEM Activity Bird Feather Cleaning

Lesson 1 How can you classify animals?

Lesson 2 How are offspring like their parents?

Lesson 3 What are the life cycles of some animals?

Investigate It! What do leaves have in common?

When a kangaroo is born, it is blind and has no fur. It is about the size of a peanut. It climbs into its mother's pouch to finish developing. The young kangaroo stays there for months to eat, sleep, and grow.

Predict What might happen if a baby kangaroo left its mother's pouch too soon?

....

....

THE BIG ? How do living things grow and change?

How can shells be classified?

☐ **1. Observe** how the shells are alike and different.

☐ **2. Classify** Sort the shells into groups and label each group.

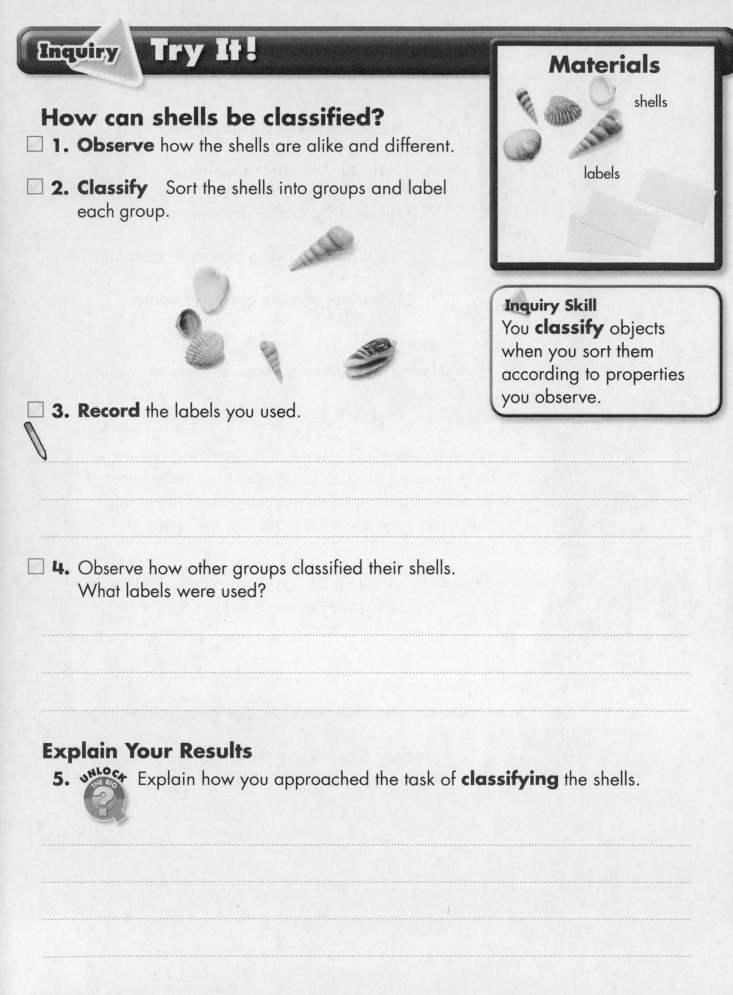

☐ **3. Record** the labels you used.

....

....

....

Inquiry Skill
You **classify** objects when you sort them according to properties you observe.

☐ **4.** Observe how other groups classified their shells. What labels were used?

....

....

....

Explain Your Results

5. UNLOCK THE BIG ? Explain how you approached the task of **classifying** the shells.

....

....

....

◉ Sequence

- **Sequence** is the order in which events take place.
- Clue words such as *first*, *next*, *then*, and *finally* can help you figure out the sequence of events.

Classify Animals

Scientists can classify animals according to their behaviors, such as how they act, and their physical characteristics, such as hair. Scientists may classify a slug such as the one below. Scientists may first identify whether or not the slug has a backbone. Next, they can find out what the slug eats. Finally, scientists can compare and contrast the slug to other animals.

Practice It!

Complete the graphic organizer to show the sequence of classifying animals.

First

Next

Finally

sea slug

Bird Feather Cleaning

Some oil leaked out. Where did it go? Oil that drips from a car washes into rivers and streams. Oil spills from a tanker leak into the ocean. Oil from these events can pollute Earth's waters. This oil is harmful to animals and plants that live in and near the water. Finding ways to clean up this oil is an ongoing engineering challenge.

As a wildlife rehabilitator, you have been asked to find a way to clean bird feathers that have been coated with oil.

Identify the Problem

☐ **1.** What problem will your cleaner help solve? _____

_____

_____

☐ **2.** Why is there a need to solve this problem? _____

_____

_____

_____

Do Research

☐ **3. Examine** a jar that contains a mixture of oil and water. **Describe** some properties of this mixture. _____

_____

☐ **4. Examine** the household cleaning-product warning label. How might the ingredients in a household cleaner impact a living animal? _____

_____

_____

Go to materials station(s). **Examine** the materials, and think about how each one may or may not be useful for your cleaner. Leave the materials where they are.

☑ **5.** What are your design constraints?

_____

_____

Develop Possible Solutions

☑ **6. List** two or three different materials you might use to clean a bird's feathers.

_____

_____

Choose One Solution

☑ **7. Tell** which material(s) you will use for your feather cleaner.

_____

_____

☑ **8.** Why did you choose these material(s)?

_____

_____

_____

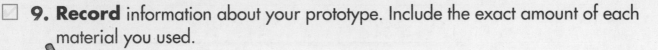

Design and Construct a Prototype

Gather a dry, clean feather and a paper towel. Collect the material(s) you chose for your cleaner in a cup. Half-fill a second cup with water. Pour a small amount of oil into the water so that a layer of oil forms on top of the water.

☐ **9. Record** information about your prototype. Include the exact amount of each material you used.

_____

_____

_____

Test the Prototype

Test your cleaner. First, dip your feather into the mixture of oil and water. **Observe** the layer of oil on the feather. Then use your cleaner to wash the feather. Use the paper towel to dry or wipe the feather. **Observe** the results.

Communicate Results

☐ **10.** How well did your cleaner work? Rate your cleaner on a scale of 1 to 3 with 1 — being poor results, 2 — being good results, and 3 — being great results. Explain why you give your cleaner this rating.

_____

_____

_____

_____

_____

Evaluate and Redesign

☐ **11.** What changes could you make to your cleaner to make it work better? Be specific as to how you will change your cleaner.

_____

_____

_____

_____

_____

☐ **12. Make** your changes and **test** your redesigned cleaner. How well did it work? Explain.

_____

_____

_____

_____

How can you classify animals?

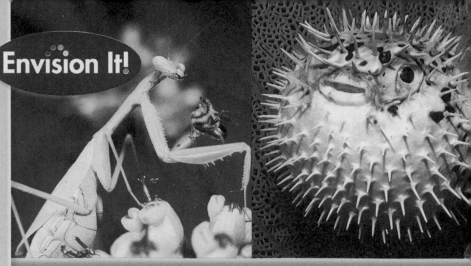

Envision It!

Tell which characteristics you think can help you classify each animal.

Inquiry **Explore It!**

How does a backbone move?

☐ **1. Make a model** of a backbone. Knot one end of a pipe cleaner.

☐ **2.** String a pasta wheel and then a jelly ring.

☐ **3.** Keep going. Use all the wheels and rings.

☐ **4.** Knot the other end of the pipe cleaner.

Explain Your Results

5. Observe how the **model** moves. Discuss and explain how a backbone moves.

....

....

....

....

....

....

Materials

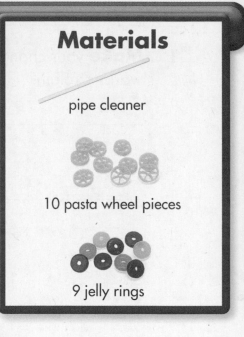

pipe cleaner

10 pasta wheel pieces

9 jelly rings

I will know how to classify animals into major groups based on characteristics and behaviors.

Words to Know

trait   invertebrate
vertebrate   arthropod

Classify Animals

Animals are classified into groups. Animals can be classified by what we want to learn about them. Animals can also be classified by ~~how they look.~~ Scientists identify body features, such as long ears or short fur, to classify animals. A feature passed on to a living thing from its parents is called a **trait.** Traits can include an animal's behavior or its physical characteristics. Animals can also be classified by where they live or how they act.

One animal can be placed into different groups. For example, a group of animals that eat mice can include snakes, hawks, and owls. A group of animals that fly can include hawks and owls but not snakes.

1. **Circle** some ways animals are classified.

2. **Suggest** What is another reason you might not classify a snake with hawks and owls?

Snakes are reptiles hawks owls are birds

Animals with Backbones

One main characteristic scientists use to classify animals is whether or not they have a backbone. An animal with a backbone is called a **vertebrate.** For example, cats, birds, and fish are vertebrates. Vertebrates may look different, but they all have a backbone and other bones. Bones grow as the animals grow. Bones support the body. This allows some vertebrates to grow very big.

3. Infer What allows a giraffe to grow so tall?

its back bone

Read the next page. Then answer these questions.

4. Differentiate What is one way reptiles and amphibians are different?

5. Circle two traits an animal can have to be classified as a mammal.

Groups of Vertebrates

Fish

Fish are vertebrates that live in water. Most fish have slippery scales, breathe through gills, and lay eggs. Fish are cold-blooded vertebrates.

6. Illustrate Draw a fish.

Amphibians

Amphibians are cold-blooded vertebrates. They have smooth, moist skin. They hatch from eggs. Frogs, toads, and salamanders are amphibians. Most young amphibians live in water. They get oxygen through their gills and skin. Most amphibians develop lungs to breathe air out of the water.

Reptiles

Snakes, lizards, turtles, and crocodiles are reptiles. Reptiles are cold-blooded vertebrates. They have dry, scaly skin. They breathe air through lungs. Most reptiles lay eggs.

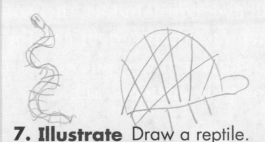

7. Illustrate Draw a reptile.

Birds

Birds are warm-blooded vertebrates with feathers and bills. Feathers help birds stay warm. Wings and light bones help most birds fly. They breathe air through lungs. All birds hatch from eggs.

Mammals

The vertebrates you probably know best are mammals. Mammals are warm-blooded vertebrates. They usually have hair that keeps them warm. Mammals breathe air through lungs and feed milk to their young. Most mammals are born alive instead of hatching from eggs.

Animals without Backbones

Most animals do not have bones or skeletons inside their bodies. Animals without backbones are called **invertebrates.** Sea stars, butterflies, and spiders are invertebrates.

Invertebrates have structures other than bones to give them their shape. A soft sac filled with liquid supports worms and sea jellies. A hard shell supports clams and lobsters. Insects have a hard covering on the outside of their bodies. These kinds of structures cannot support very big animals. Most invertebrates are smaller than most vertebrates.

You may not notice some invertebrates because many are very small. Yet invertebrates live all over Earth. In fact, there are many more invertebrates than vertebrates. For example, several million tiny roundworms may live in one square meter of soil.

8. CHALLENGE How do you think Earth can support more invertebrates than vertebrates?

....

....

....

....

....

Lightning Lab

Classify Different Animals

Draw an animal. Describe two features such as how the animal moves and what it eats. Draw another animal. Compare the features. Write how the animals are alike and different. Then classify them.

slug   orangutan

Sea Jellies

Sea jellies have soft bodies and long, stinging body parts. The body of a sea jelly is made mostly of water. A sea jelly stuns its prey before pulling it into its stomach. Most sea jellies live in the ocean.

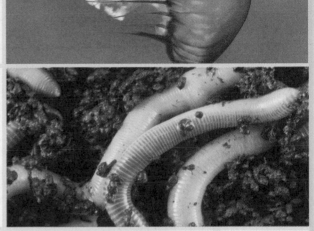

Worms

Worms are animals with long, soft bodies and no legs. Have you ever seen an earthworm in the soil? These invertebrates help keep soil healthy.

Mollusks

Mollusks are animals with soft bodies. Some mollusks include octopuses, squids, clams, and snails. Many mollusks have hard shells and eyes.

9. Illustrate Draw a mollusk.

Arthropods

Arthropods are the largest group of invertebrates. An **arthropod** is an animal that has a hard covering outside its body. The bodies of arthropods have more than one main part, and their legs have joints. Insects, spiders, and crabs are all arthropods.

10. Classify Look at the pictures to the left. How would you classify each animal?

....

....

Animal Birth

Another trait that helps scientists classify animals is the way they give birth. Most animals begin in small eggs. The eggs grow to different sizes. The young animals are then born in different ways.

Eggs

Many animals hatch from eggs. For example, all birds hatch from eggs. Most fish, amphibians, and reptiles also hatch from eggs. Crocodiles lay eggs, as most other reptiles do. After growing in the eggs for two or three months, young crocodiles hatch from the eggs.

Live Birth

Most mammals have live births. This means that the young animal is born instead of hatching from an egg. You may have seen images of a lion with her young cubs. She gave live birth to the cubs after being pregnant for about four months.

11. Classify How would you classify a turtle?

12. ⊙ Sequence What two things happen before a crocodile hatches from an egg?

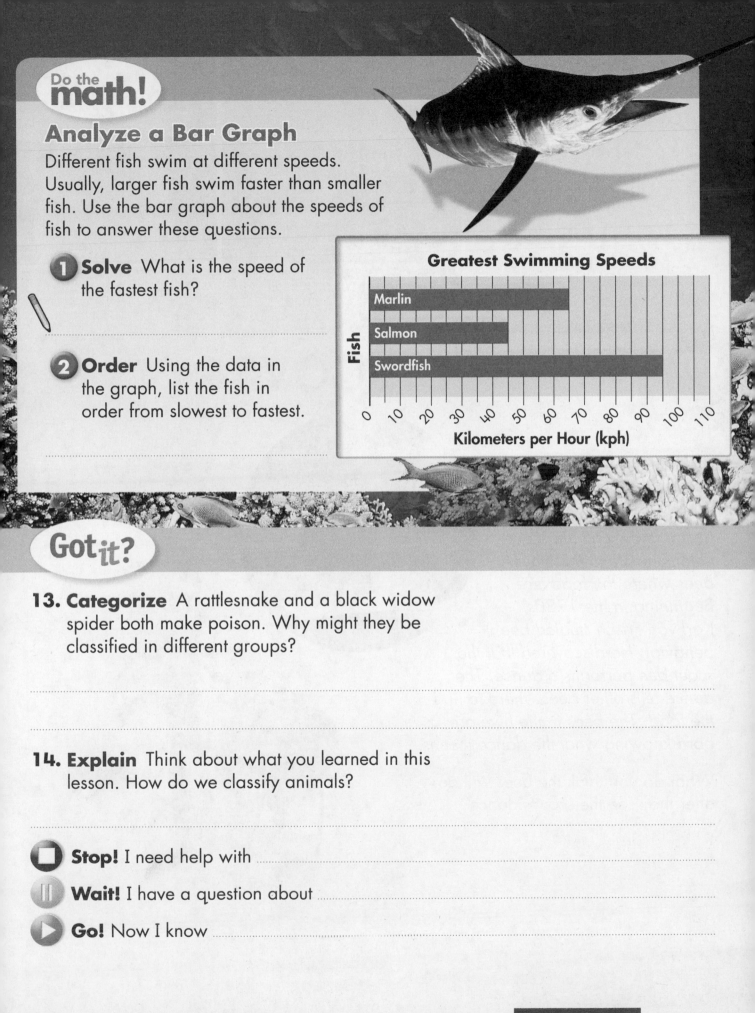

Do the math!

Analyze a Bar Graph

Different fish swim at different speeds. Usually, larger fish swim faster than smaller fish. Use the bar graph about the speeds of fish to answer these questions.

1 Solve What is the speed of the fastest fish?

2 Order Using the data in the graph, list the fish in order from slowest to fastest.

Greatest Swimming Speeds

Fish: Marlin, Salmon, Swordfish

Kilometers per Hour (kph)
0 10 20 30 40 50 60 70 80 90 100 110

Got it?

13. Categorize A rattlesnake and a black widow spider both make poison. Why might they be classified in different groups?

14. Explain Think about what you learned in this lesson. How do we classify animals?

■ **Stop!** I need help with

Ⅱ **Wait!** I have a question about

▶ **Go!** Now I know

How are offspring like their parents?

Circle the two pictures that show behaviors an animal must learn.

MY PLANET DIARY DISCOVERY

Karl von Frisch

A honey bee scout flies out of the hive to look for food. It finds flowers full of sweet nectar. How can the scout communicate to the other bees where the food is? Beginning in the 1920s, Karl von Frisch studied bee behavior. He discovered that the scout bee performs a dance. The dance tells other bees where to find the food. The bees in the hive are born knowing what the dance means.

What do you think the bees will do after they see the scout's dance?

....

....

....

UNLOCK
THE BIG
?

I will know that some characteristics and behaviors are inherited and some are learned or acquired.

Words to Know

inherit
instinct

Draw an X on the pictures that show behaviors an animal is born knowing how to do.

Both Alike and Different

Why do kittens look like cats and not like dogs? Why does a corn seed grow into a corn plant and not a tomato plant? Most young plants and animals grow to look like their parents. Some plants and animals look like their parents even when they are very young.

The young antelope in the picture shares many characteristics with its parent. For example, the young antelope has the same body shape as its parent. Its fur is about the same length too.

The young antelope is also different in some ways. For example, its horns are much smaller than its parent's horns. The young antelope's horns will grow larger as it gets older. But even then, its horns may not have the exact shape or size of its parent's horns.

1. ◉ **Compare and Contrast** Describe other ways in which the young antelope and its parent are alike and different.

....

....

....

....

....

....

Inherited Characteristics

Young plants and animals are called offspring. Why do offspring often look like their parents?

Many characteristics of plants and animals are inherited. **Inherit** means to receive from a parent. An inherited characteristic is one that is passed on from parents to their offspring. An inherited characteristic is also called a trait. Animals inherit traits such as color and the shape of their body parts. Plants inherit traits such as leaf shape and flower color. The traits of an animal or plant often help it to survive in its environment.

Humans also inherit traits. You may have inherited traits such as hair color and eye color from your parents.

2. **Underline** the words that tell what *inherit* means.

3. **Analyze** This frog's skin color is inherited. How does it help the frog survive?

....

....

Young pine trees inherit green, needlelike leaves from adult pine trees.

Acquired Characteristics

Not all characteristics are inherited from parents. Suppose a woman has her ears pierced. Her offspring will not be born with pierced ears. Pierced ears are an acquired characteristic. You acquire, or get, them during your lifetime. Only characteristics that you are born with can be passed to your offspring.

Plants and animals develop acquired characteristics through interactions with their environment. For example, a plant's leaves may turn brown if it gets too much sun. Brown leaves are an acquired characteristic. The plant's offspring will not have brown leaves.

4. **List** Look at the tree in the picture. Write one inherited characteristic and one acquired characteristic of the tree.

....

....

The scars on this elephant seal's body are from fighting other seals. The scars are an acquired characteristic.

Massive winds have helped cause this tree's slanted shape.

Inherited Behavior

Behaviors are things that animals do. A behavior that an animal is born able to do is an **instinct.** Instincts are inherited behaviors. One instinct is an animal's response to hunger. For example, baby birds open their mouths when a parent brings food. Puppies are born knowing how to suck milk.

Some animals have an instinct to move, or migrate, when the seasons change. Some butterflies migrate thousands of miles. They fly to warm places to survive the winter. Other animals, such as bats, have an instinct to hibernate during winter. When animals hibernate, their body systems slow down. This saves energy. The animals don't need as much food to survive.

Baby birds are born knowing how to open their mouths for food.

5. **Explain** Explain in your own words what *migrate* means.

....

....

6. **Apply** Dogs have many instincts. Describe a behavior of dogs that you think is an instinct. Explain why you think the behavior is inherited.

....

....

....

Most types of spiders have an instinct to build webs.

Learned Behaviors

Animals learn some behaviors from their parents or other adults. For example, chimpanzees learn how to use a stick as a tool. They use the stick to catch and eat insects. Chimpanzees are not born knowing how to use tools. They learn how to do this by watching other chimpanzees. Young chimpanzees also must learn which foods are safe to eat. Their mothers and other adults teach them.

Humans learn many behaviors from their parents or other adults. You learned how to read and do math in school. A parent may have taught you how to tie your shoelaces or eat with a spoon. You were not born knowing how to do these things.

A chimpanzee pokes a stick into an insect nest. It pulls out the stick. Then it eats the insects that are on the stick.

7. ◉ Main Idea and Details What is the main idea of this page?

8. Differentiate This girl learned how to brush her teeth. How is this learned behavior different from an instinct?

Small Differences in Traits

Offspring often look like their parents. Offspring can also look like each other. But they may not look exactly alike. Different animals of the same kind can look and act different. For example, two brown rabbits can have brown offspring. They may also have white or gray offspring.

Differences That Can Help an Animal

Some differences in the way an animal looks or acts can help it survive and reproduce. For example, rock pocket mice live in rocky habitats in desert areas. Some habitats have light brown rocks. Others have black rocks. The mice have either light brown or black fur. Scientists have found that a mouse's color often matches the rocks in its habitat. Why would this be? Owls hunt and eat mice. However, owls cannot see light brown mice on light brown rocks or black mice on black rocks.

9. Describe Write a caption for the picture above.

....

....

....

10. Circle the mouse with the fur color that helps it survive on light-colored sand. Tell what kind of habitat it may not survive in.

Differences That Can Harm an Animal

Small differences in traits can harm an animal. Some traits can make it harder for an animal to survive and reproduce.

Suppose two light brown mice have offspring. Most are light brown, but some are black. Which offspring are more likely to survive in a habitat of light brown rocks? The light brown offspring will be hard for owls to see. But black mice are easier to see on light brown rocks. The black offspring are more likely to be eaten by owls. They are less likely to survive and have offspring of their own.

11. **Apply** Tell why you think there may be few owls with poor eyesight in a habitat.

Owls are most likely to hunt and eat mice they can see easily.

Got it?

12. **Name** What are two ways an animal is able to acquire a behavior?

....

....

13. **Apply** How do webbed feet help a duck survive?

....

....

⬛ **Stop!** I need help with ....

⏸ **Wait!** I have a question about ....

▶ **Go!** Now I know ....

Lesson 3

What are the life cycles of some animals?

Label the pictures 1 through 3 to show the correct sequence in the life cycle of a bald eagle.

Inquiry **Explore It!**

What is the life cycle of a grain beetle?

☐ **1. Observe** several mealworms. **Record** a stage you see.

☐ **2.** Observe the mealworms for about 3 weeks.

☐ **3.** Draw each new stage you see.

Materials

mealworms in habitat cup

hand lens

crayons or markers

[ ] → [ ] → [ ]

Explain Your Results

4. Interpret Data How did the mealworms change?

....

....

....

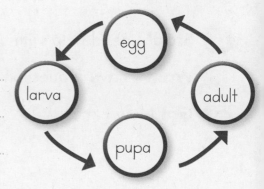

UNLOCK
THE BIG

I will know how different
animals grow and change
during their life cycles.

Words to Know

larva
pupa
metamorphosis

Life Cycles

An animal's life starts out as an egg. Sometimes
the egg develops into a young animal inside the
mother's body. Then the mother gives birth to a live
young. For other animals, the mother lays an egg
outside of her body. Eagles have their young in this
way. First, the mother eagle lays an egg. Next, the
eaglet, a young eagle, develops inside the egg.
Finally, the eaglet hatches when it is ready.

After birth, an animal begins to grow. It
develops into an adult and then it can reproduce.
Eventually, it dies. Its life cycle is complete.

*After they are born,
bear cubs grow bigger
and develop into adults.*

1. ◎ **Sequence** Complete the graphic organizer
to sequence the steps in an eagle's birth.

First

[ ]

↓

Next

[ ]

↓

Finally

[ ]

Life Cycle of a Butterfly

The life cycle of a butterfly has four stages, as shown in the diagram. A butterfly looks very different at each stage of its life. It also behaves in different ways.

For example, compare the larva and adult stages in the diagram. A **larva** is the second stage in the life cycle of some insects. A butterfly larva is called a caterpillar. It has a worm-like body. It eats plants. It must eat a lot to grow and store energy.

A **pupa** is the stage in an insect's life cycle between larva and adult. A butterfly pupa is protected inside a hard covering called a chrysalis. It does not eat, and it hardly moves.

The adult butterfly that comes out of the chrysalis looks nothing like the larva that went in. It has wings, long legs, and antennae. Some adult butterflies feed on the nectar of flowers. Some do not feed at all. After laying eggs, the adult butterfly will die.

2. **Apply** In the blank spaces, write titles for stage 2 and stage 3 in the life cycle of the butterfly.

3. **Infer** Why is it important that the butterfly larva store energy by eating a lot?

....

....

....

1 **Egg**
A butterfly begins life in a tiny egg. The egg in this picture has been magnified, or made to look bigger.

4 **Adult Butterfly**
The adult butterfly breaks out of the chrysalis. It flies away to find a mate. It will lay eggs if it is a female. Eventually, the butterfly will die.

4. Identify Draw an ✗ on the life cycle stage in which the butterfly's wings grow.

2

The butterfly larva is called a caterpillar. It hatches from the egg. The caterpillar sheds its skin several times as it grows.

3

A hard covering, or chrysalis, forms around the larva. The larva is now called a pupa. Inside the chrysalis, the insect grows wings and long legs.

Life Cycle of a Frog

Some animals change form as they develop. This change in form during an animal's life cycle is called **metamorphosis.** Many insects go through metamorphosis. Frogs do too. Frogs are amphibians. Amphibians live in water during some parts of their lives. They live on land during other parts of their lives.

A frog life cycle begins with an egg. The young frog that hatches from the egg is called a tadpole. A tadpole has body parts for living in water. It has a tail for swimming. It breathes with gills like fish do. As the tadpole grows, it develops body parts for living on land. It grows legs. The tail disappears. Lungs replace gills. Finally, an adult frog forms. It uses its legs to hop. An adult frog lays eggs in water. Some frogs reproduce many times before they die.

5. Identify Draw an ✗ on the life cycle stage in which the frog lives on land.

Eggs

Mother frogs often lay hundreds or thousands of eggs in the water. The eggs are surrounded by a jelly-like material.

Adult Frog

The adult frog lives on land and in water. It returns to the water to lay its eggs.

6. Determine the Factors List body parts and other materials from the diagram that help keep frogs alive and healthy.

....

....

....

2 **Tadpole**

A tadpole hatches from each frog egg. Tadpoles live underwater and breathe with gills.

3 **Growing Tadpole**

The tadpole changes as it grows. Its tail becomes shorter, and its legs begin to grow. It develops lungs for breathing, and its gills disappear.

Go Green

Frog Habitats
A habitat is the place where a plant or animal lives. Find out where frogs live. Make a list of things that a frog habitat must have so the frog can complete its life cycle. Then explain how you can help protect frog habitats.

Life Cycle of a Mammal

Unlike amphibians and insects, young mammals do not change very much as they become adults. Many mammals look like their parents when they are born. Like you, they grow as they get older.

7. Compare How is a young bobcat similar to an adult bobcat?

....

....

....

8. Contrast In what way is an adult bobcat different from a young bobcat?

....

....

....

1 Egg
Young bobcats develop from eggs inside the mother's body. They are born when they are ready to live outside the mother's body.

2 Kitten
Young bobcats are called kittens. The mother bobcat's body makes milk. The kittens drink the milk.

4 Adult
When the young bobcats grow to be adults, they can reproduce.

3 Growth
The young bobcats grow bigger. The mother bobcat takes care of them.

Some animals go through their entire life cycle quickly. For example, most insects live for less than one year. Other animals live much longer. The length of an animal's life is called its life span. The graph below shows the life spans of some animals.

9. Analyze What pattern do you see in the graph?

Animal Life Spans

Life Span (years)

80
60
40
20
0

Rabbit   Deer   Bear   Elephant

Animal

Got it?

10. How is a mammal's life cycle different from a frog or butterfly life cycle?

11. Describe How must a frog's body change before it can live on land?

⬛ **Stop!** I need help with

⏸ **Wait!** I have a question about

▶ **Go!** Now I know

What do leaves have in common?

Follow a Procedure

☐ **1.** Spread out the leaves. **Observe** them. Which have similar shapes?

☐ **2.** Make a yarn circle for each kind of shape. You may have from 3 to 5 groups.

☐ **3. Classify** Place leaves with similar shapes in the same circle.

Materials

10 leaves or leaf pictures

5 yarn circles

Inquiry Skill Scientists **classify** objects by observing their traits.

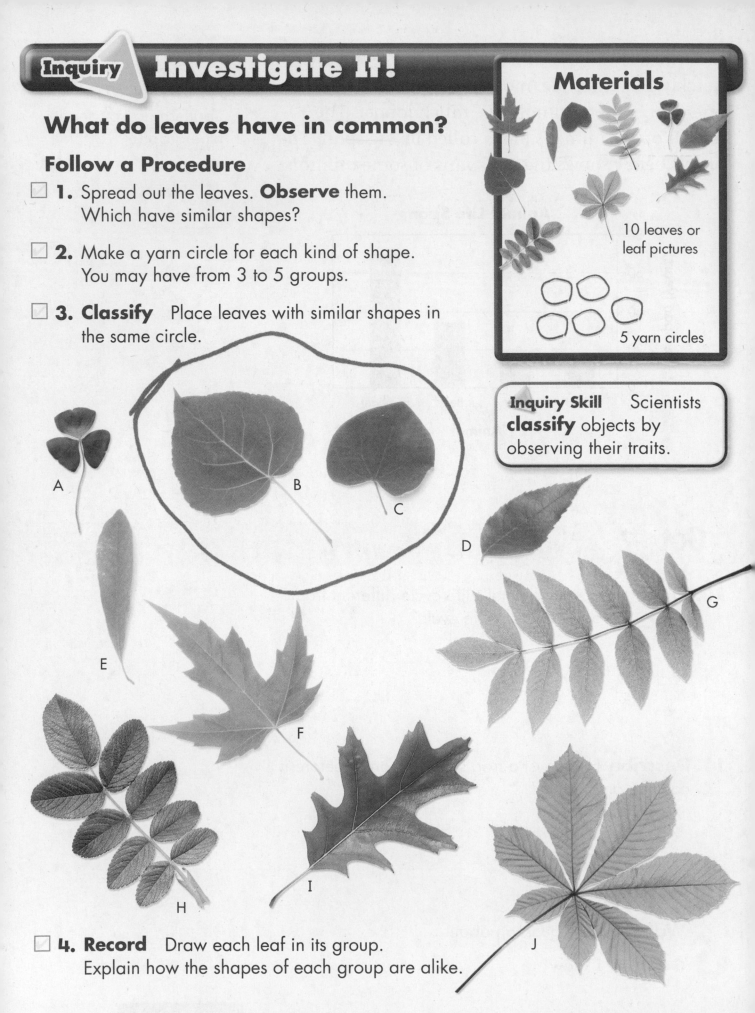

☐ **4. Record** Draw each leaf in its group. Explain how the shapes of each group are alike.

Leaf Observations

Leaf Drawings or Letters of Leaves	How Are the Leaf Shapes Alike?
Group A	
Group B	
Group C	
Group D	
Group E	

Analyze and Conclude

5. Describe another way to **classify** the leaves.

....

....

6. UNLOCK THE BIG ? Why might it be helpful to classify leaves?

....

....

STEM Shark Tracking

Science
Technology
Engineering
Math

Scientists track sharks with devices to learn where, when, and why sharks travel the ocean. How does a tracking device work? First, scientists attach the tracking device to the shark's dorsal, or back, fin. Then, when the dorsal fin breaks the surface of the ocean, a radio signal is transmitted to a satellite. Next, the satellite receives the signal and locates the shark. Last, the satellite transmits the shark's position to a central computer. Each time the tag transmits a signal, the computer plots, or marks, its position. These positions are shown on a map. They show the shark's movements over time. Engineering and technology are helping scientists study sharks.

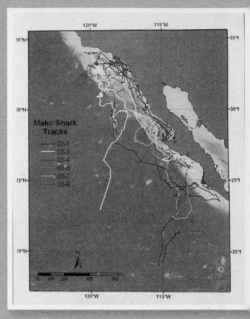

This mako shark was tracked around the Baja Peninsula for several months.

Illustrate Draw an illustration of how the signal from the tracking device goes from the shark to the central computer.

Vocabulary Smart Cards

trait
vertebrate
invertebrate
arthropod
inherit
instinct
larva
pupa
metamorphosis

Play a Game!

Cut out the Vocabulary Smart Cards.

Work with a partner. Spread out two sets of Vocabulary Smart Cards on a table. One set should show the definition, and the other should show the word.

Have your partner pick a card and find the definition that matches the word.

Have your partner repeat with another word.

arthropod
artrópodo

trait
rasgo

inherit
heredar

vertebrate
vertebrado

instinct
instinto

invertebrate
invertebrado

a feature passed on to a living thing from its parents	an animal that has a hard covering outside its body
Use a dictionary. Find as many synonyms for this word as you can.	Write a sentence using this word.
característica que pasa de padres a hijos entre los seres vivos	animal que tiene el cuerpo envuelto por una cubierta dura

Interactive Vocabulary

Make a Word Frame!

Choose a vocabulary word and write it in the center of the frame. Write the definition in the box above. Write examples in the box on the left. Write some things that are not examples in the box on the right. Write something to help you remember this word in the box below.

an animal with a backbone	to receive from a parent
Write three examples.	Write an example of an inherited characteristic.
animal que tiene columna vertebral	recibir de un progenitor

an animal with a backbone

dog, snake — **vertebrate** — worm, insect

I have a backbone.

an animal without a backbone	a behavior an animal is born able to do
What is the prefix of this word? What does this prefix mean?	Write a sentence using this word.
animal que no tiene columna vertebral	conducta que tiene un animal desde que nace

188

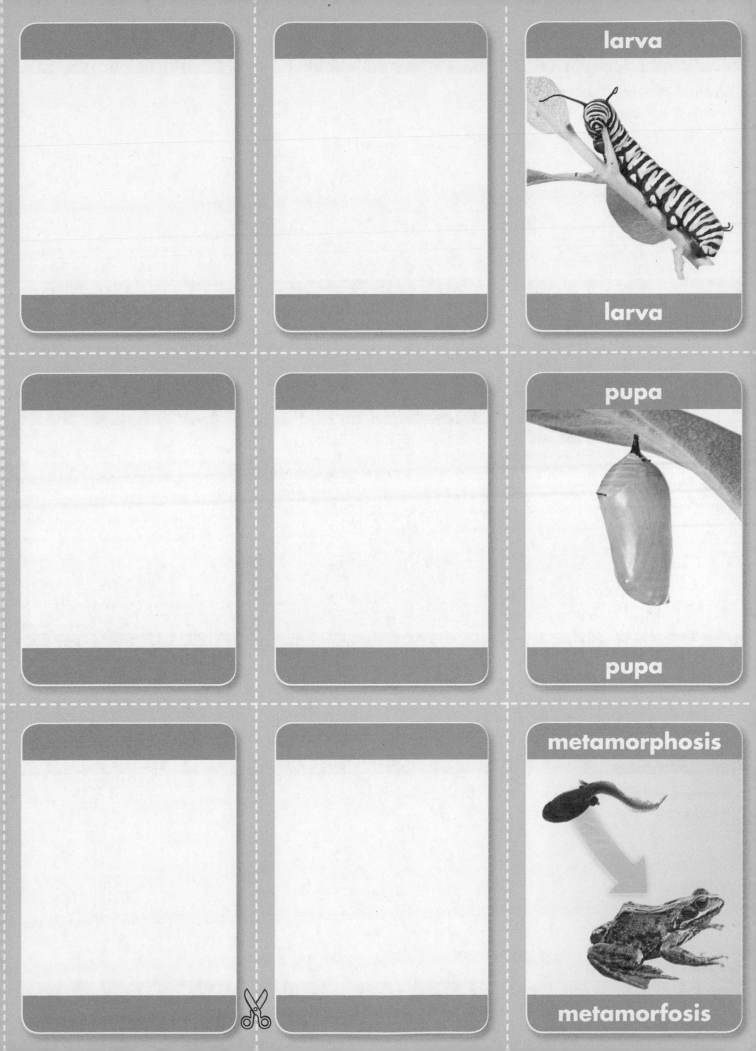

larva

larva

pupa

pupa

metamorphosis

metamorfosis

second stage of the life cycle of some insects

Write a sentence using this word.

....

....

....

....

segunda etapa del ciclo de vida de algunos insectos

---

stage of an insect's life cycle between larva and adult

Draw an example.

etapa de la vida de un insecto entre larva y adulto

---

a change in form during an animal's life cycle

Name two animals that go through metamorphosis.

....

....

....

cambio de la forma de un animal durante su ciclo de vida

Lesson 1

How can you classify animals?

- Animals can be classified according to their characteristics, such as whether or not they have a backbone.
- Some animals hatch from eggs and others have live births.

Lesson 2

How are offspring like their parents?

- Animals and plants inherit certain characteristics from their parents. Other characteristics are acquired.
- Animal behaviors can be inherited or learned.

Lesson 3

What are the life cycles of some animals?

- Some insects and amphibians change form as they develop into adults. This process is called metamorphosis.
- Mammals do not change very much as they become adults.

Chapter Review

How do living things grow and change?

Lesson 1

How can you classify animals?

1. **Vocabulary** A(n) _____ is an animal without a backbone.
   A. vertebrate
   B. whale
   C. invertebrate
   D. mammal

2. **Categorize** Why can different animals be grouped in more than one way?

Do the math!

3. What is the difference in speed between a barracuda and the southern bluefin tuna?

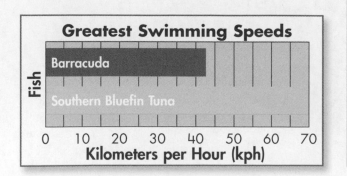

Lesson 2

How are offspring like their parents?

4. **Compare and Contrast** How are young bobcats and their parents alike and different?

5. **Identify** Which of the following is an acquired characteristic?
   A. sunburn
   B. eye color
   C. hair color
   D. height

6. **Suggest** Name one learned behavior and one inherited behavior of a chimpanzee.

What are the life cycles of some animals?

7. ⊙ **Sequence** A monarch butterfly's life cycle has four stages. What is the correct order?
   A. egg, pupa, adult, larva
   B. egg, pupa, larva, adult
   C. egg, larva, pupa, adult
   D. egg, adult, pupa, larva

8. **Vocabulary** A frog's change in form during its life cycle is called a(n) _____.
   A. amphibian
   B. metamorphosis
   C. tadpole
   D. life span

9. **Contrast** How is the birth of a baby chicken different from the birth of a baby cat?

....

....

....

....

....

10. **Write About It** Describe what happens during the pupa stage of a butterfly's life cycle.

....

....

....

....

....

....

....

....

11. APPLY THE BIG ? **How do living things grow and change?**

Describe the stages in the life cycle of a dog.

....

....

....

....

....

Read each question and choose the best answer.

1 Which animal goes through metamorphosis during its life cycle?

A duck

B cat

C butterfly

D turtle

2 Which is an example of an instinct?

A rowing a boat

B reading

C hibernating

D having curly hair

3 Animals can be divided into two groups based on whether they have _____ or not.

A backbones

B tails

C fur

D lungs

4 When a tadpole becomes an adult frog, it _____.

A grows a longer tail

B breathes with lungs

C lives underwater

D breathes with gills

5 An inherited trait is one that _____.

A you are not born with

B is passed on from parents to their offspring

C you learn how to do

D is passed on from offspring to their parents

6 Name the invertebrate group all of the following animals belong to: mosquito, spider, beetle, and crab.

....

....

Classify Local Animals

Take a look around. You might be surprised at all the animals you can find in your neighborhood. You can find tiny ants living in a crack in the sidewalk. You can see birds flying. You might even see a deer passing through your backyard.

You might look for butterflies in your yard. There are many different kinds of butterflies. Like all insects, butterflies have six legs and three body parts. However, what you are most likely to notice are their colorful wings.

You can classify animals you find. Look for animals with your parent or guardian. Find out if there are more vertebrates or invertebrates in your neighborhood. Write down your descriptions of each animal. Take or draw a picture. Then, use your school library to research these animals.

APPLY THE BIG ?

What kinds of animals are in your neighborhood? Were there more vertebrates or invertebrates? How do they change and grow?

Why does the grass need the bison?

Ecosystems

Try It! How can you recycle some materials?

STEM Activity Nothing Like a Habitat

Investigate It! What can you find in your local ecosystem?

Life Science

Apply It! How can plants survive in the desert?

American bison live on grasslands in the United States. Like many other grassland animals, they depend on grass for food.

Predict How do you think bison help grassland plants to grow and stay healthy?

....

....

....

THE BIG ? How do living things interact?

How can you recycle some materials?

Recycle, reuse, and reduce to save resources.

☐ **1. Observe** the materials.

☐ **2.** Brainstorm inventions you could make from the materials.

....

....

....

☐ **3.** Select one invention to make from the materials.

☐ **4. Make a model** by drawing a diagram of your invention.

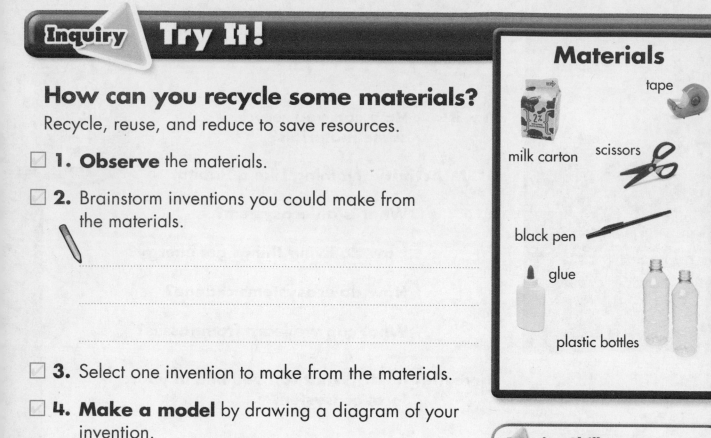

Materials

tape

milk carton   scissors

black pen

glue

plastic bottles

Inquiry Skill
You can **make a model** to illustrate your ideas.

☐ **5. Communicate** Share what your invention does.

Explain Your Results

6. UNLOCK THE BIG **? Communicate** Describe how your invention uses recycled materials to save resources.

....

....

....

Cause and Effect

Let's Read
Science!

- A **cause** is why something happens.
  An **effect** is what happens.
- When you read, sometimes clue words such as *because* and *since* signal a cause-and-effect relationship.

The Big Fire

The forest fire started when lightning struck a tree. Because the fire grew quickly, firefighters had trouble putting it out. The fire destroyed hundreds of acres of woodland. It killed trees, grasses, and other plants. Because animals could not find food and shelter, they moved to other places.

Apply It!

Use the graphic organizer below to write a cause and effect found in the example paragraph.

Cause

Effect

Nothing Like a Habitat

Do you know what organisms live around you? A habitat is an area where groups of organisms live. A habitat helps living things meet their needs. These needs include food, water, air, light, and soil. A habitat can be as big as a lake or as small as a drop of pond water. Many types of living things share the same habitat.

A scientist studying a habitat needs your help to design a way to mark off a small part of the habitat. You will collect data on the living things found there. Then you will use that data to estimate the size of each plant and animal population living in the entire habitat.

Identify the Problem

☐ **1.** What problem will your plant and animal sampler help solve? _____

_____

_____

Do Research

Examine the entire habitat.

☐ **2. Describe** the habitat. Include how big the habitat is. _____

_____

☐ **3.** How could you estimate the number of living things in the habitat?

_____

_____

☐ **4.** Determine where you want to place your sampler. **Describe** the location.

_____

_____

Go to the materials station(s). Look at each material. Think about how each one may or may not be useful for estimating the number of plants and animals in the habitat. Leave the materials where they are.

☐ **5.** What are your design constraints? _____

_____

_____

Develop Possible Solutions

☐ **6. Describe** two ways in which you could determine the size of plant and animal populations in the habitat.

_____

_____

_____

_____

Choose One Solution

☐ **7. Describe** how you will build your sampler and how you will take your sample.

_____

_____

_____

_____

_____

☑ **8. List** the materials you will need. _____

_____

_____

☑ **9. Explain** how you can use your sampler to **estimate** the number of plants and animals in the habitat. _____

_____

_____

Design and Construct a Prototype

Gather your materials. **Build** your sampler.

☑ **10. Record** information about your prototype. Be sure to include the size of your sampler. _____

_____

_____

_____

Test the Prototype

Test your sampler. **Record** your plant and animal counts in the table below. (Hint: Count grass by clumps.) Remember to look in the soil, too. Use your data to estimate how many of each plant and animal are in the whole habitat.

Plants			Animals		
Type	Number in sample	Number in Habitat	Type	Number in Sample	Number in Habitat

Communicate Results

☐ **11. Share and compare** your results with those of your classmates.

Evaluate and Redesign

☐ **12.** What changes could you make to your sampler to make it work better?

_____

_____

_____

☐ **13. Make** your changes and **draw** your revised sampler.

☐ **14.** How well did your revised prototype work? Explain. _____

_____

_____

_____

What is an ecosystem?

Circle two living things in the picture.
Draw an ✗ on two nonliving things.

my planet Diary ← Connections →

Wetlands once covered about 392 million acres (159 million hectares) in what is now the United States. Today, Alaska, Florida, Louisiana, Minnesota, and Texas have the most acres of wetlands. Alaska has lost little of its wetlands. But wetlands in many other states are disappearing. Consider Louisiana. The state loses areas of wetlands the size of a football field every 30 minutes!

You can use geography skills to understand how Louisiana's wetlands are changing. Look at the maps. The first map shows Louisiana's coast in 1839. The second map shows the same coast more than 150 years later. The green areas are areas of wetland. Notice the changes.

Draw on the 1993 map. Use a red pencil to show how you think the map would change if wetland loss continues.

1839

1993

I will know how living and nonliving things interact in an ecosystem.

Words to Know

ecosystem   population
habitat   community

Places for Living Things

How is the place where a bear lives different from the place where an earthworm lives? Each kind of living thing needs a certain environment. A living thing's environment is everything around it. An environment has living and nonliving parts. The living parts include plants, animals, and other living things.

Sunlight is a nonliving part of an environment. The sun's rays warm other nonliving parts, such as air, water, and soil. Because of the sun's heat, Earth's air, water, and soil are warm enough for living things.

1. **Apply** What parts of an environment are affected by the sun's heat?

....

....

....

2. **Describe** Explain how bears interact with living and nonliving things.

....

....

....

....

....

Parts of an Ecosystem

The living and nonliving parts of an environment interact. *Interact* means to act together. These interacting parts make up an **ecosystem.** The pictures on these pages show a marsh. A marsh is a type of wetland ecosystem.

The living parts of an ecosystem depend on nonliving parts. For example, plants need sunlight, soil, air, and water to grow. The living parts also depend on one another. For example, animals eat other living things. Some animals use plants for shelter.

3. **Identify** Draw another living thing you might find in this wetland. Tell how it interacts in the ecosystem.

Box turtles live on land near wetlands. Marsh and pond turtles live in the water.

4. **Predict** Tell what might happen to a marsh turtle if the water in the ecosystem dried up.

Water is a nonliving part of wetlands. Plants and animals need water to live and grow.

Grasses grow in marsh wetlands. They need sunlight, soil, air, and lots of water.

Great egrets eat fish, frogs, and other small animals that live in the marsh.

5. Predict How do you think turtles interact with insects in the ecosystem?

....

....

6. Describe How might this raccoon interact with living and nonliving things in this marsh?

....

....

....

....

....

Raccoons eat plants, fish, and small animals that live in the marsh. They often sleep in nearby trees.

This monkey's habitat is the trees in a rain forest.

Habitats

The place where a living thing makes its home is its **habitat.** A habitat has everything that a plant or animal needs to live. A habitat can be the water in a wetland. It can be the soil beneath a rock or even a crack in a sidewalk.

7. Describe What is the habitat of the bluespot butterflyfish in the picture below?

....

Groups Within Ecosystems

All the living things of the same kind that live in the same place make up a **population.** The coral reef ecosystem shown below includes many different populations. For example, all of the bluespot butterflyfish living around the reef make up one population. A coral reef also may have populations of crabs, clams, sharks, and other animals. These populations vary greatly in size. Being a member of these populations may have different advantages. For example, sharks may have more success hunting in groups than hunting alone.

All the populations that live in the same place make up a **community.** Populations in a community depend on each other.

8. Apply Circle a living thing that is not part of the bluespot butterflyfish population in this coral reef community.

Three bluespot butterflyfish swim over a coral reef. Staying in a group helps the fish find food and defend themselves.

Ecosystems Change

Ecosystems may change over time. When one part of an ecosystem changes, other parts are affected too. For example, a hurricane may damage the fruit trees in a forest where monkeys live. The monkeys may not be able to find enough fruit to eat. The monkey population may become smaller. Then there would be less food for animals that feed on monkeys. Their populations might become smaller too.

9. ⊙ **Cause and Effect** (Circle) one cause in the text. **Underline** one effect.

10. **Suggest** What is another way an ecosystem could be destroyed?

At-Home Lab

Local Ecosystem
Observe a terrarium ecosystem or an ecosystem in a park or your backyard. In a science notebook, list the living and nonliving parts. How do the living things get what they need from the ecosystem?

11. **UNLOCK THE BIG ?** Think about what you learned in this lesson. How do living things interact?

12. **Describe** How do living and nonliving things interact in a wetland ecosystem such as a marsh?

⏹ **Stop!** I need help with

⏸ **Wait!** I have a question about

▶ **Go!** Now I know

Lesson 2

How do living things get energy?

Envision It!

Circle a living thing that can make its own food.

Inquiry **Explore It!**

What do yeast use for energy?

Materials

watermelon slice

yeast

plastic bag

spoon

hand lens

☐ **1.** Shake $\frac{1}{2}$ spoonful of yeast on a watermelon slice.

☑ **2.** Put the watermelon slice in the bag. Seal it. Set it in a warm place. **Observe** with a hand lens.

☐ **3.** After 1, 2, and 3 hours, observe the yeast. **Record** any changes.

Yeast Observations	
Time	**Appearance of Yeast on Watermelon Slice**
After 1 hour	
After 2 hours	
After 3 hours	

Explain Your Results

4. Infer Where did the yeast get the energy to grow?

....

....

Draw an ✗ on a living thing that must eat food to get energy.

UNLOCK THE BIG ?

I will know how energy flows through ecosystems in a food chain. I will know how a food web is organized.

Words to Know

producer   decomposer
consumer   food chain

Energy Roles in Ecosystems

Every living thing needs energy to stay alive and grow. Living things get energy in different ways. Green plants use sunlight along with air and water to make sugar. The sugar is the plants' food. It gives plants the energy they need. A living thing is called a **producer** if it makes, or produces, its own food.

Many living things cannot make food. They get energy from food that they eat, or consume. A living thing that eats other organisms is called a **consumer.**

When plants or animals die, their stored-up energy is unused. Decomposers use this energy. A **decomposer** is a living thing that breaks down waste and dead plant and animal matter.

1. Label Write whether the living thing in each picture is a producer, consumer, or decomposer.

Puffins eat fish to get energy.

Mushrooms break down a dead tree for energy.

A fern plant takes in sunlight to make food.

Food Chains

Most ecosystems get energy from sunlight. Plants and other producers transform the sun's energy into food energy. This food energy from producers can be passed along a food chain. A **food chain** is the transfer of energy from one living thing to another.

In a food chain diagram, arrows show the flow of energy. The first link in the food chain on these pages is the sun. A producer, such as grass, is the next link. The producer uses the sun's energy to make food. Next, a consumer, such as a prairie dog, eats the producer. The producer passes energy to the consumer. That consumer may then be eaten by another consumer, such as an eagle. In this way, energy from a producer can be passed from one consumer to another.

The consumers in a food chain can be classified by what they eat. Some consumers eat only plants. They are called *herbivores*. Some consumers eat only other animals. They are called *carnivores*. Other consumers eat both plants and animals. They are called *omnivores*.

2. **Explain** Complete the captions in the diagram to explain how energy is transferred in this food chain.

3. **Identify** Draw an ✗ on the consumer that is an herbivore. ⟨Circle⟩ the consumer that is a carnivore.

4. **Infer** Decomposers are not shown in the diagram. Tell what role you think they play in this food chain.

Grassland Ecosystem

212

A food chain begins with energy from the ....

Golden eagles eat prairie dogs. Energy passes from the .... to the ....

Grasses use air, water, and energy from the .... to make food.

Prairie dogs eat grass. Energy passes from the .... to the ....

Food Webs

Do you eat the same food at every meal? Some animals do not always eat the same things either. Ecosystems have many food chains. Food chains combine to form a food web. A food web is a system of overlapping food chains in an ecosystem. Food webs show that energy flows in many different ways in an ecosystem. Energy can flow from one producer to many consumers. One consumer can be eaten by many other consumers.

5. **Draw** an ✗ on the consumer in this food web that is an omnivore.

6. **Identify** List the consumers in this food web that eat prairie dogs.

....

....

....

snake

golden eagle

badger

black-footed ferret

mouse

coyote

cattle

grasshopper

prairie dog

energy from the sun

grasses

This diagram shows an example of a food web from the Great Plains.

Changes in Food Webs

All of the living things in a food web are connected. If one part of a food web is removed or changed, other parts change. For example, prairie dogs build colonies on the grassy plains. But people also settle on these plains. This reduces the habitat for prairie dogs. Their numbers may decrease. With fewer prairie dogs to eat, black-footed ferrets may not have the food they need. The ferrets may die out. This change can affect the badgers who eat ferrets. Badgers may have to look for other food.

7. ◉ **Cause and Effect** <u>Underline</u> two effects in the text that may result if the number of prairie dogs is reduced.

Lightning Lab

Draw a Food Web
Choose an ecosystem such as a forest or ocean. Draw a food web that shows how energy is transferred from one living thing to another. Tell what might happen if part of the food web disappeared.

Got it?

8. ◉ **Compare and Contrast** How are food chains and food webs alike and different?

....

....

9. **UNLOCK THE BIG ?** Think about what you learned about food chains and food webs. How do living things interact?

....

....

 Stop! I need help with ....

Wait! I have a question about ....

▶ **Go!** Now I know ....

How do ecosystems change?

Envision It!

Tell how this forest fire will affect the living things in this ecosystem.

Inquiry **Explore It!**

How can pollution affect an organism?

☐ **1. Measure** Add 30 mL of water to Cup A. Add 30 mL of vinegar to Cup B.

☐ **2.** Add 1 spoonful of sugar and ½ spoonful of yeast to both cups. Stir gently.

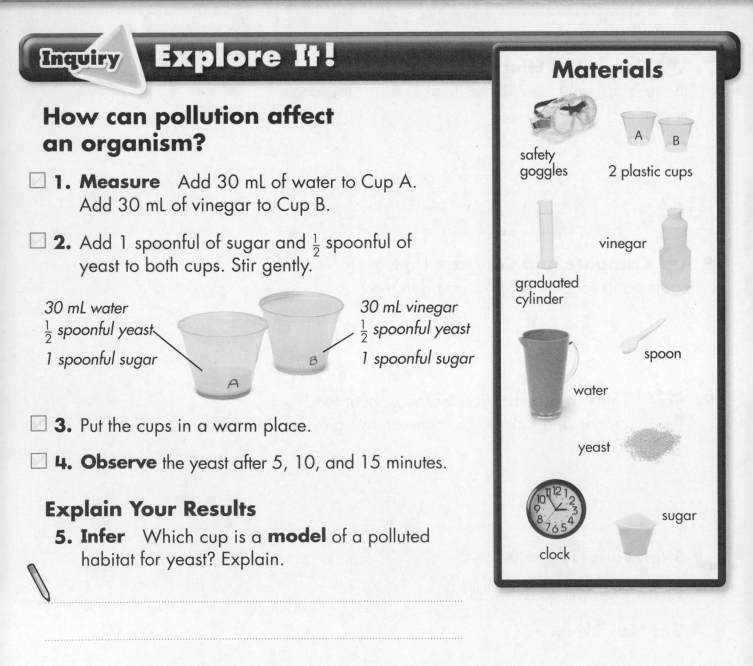

30 mL water
½ spoonful yeast
1 spoonful sugar

30 mL vinegar
½ spoonful yeast
1 spoonful sugar

☐ **3.** Put the cups in a warm place.

☐ **4. Observe** the yeast after 5, 10, and 15 minutes.

Explain Your Results

5. Infer Which cup is a **model** of a polluted habitat for yeast? Explain.

Materials

safety goggles

2 plastic cups

vinegar

graduated cylinder

spoon

water

yeast

sugar

clock

I will know how ecosystems change. I will know that some changes can help and other changes can harm the living things in an ecosystem.

Word to Know

adaptation

Tell another way that a forest ecosystem could change.

Ecosystem Change

Ecosystems are always changing. These changes can be rapid and widespread, such as when a fire burns through a forest. But even smaller changes can have many effects.

Think about what happens when a 200-year-old tree falls in a storm. Throughout its life, the tree shaded the forest floor. Now the forest floor will receive much more sunlight. Seedlings that require a lot of sunlight will have a chance to grow. Other plants that grow best in shade might not survive.

The change may affect animals too. Birds that nested in the tree may need to find a new home. But the fallen tree may provide habitat for salamanders and other animals.

A fallen tree provides shelter for a salamander.

1. ◉ **Cause and Effect** Find a cause and an effect in the text. Write them in the boxes below.

Cause

Effect

Living Things Cause Change

All living things need resources like water and food. Living things get what they need from their environments. As they do this, they cause changes in their environments. For example, people cut down trees to build homes. They clear land in order to grow food in open fields. But people are not the only living things that cause change.

Look at the groundhogs in the pictures. Groundhogs live underground in tunnels, or burrows. As they dig their burrows, they change the environment. These changes can be harmful. Groundhogs can damage crops, lawns, and the roots of trees. But some living things benefit from changes that groundhogs cause. Foxes, rabbits, and other animals often live in burrows made by groundhogs. Groundhogs also improve soil by mixing it as they dig. This benefits plants that grow in the soil.

A groundhog burrow can have many rooms and entrances.

2. **Evaluate** What is one positive effect of the changes groundhogs cause? What is one negative effect?

Read a Graph

Mexican gray wolves used to live in parts of the southwest United States. But as more people settled in this area, the wolves' ecosystem changed. Wolves had less space in which to live. Eventually, wolves disappeared from the region. In 1998, scientists began a project to raise more wolves and release them into the wild. This graph shows changes in the wolf population during the first ten years of the project.

Changes in Wolf Population

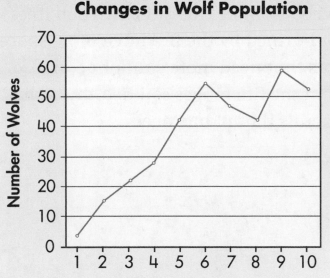

3 Summarize How did the size of the wolf population change during the first ten years of the project?

....

....

....

1 Determine During which years did the population of wolves increase each year?
A. Year 1 to Year 6
B. Year 6 to Year 8
C. Year 6 to Year 9
D. Year 1 to Year 9

4 Predict What is one factor that could stop the wolf population from growing? Explain.

....

....

....

2 Identify In which year was the wolf population the largest?

....

3. **Underline** four things in the text that can change ecosystems.

4. **Infer** In some areas, forest rangers start forest fires on purpose. Why do you think they might do this?

Natural Events Cause Change

Natural events can also change ecosystems. Fires can burn forests. Hurricanes can wash away beaches and knock down trees. They can also cause floods. Floods change ecosystems too. They kill plants and can destroy animal habitats.

Droughts can also change ecosystems. During a drought, very little rain falls. Plants die from lack of water. If animals cannot find enough water, then they may die or move to other places.

Not all living things are harmed by changes to ecosystems. A forest fire may destroy many trees and animals' homes. But the fire also clears dead plants and wood from the forest floor. Then trees that were not harmed by the fire have more space to grow. Plants that need more sunlight can also grow. Ash from the fire makes soil healthy. Ash contains minerals that plants need.

Go Green

Conserve Water
All living things need water. Droughts affect people, plants, and animals. Think about how you use water each day. Create a list of ways that you can save water. Share your list with a partner.

Plants grow in an area cleared by fire.

Seasonal Change

In some ecosystems, the cycle of the seasons brings major changes. For example, summers may be warm, but winters may be very cold and snowy. Some plants die in winter. Food may be hard to find for some animals.

Many plants and animals have adaptations that help them survive these changes. An **adaptation** is a trait that helps a living thing survive in its environment. For example, some trees shed their leaves before winter. This reduces the amount of water they need to take in during winter. Some animals, such as bats and ground squirrels, hibernate, or sleep, through the winter.

Some trees shed their leaves in winter. When spring comes, new leaves will grow.

5. **Word Structure** You can change some verbs to nouns by adding the suffix *–ion*. For example, the word *adaptation* comes from the verb *adapt*. Write the verbs that the nouns below are based on. Say a sentence using each word.

   hibernation ....

   migration ....

6. [CHALLENGE] Do you think the tree in the pictures makes food during the winter? Explain.

   ....

   ....

   ....

Some birds migrate, or move, to warmer places during winter. This golden plover will travel more than a thousand miles when it migrates.

Living Things Return

On May 18, 1980, the volcano Mount St. Helens erupted in the state of Washington. This eruption was huge. The blast changed the ecosystem. It knocked over trees. It burned whole forests and killed many animals. Rivers of mud covered large areas. The volcano released a cloud of ash into the air. Winds carried the ash around the world.

There were few signs of life after the eruption. Over time, however, wind carried the seeds of grasses, flowers, and trees to the mountain. New plants began to grow. Soon spiders and beetles arrived. Birds returned to live in the standing dead trees. Small and large mammals also returned. Each new change allowed more kinds of plants and animals to live there again. The ecosystem is not the same as it was before the eruption. But it is recovering.

Ash poured from Mount St. Helens for nine hours after the eruption.

7. Generalize What generalization can you make about ecosystems based on Mount St. Helens?

....

....

....

....

8. Infer Look at the pictures. Why do you think plants returned to Mount St. Helens before insects and other animals did?

....

....

....

Few plants and animals remained alive on Mount St. Helens after the eruption. Some animals that lived underground survived.

Got it?

9. UNLOCK THE BIG ? Give an example of how an animal can cause a change in an ecosystem that harms other living things.

....

....

10. Explain Describe two ways a forest fire can be helpful to plants.

....

....

Stop! I need help with ....

Wait! I have a question about ....

Go! Now I know ....

What can we learn from fossils?

Tell What do you think this dinosaur ate? Explain.

Inquiry Explore It!

What can a fossil tell you?

☐ **1. Make a model** of a fossil. Press a shell into clay.

☐ **2.** Make a fossil model with an object.

☐ **3.** Guess what your partner's fossil model shows.

Explain Your Results

4. How did you **infer** what your partner's fossil model showed?

....

....

5. How do fossils give clues about living things?

....

....

....

....

Materials

shell

clay

objects

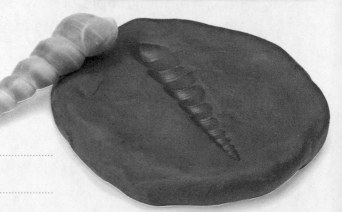

I will know the characteristics of fossils. I will know how fossils are used to learn about the past.

Words to Know

extinct
fossil

Fossils

Many kinds of plants and animals that lived long ago are no longer living on Earth. They are **extinct.** How do scientists learn about plants and animals from the past? One way is to study fossils.

A **fossil** is the remains or mark of a living thing from long ago. Fossils are often found in sedimentary rock. The pictures show one way that fossils form. Sediments cover the remains of an animal. The sediments then turn to rock over time. As the animal's body wears away, it leaves a mold in the rock in the shape of the animal's parts.

Fossils form in other ways too. Some are actual parts of living things, such as bones. Sometimes an animal's whole body becomes a fossil. For example, scientists have found the bodies of insects in hardened tree sap. Signs of living things, such as preserved footprints, are a type of fossil too.

1. Apply Tell if the fossil in the bottom picture is the actual remains of a lizard. Explain how you know.

A lizard dies and is covered by mud.

The mud becomes rock. The mold of the lizard is a fossil.

2. Infer How do you think *T. rex* used its long tail?

....

....

....

....

a fern fossil

3. Predict The fern in the fossil looks black. Do you think ferns from the past were really black? Explain.

....

....

....

....

4. Identify Look at the fern and *T. rex* fossils on these pages. Tell what characteristics you see.

Tyrannosaurus rex *could grow as long as a school bus.*

What Fossils Show

Fossils show how plants and animals have changed over time. They also help us understand how Earth has changed.

From plant fossils, scientists have learned that many of the first plants were like today's ferns. Modern ferns live in warm, moist areas. Ferns from the past probably needed the same conditions. Scientists have found fern fossils in places that today are desert-like. The fossils are a clue that the climate in those places was once warm and wet.

Scientists also use fossils to learn how animals of the past lived. Look at the skeleton of *Tyrannosaurus rex*, a dinosaur that lived more than 65 million years ago. *T. rex* is extinct now. By studying its fossils, scientists can infer how *T. rex* lived. The sharp teeth are a sign that *T. rex* ate meat. The powerful back legs show that *T. rex* walked on two legs, not four. The thick, heavy skull? It probably protected *T. rex* from the bites of other dinosaurs.

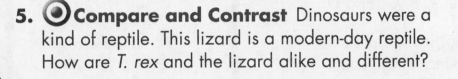

lizard

Lightning Lab

Fossil Cards
Use your school's media center to find pictures of dinosaur fossils. Draw each fossil on an index card. Add notes about what the dinosaur ate and the environment it lived in. Share the cards with a partner.

5. ◉ **Compare and Contrast** Dinosaurs were a kind of reptile. This lizard is a modern-day reptile. How are *T. rex* and the lizard alike and different?

....

....

....

Got it?

6. **Conclude** Scientists find the fossil of a large animal. The fossil shows that the animal had flippers and a tail. What can the scientists conclude?

....

....

7. **Explain** What can we learn about the past from studying fossil records?

....

....

□ **Stop!** I need help with ....

❚❚ **Wait!** I have a question about ....

▶ **Go!** Now I know ....

What can you find in your local ecosystem?

Follow a Procedure

☐ **1.** Use 2 strings to divide a square meter of land into 4 squares. **Measure** the length of each side to make sure the sections are squares. Use index cards to label the squares *A*, *B*, *C*, and *D*.

☐ **2.** Use a hand lens to look for living things in Square A. **Record** the living things you **observe.**

☐ **3.** Observe the nonliving things. Record the things you find.

☐ **4.** Repeat for each square.

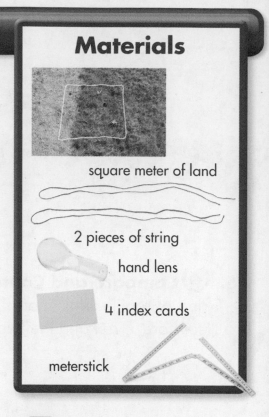

Materials

square meter of land

2 pieces of string

hand lens

4 index cards

meterstick

Be careful! **Wash your hands when finished.**

Inquiry Skill
When you record information you have **observed,** you are collecting data.

Observations		
Square	Living Things	Nonliving Things
A		
B		
C		
D		

Analyze and Conclude

5. What living things were present in the most squares?

....

....

....

6. ANSWER THE BIG ? What nonliving things did you **observe** in your investigation?

....

....

....

....

....

....

Minnesota Valley National Wildlife Refuge, Minnesota

blue-winged teal

THE NATIONAL WILDLIFE REFUGE SYSTEM

The National Wildlife Refuge System was started more than 100 years ago. Its purpose was to set aside land to save plant and animal species. Today, the system includes more than 550 refuges. There is at least one refuge in every state. In fact, there is probably a refuge close enough for you to visit.

A refuge does more than protect individual plants and animals. It also protects habitats. Different refuges protect different types of habitats. For example, Minnesota Valley National Wildlife Refuge provides wetland habitat for migrating ducks. It is one of the few urban refuges in the country. More than three million people live in the area surrounding the refuge.

white-tailed antelope squirrel

Stillwater National Wildlife Refuge, Nevada

REVIEW THE BIG ? Why is protecting habitats important to saving plant and animal species?

Parker River National Wildlife Refuge, Massachusetts

common snapping turtle

Vocabulary Smart Cards

ecosystem
habitat
population
community
producer
consumer
decomposer
food chain
adaptation
extinct
fossil

Play a Game!

Cut out the Vocabulary Smart Cards.

Work with a partner. Choose a Vocabulary Smart Card.

Write two or three sentences using the vocabulary word.

Have your partner repeat with another Vocabulary Smart Card.

community

comunidad

ecosystem

ecosistema

producer
productor

habitat

hábitat

consumer
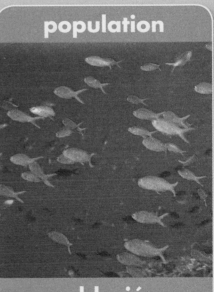
consumidor

population
población

the living and nonliving things that interact in an environment

Write an example of this word.

....

....

todos los seres vivos y las cosas sin vida que interactúan en un área determinada

---

all the populations that live in the same place

Write a sentence using this word.

....

....

....

todas las poblaciones que conviven en el mismo lugar

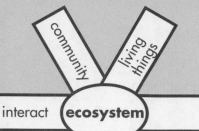

Make a Word Wheel!

Choose a vocabulary word and write it in the center of the Word Wheel graphic. Write synonyms or related words on the wheel spokes.

---

the place where a living thing makes its home

Draw an example.

el lugar donde un ser vivo establece su hogar

---

a living thing that makes, or produces, its own food

Write a sentence using this word.

....

....

....

ser vivo que genera, o produce, su propio alimento

---

all the living things of the same kind that live in the same place

What is the suffix of this word?

....

....

....

todos los seres vivos de la misma especie que viven en el mismo lugar

---

a living thing that eats other organisms

Write the verb form of this word.

....

....

....

ser vivo que se alimenta de otros organismos

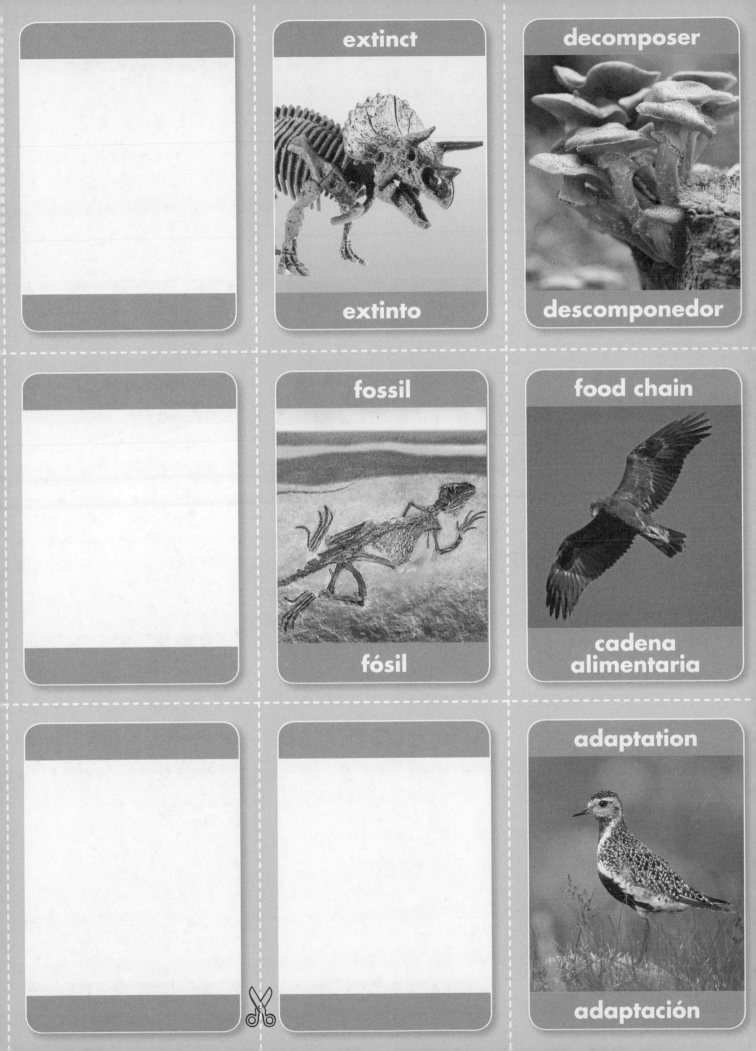

extinct

extinto

decomposer

descomponedor

fossil

fósil

food chain

cadena alimentaria

adaptation

adaptación

a living thing that breaks down waste and dead plant and animal matter

Write an example of this word.

....

....

ser vivo que destruye residuos y materia de animales y vegetales muertos

---

no longer lives on Earth

Write as many antonyms as you can think of.

....

....

....

....

que ya no existe en la Tierra

....

....

....

....

---

the transfer of energy from one living thing to another

Draw an example.

transmisión de energía de un ser vivo a otro

---

remains or mark of a living thing from long ago

Write a sentence using this word.

....

....

....

restos o marca de un ser vivo que existió hace mucho tiempo

....

....

....

....

---

a trait that helps a living thing survive in its environment

Write an example of this word.

....

....

....

rasgo de los seres vivos que los ayuda a sobrevivir en su medio ambiente

---

....

....

....

....

....

Lesson 1

What is an ecosystem?

- An ecosystem is all the living and nonliving things that interact in an environment.
- Populations and communities are groups within ecosystems.

Lesson 2

How do living things get energy?

- The sun's energy flows to living things through a food chain.
- A food web is a system of overlapping food chains in an ecosystem.

Lesson 3

How do ecosystems change?

- Living things can cause changes in their environment.
- Changes can help some living things and harm others.
- Natural events, such as droughts, can change ecosystems.

Lesson 4

What can we learn from fossils?

- A fossil is the remains or mark of a plant or animal that lived long ago.
- Fossils show how plants and animals have changed over time.
- Fossils help scientists learn about plants and animals that are extinct.

Lesson 1

What is an ecosystem?

1. **Vocabulary** All the populations living in the same place form a(n)_____.
   A. community
   B. resource
   C. ecosystem
   D. habitat

2. **Predict** Desert snakes eat kangaroo rats. What do you think would happen to the population of rats if the population of snakes grew larger? Why?

3. **Write About It** Describe how a raccoon in a marsh interacts with a living part and a nonliving part of the ecosystem.

Lesson 2

How do living things get energy?

4. **Vocabulary** A living thing that breaks down waste and dead plant and animal matter is called a ___.
   A. carnivore
   B. producer
   C. consumer
   D. decomposer

5. **Identify** Which of the following is an example of an herbivore?
   A. coyote
   B. golden eagle
   C. grasshopper
   D. snake

6. **Suggest** List three living things that might be part of a prairie food chain. Explain how they get energy.

Life
Science

Lesson 3

How do ecosystems change?

Do the math!

7. Look at the graph below. Describe the overall change in the wolf population from Year 5 to Year 10.

....

....

....

Changes in Wolf Population

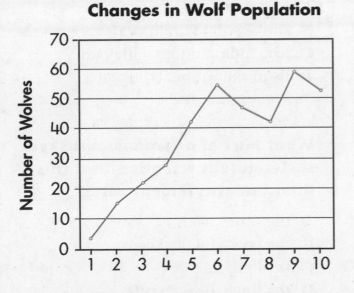

8. Give an Example Describe an adaptation that helps an animal survive seasonal changes in its ecosystem.

....

....

Lesson 4

9. Identify Which of the following is an example of a fossil?
   A. a bone that has turned to stone
   B. the body of an insect trapped in tree sap
   C. a footprint preserved in rock
   D. all of the above

10. Vocabulary An extinct animal is one that _____
   A. eats only meat.
   B. eats only plants.
   C. no longer lives on Earth.
   D. walks on its hind legs.

11. Write About It How do fossils help scientists learn how plants and animals have changed over time?

....

....

....

....

....

....

....

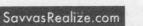 **237**

Benchmark Practice

Life Science

Read each question and choose the best answer.

1 Which of the following is an example of a decomposer?

A the sun
B a grasshopper
C a mushroom
D a bear

2 What do sunlight, soil, air, and water all have in common?

A They are nonliving parts of an ecosystem.
B They are a community.
C They are living parts of an ecosystem.
D They are part of a population.

3 Which statement is true about how changes in the environment affect the living things in an ecosystem?

A Changes harm all living things.
B Changes benefit all living things.
C Changes harm some living things and benefit others.
D Changes are not harmful.

4 Some trees shed their leaves before winter. What is this an example of?

A an adaptation
B a competition
C an ecosystem
D a population

5 Which of the following is an example of an interaction between a living part of an ecosystem and a nonliving part?

A bird nesting in a tree
B snake eating an insect
C frog hiding under a lily pad
D fish finding shelter in water

6 What part of a *Tyrannosaurus rex* skeleton tells scientists that this dinosaur was a meat-eater?

A the sharp teeth
B the powerful back legs
C the long tail
D the thick, heavy skull

Zoo Designer

Have you ever wondered who designs zoos? A zoo designer plans new zoos or improves older ones. Zoo designers build safe environments that meet the animals' needs. Animals in a zoo come from many different places. Each kind of animal is adapted to a specific environment. Some animals have special adaptations to help meet their needs. A zoo designer has to understand each animal's adaptations.

For example, a polar bear has thick fur that keeps it warm in an arctic environment. A zoo designer needs to make a cold-weather environment that meets the polar bear's adaptation. Some zoo designers design a space based on an animal's adaptation to seasons. For example, penguins are from Antarctica. The lighting of penguin exhibits mimics the amount of light in Antarctica in different seasons.

Name an animal. How do you think a zoo designer would build a habitat to meet the needs of this animal?

....

....

....

....

Materials

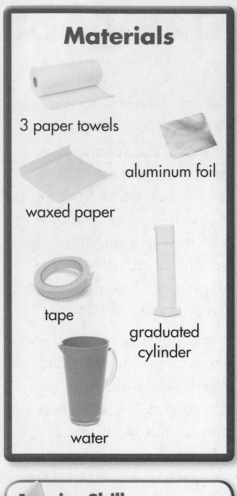

3 paper towels

aluminum foil

waxed paper

tape

graduated cylinder

water

Inquiry Skill
Every experiment must have a **hypothesis,** a testable statement.

How can plants survive in the desert?

Some plants have flat leaves. Many cactus plants have leaves shaped like needles. Some leaves have a waxy coating. The shape of the leaf helps the plant survive.

Ask a question.
How can a leaf's structure help a plant hold water?

State a hypothesis.
1. Write a **hypothesis.** Circle one choice and finish the sentence. If a leaf is narrow and thin and has a waxy coating, it will lose water
(a) *more slowly*
(b) *more quickly*
than flat leaves or leaves without a waxy coating because

....

....

....

Identify and control variables.
2. In an **experiment** you change only one **variable.** Everything else must remain the same. What must stay the same? Give one example.

....

....

3. Tell the one change you will make.

....

....

Design your test.

☐ **4.** Draw how you will set up your test.

☐ **5.** List your steps in the order you will do them.

Do your test.

☐ **6.** Follow the steps you wrote.

☐ **7. Record** your results in the table.

Collect and record your data.

☐ **8.** After one day, describe your towels in the chart below.

> **Work Like a Scientist**
> It is important to make careful observations. Record all of your observations. Use charts or graphs to help you record.

Interpret your data.

☑ **9.** Compare how damp the towels were after one day.

☑ **10.** How does the shape and size of a leaf affect how fast a leaf loses water? Why?

☑ **11.** How does a waxy coating help a plant?

State your conclusion.

12. You conducted an **experiment** to test your **hypothesis.** Compare your hypothesis with your results. **Communicate** your conclusions.

----

13. Infer What are 2 adaptations cactuses have that help them survive in the desert?

Performance-Based Assessment

Germinating Seeds

Seeds need the right conditions to germinate and grow. Use plastic cups, potting soil, and bean seeds to find out how well seeds germinate and grow with different amounts of water.

- What happened when you watered the seeds too much?
- What happened when you watered the seeds too little?

Animals and Seasons

Different animals respond to seasons and temperatures in different ways. Think about three animals in your area. Draw pictures of how they look and where they live during summer. Then draw pictures of how they look and where they live during winter. Write a description of the ways that the animals in your area respond to changing seasons.

- Why do you think animals respond to changing seasons?

Science and Engineering Practices

1. Ask a question or define a problem.
2. Develop and use models.
3. Plan and carry out investigations.
4. Analyze and interpret data.
5. Use math and computational thinking.
6. Construct explanations or design solutions.
7. Engage in argument from evidence.
8. Obtain, evaluate, and communicate information.

Life Cycle Poster

Choose an animal that lives in your state. Make a poster that shows the stages in the animal's life cycle. The poster should include:

- pictures of what the animal looks like at each stage of development,
- captions describing how the animal changes at each stage, and
- arrows connecting the stages in the correct sequence.

Matching Traits

Work with a partner. Use magazines or the Internet to find many pictures of the same type of animal. Look for pictures of both parents and their offspring. For each set of pictures, circle a trait on the parent and the matching trait on the offspring. For example, you might circle the long ears of a parent rabbit and those of its offspring. Write the trait on a sheet of paper or next to the photo. Then give your partner the photo to place an X on another pair of matching traits. Continue to take turns identifying matching traits with circles and Xs and writing the traits. Try to identify at least eight matching traits.

- What evidence did you see that animals inherit traits from their parents?
- What else might affect an animal's traits?

Why is there snow up here and not down here?

Weather Patterns

Try It! How does water temperature affect evaporation?

STEM Activity Runaway Water!

Investigate It! How are clouds and the weather related?

Earth Science

Apply It! Does the salt in salt water evaporate?

Some of the hottest places on Earth have mountains that are covered in snow.

Predict What makes the weather at the top of the mountain different from the weather at the bottom of the mountain?

....

....

 How does weather change over time?

How does water temperature affect evaporation?

When water changes from a liquid to a gas, it evaporates.

☐ 1. **Predict** how water temperature affects evaporation.

....

....

☐ 2. Choose a water and fill the plastic cup halfway. Write your temperature on the cup.

☐ 3. Put the lid on the cup.

☐ 4. Put an ice cube on the lid.

☐ 5. **Observe** Describe what you see in your cup. Compare your results with other groups.

....

....

....

....

Explain Your Results

6. **Draw a Conclusion** How did water temperature affect evaporation?

....

....

Materials

plastic cup

lid

ice cube

water (cold, room temperature, warm)

Inquiry Skill
You use what you observe to help **draw a conclusion.**

◉ Sequence

The order in which events happen is the **sequence** of those events. Sequence can also mean the steps you follow to do something.

Tornado!

The air was humid on that day, and the sky looked dark and greenish. First, the tornado sirens began to wail. People took cover underground. Next, hailstones started to fall. The wind began knocking down trees and poles. Finally, the tornado arrived. It sounded like a freight train as it ripped off roofs, pulled up trees, and overturned cars.

Practice It!

Use the graphic organizer to list the sequence of events in the paragraph above.

First

....

....

Next

....

....

Finally

....

....

Runaway Water!

Do you know how powerful water is? It's a powerful natural resource! The flow of water can be difficult to control. Dams can help humans control water and use it for many purposes. Dams can prevent flooding. They also can provide a source of drinking water. Dams can convert the energy of falling water into other types of energy. Dams also provide people with places to swim, fish, and boat. Your state government has hired you to design a dam to stop or change the flow of water.

Identify the Problem

☐ **1.** What problem will your design help solve? _____

_____

_____

Do Research

☐ **2. Examine** several pictures of dams. What functions do these dams provide?

_____

_____

☐ **3.** What are some properties of water that provide challenges when building a dam?

_____

_____

☐ **4.** How might the location of a dam affect its design?

_____

_____

Go to the materials station(s). Look at each material. Think about how it may or may not be useful for building your dam. Leave the materials where they are.

☑ **5.** What are your design constraints?

_____

_____

Develop Possible Solutions

☑ **6. Describe** two ways in which you could use the materials to build a dam.

_____

_____

Choose One Solution

☑ **7. Describe** your dam and how you will build it. _____

_____

_____

☑ **8. List** the materials you will need. _____

_____

_____

☑ **9.** Why did you choose these materials? _____

_____

_____

Design and Construct a Prototype

Gather your materials plus a ruler. Use your design to build a dam in a stream table. Measure the dimensions of your dam and the space it fills.

☑ **10. Record** the measurements of your prototype. ✎ _____

_____

_____

Test the Prototype

Test your design. Pour water into the stream table so that it flows toward the dam. **Observe** how the dam affects the flow of water. Start with a small amount of water. Increase the flow of water. What happens when you increase the flow of water?

Communicate Results

☑ **11.** Did your dam solve the problem you identified? Rate your design on a scale of 1 to 3 with 1 being poor results, 2 being good results, and 3 being great results. Explain why you give your dam this rating.

_____

_____

_____

Evaluate and Redesign

☑ **12.** What changes could you make to your design to make it work better?

_____

_____

☑ **13. Record** the new measurements. Make your changes.

_____

_____

☐ **14.** How well did your revised prototype work? Explain. ✎

_____

_____

What is the water cycle?

Envision It!

Circle the places where you think there is water.

MY PLANET DIARY

Connections

You can use a map and your geography skills to help you understand why some places have a lot of storms. Did you know that New Orleans, Louisiana, is the third wettest city in the United States? This city gets about 162 cm (64 in.) of rain each year. Why does New Orleans get so much rain? Blame it on the Gulf of Mexico. Storms from the Atlantic Ocean pick up moisture from the warm waters of the Gulf. These storms then drop heavy rainfall as they move over land.

Look at the map. What other places might get a lot of rain? Explain why.

....

....

....

Houston Baton Rouge Biloxi Mobile Pensacola Tallahassee
New Orleans

Corpus Christi

Tampa
Fort Myers

Gulf of Mexico

I will know the processes of the water cycle.

Words to Know

water cycle
precipitation

Water on Earth

The water on Earth is found in different forms. It can be found in many places. Water can move from one place to another.

Suppose you follow a particle of water for a year. First, you might find the water particle crashing on a beach in an ocean wave. Next, you might find it drifting high as part of a cloud. Finally, you might find the water particle floating down as snow.

Water covers about three fourths of Earth's surface.

1. ◉ **Sequence** Read the second paragraph again. Complete the graphic organizer to show the cycle of a water particle.

First

> ⌇ ....

↓

Next

> drifting high as part of a cloud

↓

Finally

> ....

Go Green

Reduce Water Use

There is only a certain amount of fresh water on Earth. It must be used again and again. Think about how you use water. Describe three ways that you could use less water.

Condensation

The water vapor rises into the air and cools. As it cools, the vapor changes into tiny water droplets. This change from a gas into a liquid is called condensation. The water droplets collect and form clouds.

2. **Underline** the word in the caption that describes the process of water vapor becoming a liquid.

Evaporation

The sun's warmth causes water on Earth's surface to evaporate. Evaporation is the change from liquid water to water vapor, a gas.

Water Cycle

The movement of water from Earth's surface into the air and back again is the **water cycle.** The water cycle is important because it gives Earth a constant supply of fresh water. Most of Earth's water is salty ocean water that you cannot drink.

Water changes form, or state, as it moves through the water cycle. After water moves through the stages of the water cycle, the cycle begins again. Read the captions and follow the arrows to find out more.

Precipitation

Water particles in the clouds join together. When they become heavy, they fall to Earth as rain, snow, sleet, or hail. Water that falls to Earth is called **precipitation**.

Storage

Some precipitation seeps into the ground. Other precipitation, called runoff, flows over the land and collects in streams, lakes, and the ocean.

Got it?

3. Identify List the steps of the water cycle.

Evaporation oder pee ci pite ton

4. Conclude Why is the sun important to the water cycle?

the sun is import because it helps the water to evapoat

⬛ **Stop!** I need help with it

⏸ **Wait!** I have a question about it

▶ **Go!** Now I know it

What are weather and climate?

Tell how the weather patterns in these two places are different.

Inquiry **Explore It!**

What is the daily temperature?

Materials

thermometer

☐ **1.** Place your thermometer outside. Wait 5 minutes.

☐ **2.** **Measure** the temperature. **Record.**

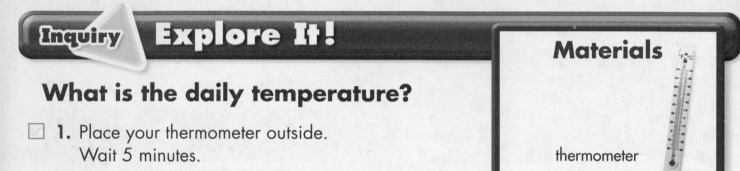

Temperature for 3 Days	
Day	Temperature (°C)
Day 1	
Day 2	
Day 3	

☐ **3.** Repeat Step 2 for two days at the same time every day.

Explain Your Results

4. **Infer** Would your data be the same all year? Would it be the same a year from now? Explain.

....

....

I will know the difference between weather and climate. I will know how to describe climate patterns by using weather data.

Words to Know

weather

climate

Weather

What will the weather be this weekend? Will it be sunny or rainy? **Weather** is what the air is like outside. Weather includes the kinds of clouds in the sky and the amount of water in the air. It includes the temperature of the air and how the wind is blowing.

Clouds are made of water or ice particles in the air. Different kinds of clouds may form in different weather. Because of this, clouds can help predict what the weather will be or how it will change. For example, you often see white, fluffy clouds on sunny days.

1. Describe Write what the weather is like today. Include at least two facts.

....

....

....

....

2. Predict Look at the picture of the dark clouds. Write a caption that tells what weather you think they may bring.

....

....

....

Climate

You can describe the weather where you are. Can you describe the climate? Weather and climate are not the same thing. Weather is what the air is like in a place at a single moment. **Climate** is the pattern of weather in a place over many years.

Climate includes the average temperatures in an area. It also includes the average amount of precipitation. The climate of a place can change, but it takes many years. Weather can change every day.

3. Infer Look at the picture on these pages. It shows Oklahoma City, Oklahoma. What can you infer about Oklahoma's climate?

Lightning Lab

Local Climate
Discuss your local climate with a partner. List words that describe it. Compare it to the climates of the cities shown on the map. Which city has a climate most like yours?

Phoenix, Arizona

Average Temperature		Average Yearly Precipitation
January	July	
12°C (54°F)	35°C (95°F)	21 cm

Different parts of the United States have different climates. Look at the map below. Each color on the map represents a different type of climate.

The charts show climate data for three cities. You can use these data to describe the climate patterns for the cities. For example, Oklahoma City has a humid climate, with cool winters and hot summers. The climate in Bismarck is much drier, with cold winters and warm summers.

4. **Apply** Draw an X on the map in a place where you would expect the climate to be similar to the climate in Bismarck, North Dakota.

5. **Describe** How does the climate of Phoenix compare to the climate of Oklahoma City?

Bismarck, North Dakota

Average Temperature		Average Yearly Precipitation
January	July	
−12°C (10°F)	21°C (70°F)	43 cm

Oklahoma City, Oklahoma

Average Temperature		Average Yearly Precipitation
January	July	
4°C (40°F)	28°C (83°F)	94 cm

Factors That Affect Climate

Why do different places have different climates? One factor is the amount of sunlight a place receives. Sunlight hits Earth most directly at the equator. The equator is an imaginary line that circles Earth halfway between the North Pole and South Pole. Places near the equator usually have warmer climates than places farther from it.

The ocean is another factor that affects climate. Places near the ocean often have milder temperatures than places inland. They also may receive more precipitation. The diagram below of the California coast shows how winds from the ocean can affect climate.

6. Explain Look at the diagram. Tell how the ocean affects the climate on the western side of the mountain.

....

....

....

....

....

Along the Pacific coast, the air normally moves from west to east. Warm, moist air over the ocean moves over the land.

Mountains force the air to rise and cool. Water vapor condenses and forms lots of clouds. Then, the rain falls. These factors bring a pattern of mild, wet weather to the west side of the mountains.

Landforms Affect Climate

Mountains and other landforms may affect climate too. The diagram shows why places on opposite sides of a mountain may have different weather patterns. The west side of the mountain has mild, wet weather. The other side of the mountain has dry weather.

Altitude is another factor. Altitude is the height above sea level. The higher the altitude of a place, the colder the air. Temperatures at the mountain top would be colder than temperatures at the bottom.

7. **Draw** an ✗ on the land area that receives the least amount of rain.

8. CHALLENGE Explain why the west side of the mountain has the most trees.

....

....

....

....

....

The air does not have much moisture after it has crossed the mountains. Little rain or snow falls. The eastern side of the mountain has a pattern of dry weather.

As clouds move east, they rise higher up the side of the mountain. The air is colder, and snow falls.

winter

spring

Seasonal Weather Patterns

You might describe a climate as hot. But does that mean the weather in that place is always hot? You know that weather can change every day. Weather also changes from one season to the next.

Many parts of the world have four seasons: spring, summer, fall, and winter. Each season may have its own weather patterns. Areas close to the equator may have only two seasons: a dry season and a wet season. Temperatures in these areas may stay warm year-round.

9. Analyze Do you think the place in the pictures is near the equator? Explain.

....

....

Do the math!

Interpret a Graph

The graph shows average monthly temperatures for two cities. Use the graph to answer the questions.

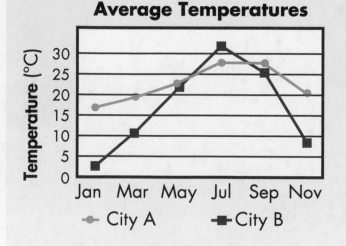

Average Temperatures

City A
City B

1 Which city is usually colder in January?

....

2 Which city is usually warmer in July?

....

3 One city is close to the ocean. The other is far from the ocean. Which city is close to the ocean? Tell how you know.

....

Seasonal Weather Data

You can use recorded weather data to tell about the climate patterns for a place. The table below shows monthly weather data for Boise, Idaho.

10. Describe Tell about the climate patterns in Boise from January to November.

Average Monthly Weather for Boise, Idaho						
	Jan.	March	May	July	Sept.	Nov.
High temperature	3°C (37°F)	12°C (54°F)	22°C (72°F)	32°C (90°F)	25°C (77°F)	9°C (48°F)
Low temperature	–4°C (25°F)	1°C (34°F)	8°C (47°F)	16°C (61°F)	11°C (52°F)	0°C (32°F)
Average precipitation	4 cm	4 cm	3 cm	1 cm	2 cm	4 cm

Got it?

11. Describe How are weather and climate different?

....

....

12. Analyze Two cities are at the same altitude but have different climates. What is one possible reason?

....

....

⬛ **Stop!** I need help with ....

⏸ **Wait!** I have a question about ....

▶ **Go!** Now I know ....

Lesson 3

What tools are used to measure weather?

Envision It!

Describe the weather in the picture.

Inquiry **Explore It!**

How does an anemometer work?

☐ 1. Make an anemometer like the one in the picture.

☐ 2. Use your anemometer to **measure** the wind in different places. **Observe.**

Explain Your Results

3. **Communicate** Tell how your anemometer works.

....

....

....

....

Materials

safety goggles

paper cups with holes

straw

push pin

unsharpened pencil

Be careful! Wear safety goggles.

I will know how tools are used to measure and describe weather conditions.

Word to Know

atmosphere

Why We Measure Weather

How would you describe the weather today? You might say it is too hot or too cold. Someone else might not agree. That person might like the weather. Words like *hot* and *cold* mean different things to different people.

You could also describe the weather by saying that the temperature is 34° Celsius, or 93° Fahrenheit. Celsius and Fahrenheit are scales used to measure temperature. Scientists measure weather so that they can describe its characteristics exactly. If a scientist reports that the temperature is 34° Celsius, people everywhere can understand what that means.

1. **Underline** the sentence that tells why scientists measure weather.

2. **Measure** Look at the thermometer. If the temperature got colder, would the red line move up or down?

_____

A thermometer is a tool used to measure the temperature of the air. Do you think this thermometer shows the temperature in the picture?

Measure and Record Temperatures

Place a thermometer outside. Wait 10 minutes. Read the thermometer. Record the temperature in degrees Celsius and Fahrenheit. Repeat every morning, at the same time, for a week. Graph the temperatures. Describe what you observed to a partner.

Tools for Measuring Weather

Scientists use a number of tools to help them measure and describe weather. When scientists measure the weather in different places at different times, they can better predict what the weather will be like.

An anemometer measures wind speed. A wind vane shows the direction from which the wind is blowing. Both wind speed and direction affect the weather.

Scientists use a hygrometer to measure how much water vapor is in the air. The amount of water vapor in the air is called humidity. The humidity is low when air is dry. The humidity is high when air has more water vapor in it.

A rain gauge measures water too. A rain gauge measures how much rain has fallen.

3. **Circle** the two tools used to measure wind.

4. **Draw** an ✗ on the two tools used to measure water.

rain gauge

wind vane

anemometer

hygrometer

Air Pressure

Most weather tools help scientists describe the atmosphere. The **atmosphere** is the blanket of air that surrounds Earth. The atmosphere is made up of gases that have no color, taste, or odor. These gases have weight. The weight of the atmosphere presses down on Earth. This pressing down is called air pressure.

Scientists can measure air pressure with a tool called a barometer. Changes in air pressure are clues to the kind of weather that is on the way. Low air pressure often means the weather will be cloudy or rainy. High air pressure often means fair weather with sunny, clear skies.

5. Predict Look at the barometer. If the air pressure becomes lower, how might the weather change?

barometer

Got it?

6. Compare How are a wind vane and an anemometer the same? How are they different?

7. Infer A hygrometer shows that the humidity has changed from high to low. How has the air changed?

⏹ **Stop!** I need help with

⏸ **Wait!** I have a question about

▶ **Go!** Now I know

How can you stay safe in severe weather?

Envision It!

Tell what you think you should do if you see lightning.

Inquiry Explore It!

What do tornadoes look like?

☑ 1. **Make a Model** Put the tops of the bottles together. Seal with duct tape.

☑ 2. Flip the bottles.
The water is now on top.

☑ 3. Swirl. **Observe** the top bottle.

Explain Your Results

4. How is your **model** like a tornado?
How is it different?

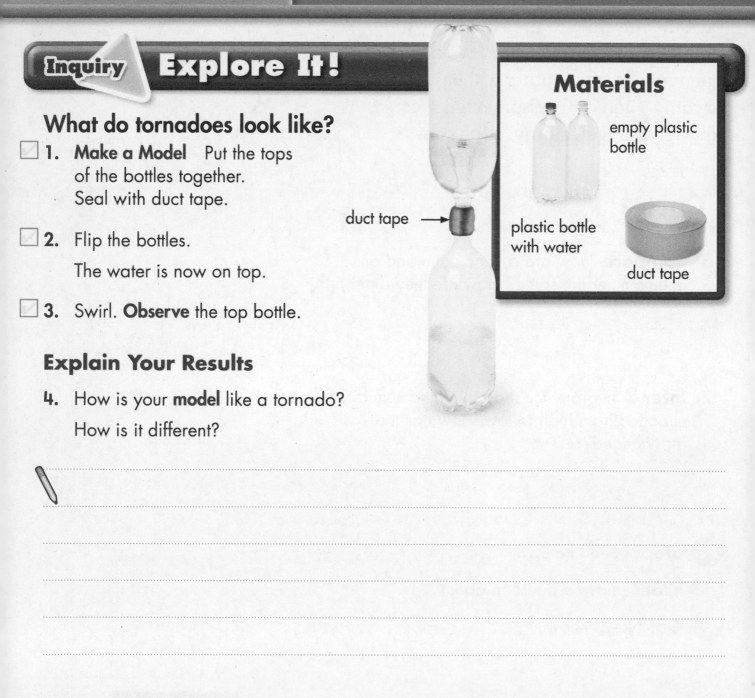

duct tape →

Materials

empty plastic bottle

plastic bottle with water

duct tape

Words to Know

severe weather

Thunderstorms

Severe weather is dangerous weather. A thunderstorm is one kind of severe weather. A thunderstorm is heavy rain with thunder and lightning. Sometimes thunderstorms have hail and strong winds too.

Other kinds of severe weather include blizzards, tornados, and hurricanes. A blizzard is a storm with heavy snow and strong winds.

Hail is pieces of ice that fall from clouds.

1. Underline two details about thunderstorms.

Thunderstorm Safety

- Find shelter in a sturdy building.

- Keep away from windows, water, and trees.

- Keep away from metal objects.

- Keep away from things that use electricity.

Tornadoes

Tornadoes can happen during thunderstorms. A tornado is a small but very strong wind that comes down from thunderstorm clouds.

Tornadoes form very quickly. It is hard to predict when tornadoes will happen. A tornado can destroy things in its path.

2. Write why it is important to be ready for severe weather.

....

....

....

....

....

Tornado Safety

• Go to the basement or an inside room.

• Crouch under the stairs or near an inner wall.

• Stay away from windows.

• Cover your head.

3. Draw an ✗ on the place where the tornado in this picture came down from.

At-Home Lab

Safe Places
Work with an adult. Identify one kind of severe weather. Make a plan to stay safe. Tell where safe places are. Tell what things you will need.

Hurricanes

A hurricane is a large storm that starts over warm ocean water. A hurricane has heavy rains. The rains can cause floods. A hurricane has very strong winds. The winds can knock down trees and buildings.

4. Compare and Contrast Write how tornadoes and hurricanes are alike and different.

....

....

....

Got it?

5. Explain How are a thunderstorm and a tornado related?

....

6. Infer Why should you stay away from windows during severe weather?

....

Stop! I need help with ....

Wait! I have a question about ....

Go! Now I know ....

5. Draw an arrow to show which way the wind is blowing.

Hurricane Safety

- Move away from the ocean.

- Bring loose objects inside.

- Stay inside and away from windows.

- Store extra food and water in your home.

How are clouds and the weather related?

Follow a Procedure

☐ 1. **Observe** the weather daily. Make your observation at the same time each day.

☐ 2. Describe the clouds. **Record.**

☐ 3. Complete the Weather Word Bank. Use words that describe weather.

☐ 4. Record the temperature and kind of weather. Use the words from the Weather Word Bank.

Materials

outdoor thermometer

 Be careful! **Do not look directly at the sun.**

Inquiry Skill
Scientists observe carefully and **record** their observations.

Weather Word Bank		
fair		
warm		
thunderstorm		

5. Use your journal notes to complete the chart.

Cloud and Weather Observations			
Day	Cloud Type	Kind of Weather	Temperature (°C and °F)
1			
2			
3			
4			
5			
6			
7			
8			
9			

Analyze and Conclude

6. Interpret Data How are cloud type and kind of weather related?

....

....

....

7. UNLOCK THE BIG ? Clouds are made of tiny droplets of water. How does water help create weather patterns?

....

....

....

....

Air Traffic Controller

You are in the control tower at an airport. You can see all the planes and runways. As an air traffic controller, your job is to make sure the planes take off and land safely.

Computers tell you the height, speed, and course of all the aircraft. Computers also tell how the weather is changing, minute by minute. You need to interpret this information and give pilots directions. Has the wind suddenly changed direction? Is the weather foggy, making it hard for pilots to see? Is a thunderstorm approaching? You give pilots directions to help them avoid bad weather and keep their planes a safe distance from other planes.

People who become air traffic controllers usually attend four years of college. They take classes to learn about weather and meteorology. What they learn about weather will help them be good controllers.

Do air traffic controllers give pilots information about weather or climate? Explain.

Vocabulary Smart Cards

water cycle
precipitation
weather
climate
atmosphere
severe weather

Play a Game!

Cut out the Vocabulary Smart Cards.

Work with a partner. Choose a Vocabulary Smart Card.

Say as many words as you can think of to describe the vocabulary word.

Have your partner guess the word.

Have your partner repeat with another Vocabulary Smart Card.

climate

clima

water cycle

ciclo del agua

atmosphere

atmósfera

precipitation

precipitación

severe weather

tiempo severo

weather

tiempo atmosférico

279

the movement of water from Earth's surface into the air and back again

Draw one part of the water cycle. Label it.

movimiento de ida y vuelta que realiza el agua entre el aire y la superficie de la Tierra

---

the pattern of weather in a place over many years

Write a sentence using this word.

....

....

....

patrón que sigue el tiempo atmosférico de un lugar a lo largo de muchos años

---

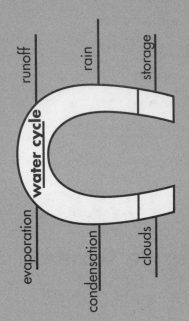

Make a Word Magnet!

Choose a vocabulary word and write it in the Word Magnet. Write words that are related to it on the lines.

---

water that falls to Earth

Write the verb form of the word.

....

....

....

agua que cae a la Tierra

---

the blanket of air that surrounds Earth

What suffix does this word have?

....

....

....

capa de aire que rodea la Tierra

---

what the air is like outside

Write a sentence using this word.

....

....

....

....

las condiciones al aire libre

---

dangerous weather

Write an example of this phrase.

....

....

....

....

tiempo peligroso

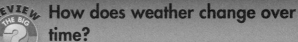

Lesson 1

What is the water cycle?

- The movement of water from Earth's surface into the air and back again is called the water cycle.
- Evaporation and condensation are some parts of the cycle.

Lesson 2

What are weather and climate?

- Weather is what the air is like outside.
- Climate is the weather pattern in a place over many years.
- Landforms and oceans are factors that affect climate.

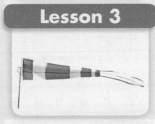

Lesson 3

What tools are used to measure weather?

- You can use weather tools to measure and describe weather.
- A hygrometer is a weather tool that measures humidity, or the amount of water vapor in the air.

Lesson 4

How can you stay safe in severe weather?

- Thunderstorms, tornadoes, and hurricanes are examples of dangerous, severe weather.
- You can make a plan to stay safe in severe weather.

Lesson 1

What is the water cycle?

1. **Vocabulary** Precipitation that flows over the land and collects in streams, lakes, or the ocean is called _____.
   A. evaporation
   B. runoff
   C. condensation
   D. water vapor

2. **Explain** Describe what causes water on Earth's surface to evaporate.

   _____

   _____

   _____

3. **Write About It** What happens when water vapor rises into cooler air?

   _____

   _____

   _____

   _____

Lesson 2

What are weather and climate?

Do the math!

Average Temperatures		
	January	July
Macon, Georgia	7°C (45°F)	27°C (81°F)
Phoenix, Arizona	12°C (54°F)	35°C (95°F)

4. Look at the table. Which city has the bigger difference between average January temperature and average July temperature?

   _____

5. ◉ **Sequence** Tell how the weather changes from season to season where you live.

   _____

   _____

   _____

6. **Vocabulary** The pattern of weather in a place over many years is called _____.
   A. weather
   B. condensation
   C. altitude
   D. climate

Lesson 3

What tools are used to measure weather?

7. **Predict** The air pressure in your area is rising. How do you think the weather will change?

8. **Analyze** If you had the tools shown here, what information about weather could you collect?

9. **Determine** What tool would you use to measure the speed of the wind?

Lesson 4

How can you stay safe in severe weather?

10. **Compare and Contrast** How are a tornado and a hurricane similar? How are they different?

11. **APPLY THE BIG ?** **How does weather change over time?**

A friend of yours visits Australia for five days. The weather is cold and rainy each day she is there. Can your friend conclude that Australia has a cold, wet climate? Explain.

Benchmark Practice

Read each question and choose the best answer.

1 Look at the table. Which <u>best</u> describes the climate in Miami?

DATA FOR MIAMI, FLORIDA

Average Temperature		Average Yearly Precipitation
January	July	
20°C (68°F)	29°C (84°F)	149 cm

A cold winters, hot summers

B cold winters, cool summers

C warm winters, hot summers

D always cold

2 Which of the following describes what the air is like outside?

A climate

B altitude

C weather

D runoff

3 A place near the ocean <u>most</u> <u>likely</u> has what type of climate?

A very cold and wet

B mild and wet

C very cold and dry

D hot and dry

4 Which of these would you use to measure precipitation?

A hygrometer

B rain gauge

C barometer

D anemometer

5 Clouds form during which stage of the water cycle?

A precipitation

B runoff

C evaporation

D condensation

6 Which kind of severe weather is hard to predict because it can form very quickly?

A rain

B thunderstorm

C tornado

D hurricane

Studying Clouds From Space

BigWorld My World

My World

Big World

Have you ever lain on your back and looked at the clouds? Clouds can form interesting shapes. They also can tell you things about the weather. For example, cirrus clouds are thin, feathery clouds high in the air. Cirrus clouds are a sign of fair weather. Stratus clouds cover the sky like a blanket. They often bring rain or snow.

Some scientists study clouds from space using satellites. They are trying to understand how clouds affect Earth's climate. Some satellite tools measure the sunlight that bounces off clouds. Scientists are finding that low, thick clouds reflect sunlight back into space. These clouds have a cooling effect on Earth.

Cirrus clouds are different. They allow sunlight to pass to Earth. The heat is then trapped. These clouds have a heating effect.

APPLY THE BIG ? How do clouds cause weather to change?

_____

_____

_____

Inquiry Apply It! Using Scientific Methods

Materials

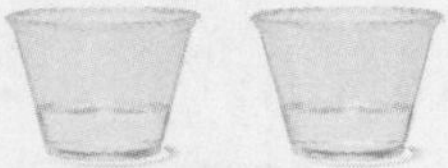

2 cups water

salt

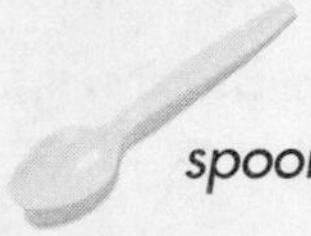

spoon

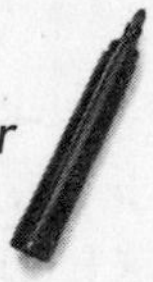

marker

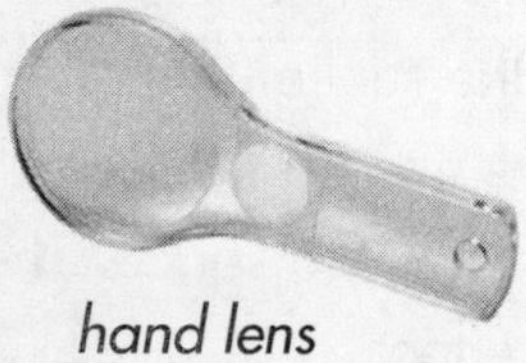

hand lens

Inquiry Skill
You collect data when you record what you **observe.**

Does the salt in salt water evaporate?

When water evaporates, it changes into gas. Salt water and fresh water both evaporate.

Ask a question.

Does salt in water evaporate?

Make a prediction.

1. Will the salt in salt water evaporate?

Design your Investigation.

☐ **2.** List your steps.

Do your Investigation.

☐ **3.** Follow your steps. Ask questions about what you see.

Collect and record data.

4. Fill in the chart.

Observations of Evaporation	
Observation 1	
Observation 2	
Observation 3	
Observation 4	

Tell your conclusion.

5. Infer What do you think is the white material on the saltwater cup? Why do you think this?

....

....

6. Infer Does the salt in the ocean evaporate? Explain

....

....

How to Stay Safe

Make a Poster

Severe weather can damage buildings and harm people. Work with a partner to make a poster about how to stay safe during thunderstorms, tornadoes, or hurricanes. Include a title for your poster. Add captions and images that you draw or find in magazines.

- Summarize the information in your poster. How can you stay safe during severe weather?
- What are some actions you can practice before severe weather hits?

Make a Booklet

In most places, the weather changes every day. Make a booklet about the weather in your area. Draw a picture of what the weather is like each day for a week. Include people in your pictures. They should be doing activities and wearing clothing that is appropriate for the weather.

- Did the weather in your area change very much this week? Explain.
- How did the weather affect your daily activities?

Science and Engineering Practices

1. Ask a question or define a problem.
2. Develop and use models.
3. Plan and carry out investigations.
4. Analyze and interpret data.
5. Use math and computational thinking.
6. Construct explanations or design solutions.
7. Engage in argument from evidence.
8. Obtain, evaluate, and communicate information.

Model the Water Cycle

In the water cycle, water moves from Earth's surface to the air and back again. Use simple materials to model parts of the water cycle. In a clear container, make a model hill out of pebbles. With your teacher's help, add a couple drops of blue dye to some water. Pour the water into a spray bottle. Spray the water on the model hill. Cover the container with plastic wrap. Place your model in a sunny location. Observe what happens.

• What parts of the water cycle did you model?

• How could you use the same materials to model other parts of the water cycle?

Measure Rainfall

Make your own rain gauge to measure how much rain falls in your area.

• Use a marker and a metric ruler to make a scale on the outside of a plastic container.

• Put a funnel into the container. You've made a rain gauge!

• Place your rain gauge outside in a flat open area. Put rocks around the container so that it will not blow over.

• Measure and record the rainfall each day for a week.

• Make a bar graph to show your results.

• Describe the pattern you observe.

If no rain falls for the week, use news reports of a place that had rain during the past week. Graph those results and describe the pattern.

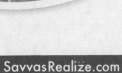

What can you ask about lake water?

The Nature of Science

Try It! Why is it important to communicate clearly?

STEM Activity Can You Hear Me?

Lesson 1 What questions do scientists ask?

Lesson 2 What skills do scientists use?

Lesson 3 How do scientists answer questions?

Lesson 4 How do scientists communicate?

Lesson 5 How do scientists use tools and stay safe?

Investigate It! How does a microscope help you make observations?

These student scientists are studying the quality of lake water. They are using tools and recording their observations. They could analyze their data in the boat or back at school.

Predict What type of observations about water do you think they are making?

....

....

THE BIG ? What is science?

Why is it important to communicate clearly?

Materials

gram cubes

folder

☐ **1.** Work with a partner. Take 6 cubes each. Set up a folder so that you cannot see each other's work.

☐ **2.** **Design** and build a simple structure.

Inquiry Skill
Scientists **communicate** when they explain how to do something.

☐ **3.** **Communicate** Tell your partner how to build your structure.

☐ **4.** Take the folder down. Compare the structures.

☐ **5.** Trade jobs and repeat.

Explain Your Results

6. **UNLOCK THE BIG ?** Think about the words you used in **communicating** your **design** to your partner. List the words that were most helpful in communicating clearly.

....

7. Why was it important to communicate clearly with your partner? **Infer** why it is important for scientists to communicate clearly with one another.

....

....

Text Features

Text features, such as headings, highlighting, pictures, and captions, give you clues about what you will read.

A **heading** tells what the content that follows is about.

A **picture** shows something you will read about.

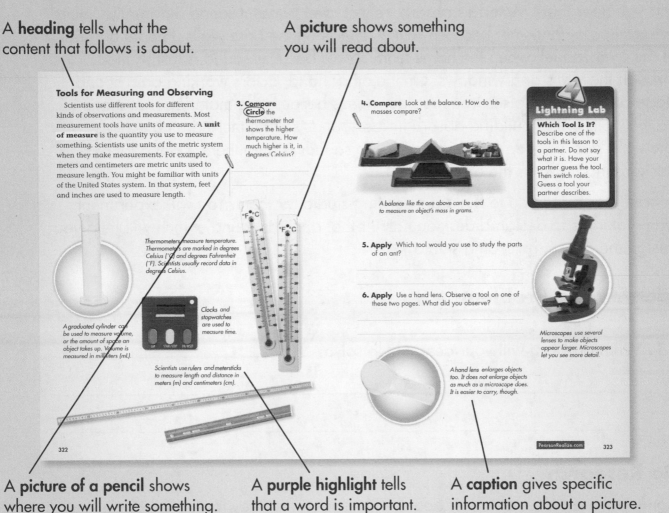

Tools for Measuring and Observing

Scientists use different tools for different kinds of observations and measurements. Most measurement tools have units of measure. A **unit of measure** is the quantity you use to measure something. Scientists use units of the metric system when they make measurements. For example, meters and centimeters are metric units used to measure length. You might be familiar with units of the United States system. In that system, feet and inches are used to measure length.

3. **Compare** Circle the thermometer that shows the higher temperature. How much higher is it, in degrees Celsius?

Thermometers measure temperature. Thermometers are marked in degrees Celsius (°C) and degrees Fahrenheit (°F). Scientists usually record data in degrees Celsius.

A graduated cylinder can be used to measure volume, or the amount of space an object takes up. Volume is measured in milliliters (mL).

Clocks and stopwatches are used to measure time.

Scientists use rulers and metersticks to measure length and distance in meters (m) and centimeters (cm).

4. **Compare** Look at the balance. How do the masses compare?

A balance like the one above can be used to measure an object's mass in grams.

5. **Apply** Which tool would you use to study the parts of an ant?

6. **Apply** Use a hand lens. Observe a tool on one of these two pages. What did you observe?

A hand lens enlarges objects too. It does not enlarge objects as much as a microscope does. It is easier to carry, though.

Lightning Lab

Which Tool Is It?
Describe one of the tools in this lesson to a partner. Do not say what it is. Have your partner guess the tool. Then switch roles. Guess a tool your partner describes.

Microscopes use several lenses to make objects appear larger. Microscopes let you see more detail.

PearsonRealize.com

322   323

A **picture of a pencil** shows where you will write something.

A **purple highlight** tells that a word is important.

A **caption** gives specific information about a picture.

Practice It!

Read the text features in the chart below. Write a clue that each one gives you about the content.

Text feature	Clue
picture	
caption	
heading	

Can You Hear Me?

Did you hear that? Materials absorb, reflect, and transmit sound differently. Sound echoes in a gymnasium because sound reflects off the bare walls. People outside of the gym can tell when the home team scores because sound is transmitted through the walls and windows. On the other hand, actors working on a sound stage cannot hear noises from outside. This is because the materials that make up the walls of the building absorb inside sounds so that there are no echoes. The walls also provide a barrier to outside sounds so that there is not a lot of background noise as the actors work.

A band has hired you to build a recording studio for them. You will experiment with materials to design a desktop barrier that absorbs sound, which will help you design the band's recording studio.

Identify the Problem

☑ **1.** What problem will your design help solve? _____

_____

_____

Do Research

Connect three pieces of poster board with tape so that they form a 3-paneled desktop barrier. Get behind your barrier so that you are speaking directly into it. Ask a classmate on the other side of your barrier a question in a normal speaking tone.

☑ **2.** Did your classmate hear you? How clearly? _____

_____

_____

Now have your classmate ask you a question in a normal speaking voice while you are behind your barrier.

☐ **3.** Did you hear your classmate? How clearly? _____

_____

_____

Examine the pictures of soundproof walls.

☑ **4.** How are these walls soundproofed? _____

_____

_____

Go to the materials station(s). Look at each material. Think about how it may or may not be useful for soundproofing your desktop barrier. Leave the materials where they are.

☐ **5.** What are your design constraints?

_____

_____

Develop Possible Solutions

☐ **6. Describe** two ways you could use the available materials to soundproof your desktop barrier.

_____

_____

_____

_____

Choose One Solution

☐ **7.** Choose one way to soundproof your barrier. **Draw** your design, and **label** all of the parts. Include a description of how you will attach the material(s) you choose for your barrier.

_____

_____

_____

☐ **8.** Why did you choose this material(s)? _____

_____

_____

Design and Construct a Prototype

Gather your materials. Use appropriate tools and units of measurement to determine the material you chose. Include measurements of the thickness of the material that is applied to your barrier.

☐ **9.** Material: _____ Amount: _____

Test the Prototype

Test your design. Again ask a classmate a question from behind your barrier and have him or her ask you a question.

☐ **10. Compare** the level and clarity of sound you now hear with what you heard before the barrier was covered. **Describe** any differences that you observe.

_____

_____

Communicate Results

☐ **11.** Did your soundproofing have the desired effect? Rate your design on a scale of 1 to 3 with 1 being no sound reduction, 2 being some sound reduction, and 3 being excellent sound reduction. **Explain** why you give your soundproofing this rating.

_____

_____

_____

Evaluate and Redesign

☐ **12.** What could you do to further soundproof your barrier? _____

_____

_____

☐ **13. Record** the new design plans, then make your changes. _____

_____

_____

☐ **14.** How well did your revised prototype work? Explain. _____

_____

Lesson 1

What questions do scientists ask?

Envision It!

Tell a question that a scientist could ask about these orange trees.

my planet diary

DISCOVERY

Have you ever heard of moon trees? Moon trees do not come from the moon. They are trees grown from seeds taken to the moon.

NASA astronaut Stuart Roosa took seeds to the moon on the Apollo 14 mission in 1971. When he brought the seeds back to Earth, NASA scientists examined them. Scientists wanted to learn if space travel changed the seeds. Then they planted the seeds. No one knew what the trees would look like or if the seeds would grow.

As the seeds grew, NASA scientists made observations. These observations helped scientists learn how space travel affects seed growth.

Moon trees grow around the United States.

How might you tell if the seeds that went to the moon changed?

....

....

....

....

....

Words to Know

scientist   inquiry
investigate

Scientists

What type of soil works best to grow corn and soybeans? That is a question a scientist might ask. A **scientist** is a person who asks questions about the natural world. Scientists collect observations in an organized way to investigate their questions. To **investigate** means to look for answers. Then scientists explain their answers.

Everyone can be a scientist. You are a scientist when you ask questions and investigate. What questions do you ask about the natural world?

1. ◎ **Text Features** Look at the text features on this page. Identify two text features and the clues they give you.

This scientist is studying crop fertilizers. He might ask a question about what kind of fertilizer will help plants grow the largest.

Text feature	Clue
Picture	tells what re talling
headins	will what we read adot

Questions

Science begins with inquiry. **Inquiry** means the process of asking questions. Scientists ask questions that they can investigate. The questions might come from something scientists observe or a problem they know. What type of soil works best to grow corn and soybeans? How can I grow bigger crops? How can I keep insects from eating crops? These are some questions scientists might ask.

Questions That Science Cannot Answer

Some questions cannot be answered by investigating. What is the prettiest flower? What juice tastes best? The answers to these questions are opinions. You might think apple juice tastes best. Another student might think orange juice tastes best. Collecting observations would not help a scientist decide which of you is right. Science cannot answer questions about tastes or personal opinions.

2. Identify Underline the question below that science cannot answer.

Do plants need water to grow?

Is baseball a better sport than basketball?

3. Generate What other question might the boy in the picture ask?

How much soil is need?

Which soil works best?

How much water do these plants need?

Lightning Lab

Questions and Answers

Think about something you would like to investigate. List the questions you would ask. Talk with a partner. How would your questions help you look for answers?

Alone or in Teams

Sometimes scientists work alone, but sometimes scientists can learn more by working together. When scientists work together they can share information and discoveries. Scientists who are investigating how to keep insects from eating crops might each try different methods and then compare their results. Scientists might take turns caring for their crops.

4. **Describe** What is another way scientists might work together?

....

....

These students use hand lenses to observe.

Got it?

5. ⊙ **Draw Conclusions** If you were acting like a scientist in class, what would you be doing? Write three things.

....

....

6. **UNLOCK THE BIG ?** A student asks the question, "What is the best color for a bike?" Can science answer this question? Explain.

....

....

⏹ **Stop!** I need help with ....

⏸ **Wait!** I have a question about ....

▶ **Go!** Now I know ....

What skills do scientists use?

Envision It!

Look at the time-elapsed photo of a hurricane.
Tell what you can observe about hurricanes.

Inquiry **Explore It!**

How can observations help you make an inference?

☐ **1.** Place the clear blue sheet over the color wheel. **Observe.**

☐ **2.** Repeat Step 1 with the clear red sheet and then the clear yellow sheet.

☐ **3.** Discuss the changes you observed.

Materials

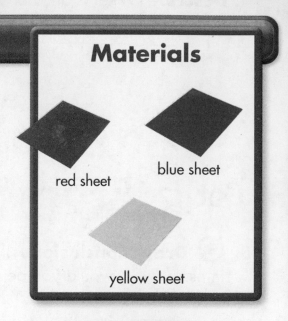

red sheet

blue sheet

yellow sheet

Explain Your Results

4. Infer How are blue, red, and yellow different from purple, orange, and green?

there are
mupplef rcncu es

5. Tell how your **observations** helped you make your inference.

I will know how to use process skills such as observation, prediction, and measurement.

Word to Know

infer

Science Skills

Scientists use process skills to learn about objects, places, or events. Observation is a process skill. When you use your five senses to find out about something, you observe. Your senses include sight, hearing, touch, taste, and smell.

Scientists often use tools to make observations. A satellite is a tool that helps scientists observe Earth's weather. Data from satellites are often displayed on weather maps. The weather map below shows hurricanes, which are strong storms.

1. **Observe** Look at the picture below. What is one observation you can make?

....

....

....

....

At-Home Lab

Estimate Length
Estimate the length of an object in centimeters. Then measure it with a ruler. Estimate the length of another object. Measure it. Did your estimation skills improve?

Estimate and Measure

Scientists sometimes estimate when they make observations. To estimate means to make a careful guess. A scientist standing on the pier in the picture might feel the wind pushing hard against his body. He might estimate that the wind is blowing about 70 or 80 kilometers per hour.

To find the exact wind speed, the scientist would make a measurement. A measurement is a number that tells how much or how many. Scientists often use tools to measure. An anemometer is a tool that can measure the speed of the wind.

2. CHALLENGE Suppose the pier in the picture is 20 feet high. Explain how you could use this information to estimate the height of the waves.

....

....

....

....

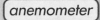
anemometer

Infer and Predict

Some data and observations are facts. For example, the statement "The wave crashed into the pier" is a fact. You can use facts to **infer,** or draw a conclusion. Scientists infer what they think is happening based on what they observe or based on prior knowledge. For example, a scientist observing the waves in the picture might infer that a hurricane is coming on shore.

Observations also can help you to predict. When you predict, you tell what you think will happen in the future. For example, a scientist might predict that the waves will get bigger as the hurricane gets closer to shore.

3. Predict What is another prediction you could make based on your observations of this picture?

....

....

....

....

Do the math!

Classify

Classify means to sort objects, events, or living things based on their properties. When you classify, you put similar things into groups or categories. Scientists use the Saffir-Simpson Hurricane Scale to classify and compare hurricanes. The scale groups hurricanes into categories according to wind speed.

Saffir-Simpson Hurricane Scale		
Category	**Wind Speed**	
	miles per hour	**kilometers per hour**
5	more than 155	more than 249
4	131–155	210–249
3	111–130	178–209
2	96–110	154–177
1	74–95	119–153

1. **Classify** A hurricane has a wind speed of 158 kilometers per hour. What is the hurricane's category?

....

2. **Compare** Hurricane A has a wind speed of 137 kilometers per hour. Hurricane B has a wind speed of 135 miles per hour. Are the two hurricanes in the same category? Explain.

....

....

....

3. **Analyze** The graph below shows wind speeds for Hurricane C in miles per hour (mph). How did the hurricane change on Day 4? Use the word *category* in your answer.

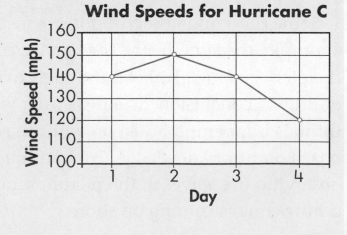

Wind Speeds for Hurricane C

....

....

....

Interpret and Explain Data

Scientists work together to interpret their data and form scientific explanations. A good explanation uses observations, inferences, prior knowledge, measurements, and data from an investigation. Scientists use all this information to explain how things happen naturally.

For example, scientists are trying to develop the ability to forecast when hurricanes will form. They use observations, weather data, and their knowledge of past storms to predict where hurricanes will strike and how strong they will be. This information can help people stay safe.

4. **Underline** five things that a good explanation uses.

HURRICANE CENTER
PREDICTION CENTER
NATIONAL UNIVERSITY
noaa

Got it?

5. Apply Name a process skill. How can it help scientists learn about hurricanes?

....

....

6. Predict What might happen if a person building a house estimated but did not measure the length of a piece of wood?

....

....

....

⬛ **Stop!** I need help with ....

⏸ **Wait!** I have a question about ....

▶ **Go!** Now I know ....

How do scientists answer questions?

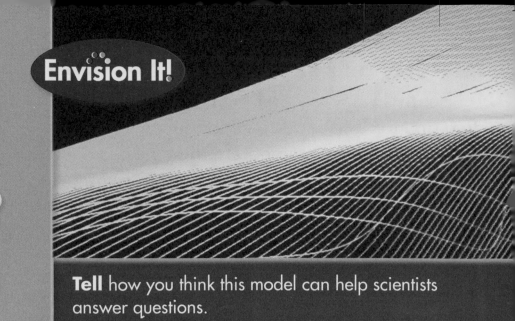

Tell how you think this model can help scientists answer questions.

Inquiry Explore It!

How can a model help answer questions?

☐ **1.** Spread out your fingers and put your hand flat on a piece of paper. **Measure** the length of the longest finger. Measure its height. **Record.**

☐ **2.** **Make a model** by tracing your hand. Measure the length of the longest finger on your model. Measure its height. Record.

Explain Your Results

3. Scientists use models to help them answer questions, but models have limitations. Does your **model** account for all your **observations** of your real finger? Explain.

_____

_____

_____

_____

Materials

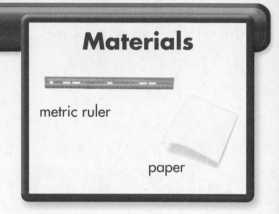

metric ruler

paper

Measurements

	Length (mm)	Height (mm)
Finger		
Model of a finger		

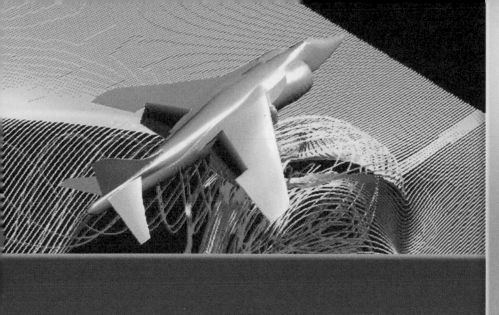

I will know how scientists use experiments and other types of investigations to answer questions.

Word to Know

model

Kinds of Investigations

Scientists are like detectives. They investigate, or look for answers, using organized steps. Different questions require different kinds of investigations. Some investigations involve observing and describing things or events. Other investigations may involve collecting samples or building models. An investigation can be any organized way of looking for answers.

An experiment is an investigation carried out under carefully controlled conditions. A scientist might do an experiment to find out if a new medicine works better than an old medicine.

1. **Text Features** What does the heading tell about this page?

....

....

....

....

2. **Analyze** These students are observing and describing flowers. Write what question you think they are investigating.

what kind of plant is this

....

....

Scientific Methods

Suppose you want to classify animals by how they keep warm. You might do an experiment to test fur's ability to keep heat in water. When scientists do an experiment, they use scientific methods. Scientific methods include the steps shown below.

3. Hypothesize Write another hypothesis for the question.

if we rap the jar in dark mltenr then the water will stay warm it aogs to

4. CHALLENGE How do you know your answer to question 3 is a good hypothesis?

we dark clors absorb heat from the sun

Ask a question.
You might have a question about something you observe.

What material is best for keeping heat in water?

State your hypothesis.
A hypothesis is a possible answer to your question. Hypotheses can be tested.

If I wrap the jar in fake fur, then the water will stay warm the longest because fake fur will keep heat in.

Identify and control variables.
Variables are things in an experiment that can change. For a fair test, you choose just one variable to change. Keep all other variables the same.

Test other materials. Put the same amount of warm water in other jars that are the same size and shape.

Test your hypothesis.

Make a plan to test your hypothesis. Include multiple trials by doing your test many times. That way, if one measurement is off, the data you collect will still be useful. Gather materials and tools. Then follow your plan.

Collect and record your data.

Keep records of what you do and find. Records can be notes, pictures, charts, or graphs.

Interpret your data.

Organize your notes and records.

State your conclusion.

Your conclusion is a decision you make based on your data. Communicate what you found. Tell whether or not your data supported your hypothesis.

Fake fur kept the water warm longest because fake fur kept the heat in. My data supported my hypothesis.

Go further.

Use what you learn from your experiment to do more experiments. Think of new questions to test.

5. ◉ **Compare and Contrast** What is the same about all three jars?

the three jac
s reallwesr
i2 some

What is different?

tefeere
diffen mite

6. **Identify** (Circle) the tool that is used in this experiment.

7. **Apply** Use the results of this experiment to ask another question that could be tested.

bo work
better
hot or
feels

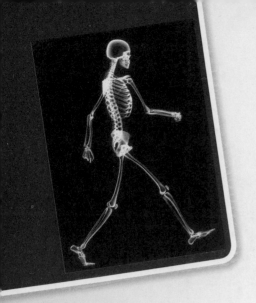

This computer model shows how the skeleton moves as the human body walks.

Models

Another way scientists investigate is with models. A **model** is a copy of something. Models help scientists understand how things work. Models also help scientists study things that are very small, large, or difficult to understand.

Some models are built out of materials such as paper and plastic. Other models are made using a program on a computer. For example, scientists have used computers to build models of the human body. These computer models help scientists better understand how different parts of the body, such as the heart and the skeletal system, work. The models can also be used to train doctors.

Models are useful, but they are not the same as the real thing. For example, a computer model might show how a person's body fits together. But it might not show how well the body will function.

8. Infer How do you think this model of the human body can help scientists?

....

....

....

9. Explain How can this model help you understand the real solar system?

....

....

....

This model is a copy of the solar system, a large group of objects in space.

Surveys

Scientists also use surveys to investigate. A survey is a list of questions or choices. Scientists can give the list to many people and learn from their answers. For example, scientists give surveys to patients to learn about their symptoms. Then scientists can interpret the data and draw inferences. The surveys and data can help scientists make new medicines.

10. Infer How are surveys a type of investigation?

....

....

Go Green

Recycling Survey
Write a survey to find out what materials people recycle in their homes. Ask about materials such as paper, plastic, glass, and metal cans. Ask your survey questions to ten people. Record the results. Do you see a pattern in the data?

Got it?

11. Summarize Name three ways scientists investigate.

....

12. Investigate Grass does not grow well under a tree. Write a hypothesis that explains why this might be true. How can you test your hypothesis?

....

....

....

⬛ **Stop!** I need help with ....

⏸ **Wait!** I have a question about ....

▶ **Go!** Now I know ....

Lesson 4

How do scientists communicate?

Tell how keeping records can help these scientists share information.

Inquiry **Explore It!**

How can scientists communicate what they learn?

☐ **1.** Conduct a survey. Think of a question you want to ask, such as "What is your favorite color?"

☐ **2.** Write your question in the chart.

☐ **3.** **Record** your data. Use tally marks.

☐ **4.** **Communicate** Make a bar graph using your data. Share this with your class.

Explain Your Results

5. How did your bar graph help you **communicate** what you learned?

....

....

....

....

Bar Graph

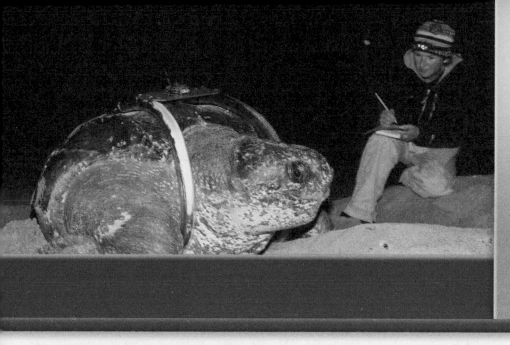

I will know how to describe a procedure and record data. I will know how scientists communicate.

Words to Know

procedure   bar graph
chart

Communication

Communication is an important part of science investigations. Scientists communicate with each other to share what they learn. They also question and check each other's work. When scientists share information in this way, their explanations are more thorough and better informed.

One way scientists check each other's work is to replicate, or repeat, an experiment. A good experiment can be repeated. For this reason, scientists must keep careful records of their experiments. Other scientists can repeat the same procedure if they know exactly how it was done.

1. **Infer** The scientists in the picture are investigating algae, a group of living things usually found in water. What kind of records do you think the scientists are keeping?

....

....

....

....

....

2. **Identify** Look at the procedure. (Circle) the units that were used to make measurements.

3. **Analyze** The person who wrote this procedure knew that warm water loses heat over time. What was the person trying to find out?

what materil would kee the wager warm.

4. **Describe** What words could be added to help describe the procedure?

Plan an Experiment

When you plan an experiment, you write a procedure. A **procedure** is a plan for testing a hypothesis. It describes the materials you will use and the steps you will follow. Write the procedure clearly so someone else can follow your steps and get the same results. Tell what units you will use in your measurements.

As you plan an experiment, think carefully about the question you are trying to answer. Figure out what you know and what you want to find out.

A procedure describes exactly how an experiment is done.

Question: What material is best for keeping heat in water?

Hypothesis: If I wrap a jar in fake fur, then it will keep the water warm the longest.

Materials: 1 jar covered in fake fur, 1 jar covered in brown paper, 1 jar covered in blue paper, warm water, 3 thermometers, plastic wrap, 3 rubber bands, clock

Procedure:
1. Label the jars A, B, and C.
2. Add a thermometer to each jar.
3. Fill each jar with the same amount of warm water.
4. Quickly cover the jars with plastic wrap and rubber bands.
5. Measure the starting temperature in degrees Celsius.
6. Measure and record how many minutes it takes for the temperature to change in each jar.
7. Empty the jars. Repeat steps 2 through 6.

Keep Records

When scientists investigate, they do the same experiment several times. Each time is called a trial. Scientists keep careful records of their results for each trial.

You can keep records in many ways. You can use numbers or words. Sometimes an easy way to record what happens is to draw a picture or a map. A chart is a way to organize what you record. A **chart** is a kind of list. You can also use a graph to organize data. A **bar graph** is a graph that helps you compare data and see patterns.

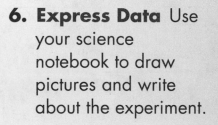

5. **Explain** Why are there two rows for each type of material in the chart below?

....

....

....

6. **Express Data** Use your science notebook to draw pictures and write about the experiment.

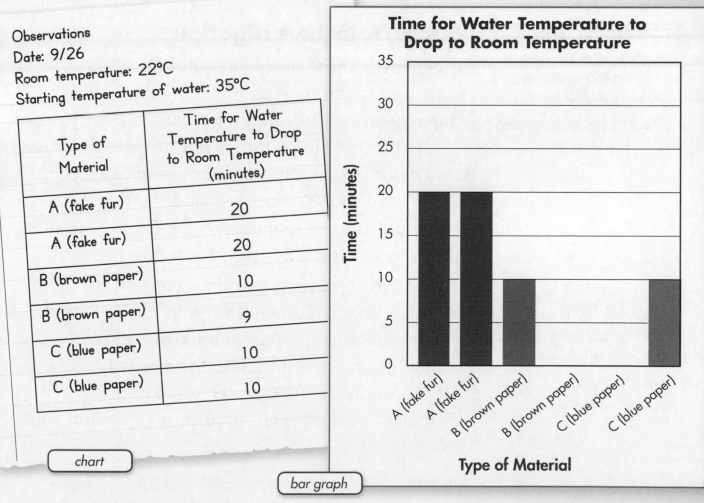

Observations
Date: 9/26
Room temperature: 22°C
Starting temperature of water: 35°C

Type of Material	Time for Water Temperature to Drop to Room Temperature (minutes)
A (fake fur)	20
A (fake fur)	20
B (brown paper)	10
B (brown paper)	9
C (blue paper)	10
C (blue paper)	10

chart

Time for Water Temperature to Drop to Room Temperature

bar graph

7. **Communicate Data** Complete the missing bars in the bar graph above.

SavvasRealize.com

8. Interpret The boy in the picture is communicating. What might he be telling his classmates?

....

....

....

9. Recall Why is it important for scientists to communicate with each other?

....

....

....

....

Share Your Investigation

Scientists share procedures, data, and conclusions with one another. They do this in different ways. They might talk about their work at a scientific meeting. Or they might write an article that describes their investigation and conclusions. Scientists also use computers and the Internet to communicate. By keeping records on a computer, they can easily send their data to other scientists.

You can communicate about your own science investigations in different ways too. For example, you might write a report or a journal entry. You might give a presentation in front of your class. Or you might create a poster, an exhibit, or a portfolio to display your procedure and what you have learned.

Repeat an Investigation

Scientists check each other's work. One scientist will repeat another scientist's experiment so they can compare evidence and explanations. An explanation is only considered true if another person can follow the procedure and get similar results.

If two scientists follow the same procedure and get different results, they can discuss why. They can use this information to make the procedure better for the next scientist.

10. Analyze Why would scientists want other scientists to repeat their experiment?

....

....

Lightning Lab

Construct a Chart
Go outside. Look at plants you see. Classify the plants in two ways. Make a chart to record your data. Discuss your chart with a partner.

Got it?

11. Summarize Name four ways scientists keep records.

....

12. Describe What information should a procedure include?

....

....

....

⬛ **Stop!** I need help with ....

⏸ **Wait!** I have a question about ....

▶ **Go!** Now I know ....

How do scientists use tools and stay safe?

Envision It!

Tell how you think microscopes help you view small objects, such as insects.

Inquiry Explore It!

How can a tool help scientists observe?

☐ 1. Find how much water is in a cup. First, **measure** 50 mL of water from the cup into a graduated cylinder. **Record** the measurement.

Then, empty the graduated cylinder into the second cup. Repeat until you have measured all the water from the first cup.

☐ 2. Calculate the total amount that was in the first cup at the start.

Explain Your Results

3. Compare your total with the amount other groups **measured.** Are the totals the same? Discuss.

4. How did the graduated cylinder help you make your comparisons?

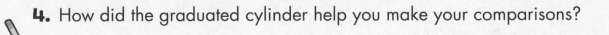

Materials

funnel

graduated cylinder

plastic cup

plastic cup with water

Volume in Cup (mL)	
Measurement	**Volume (mL)**
1st	
2nd	
3rd	
Total	

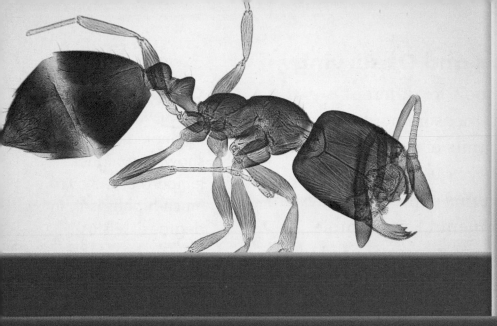

Words to Know

tool
unit of measure

Science Tools

Scientists use many different kinds of tools. A **tool** is an object used to do work. You can use tools to observe. Tools can help you measure volume, temperature, length, distance, and mass. Tools can help you collect and record data. Data are facts and information that you observe. You can record data on a computer. Computers can also help you share observations with others and find new information. Taking pictures with a camera is another way of using a tool to record data.

Some tools you use to observe make objects appear larger. Binoculars are a tool that helps you see things that are far away. For example, binoculars help you see birds nesting in trees.

1. **Underline** four things you can do with tools.

2. **Apply** How might you use binoculars like these?

....

....

....

....

Tools for Measuring and Observing

Scientists use different tools for different kinds of observations and measurements. Most measurement tools have units of measure. A **unit of measure** is the quantity you use to measure something. Scientists use units of the metric system when they make measurements. For example, meters and centimeters are metric units used to measure length. You might be familiar with units of the United States system. In that system, feet and inches are used to measure length.

3. Compare (Circle) the thermometer that shows the higher temperature. How much higher is it, in degrees Celsius?

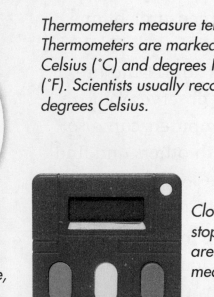

Thermometers measure temperature. Thermometers are marked in degrees Celsius (°C) and degrees Fahrenheit (°F). Scientists usually record data in degrees Celsius.

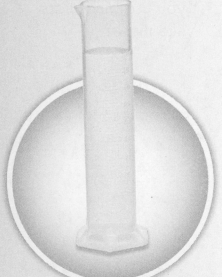

A graduated cylinder can be used to measure volume, or the amount of space an object takes up. Volume is measured in milliliters (mL).

Clocks and stopwatches are used to measure time.

Scientists use rulers and metersticks to measure length and distance in meters (m) and centimeters (cm).

4. Compare Look at the balance. How do the masses compare?

....

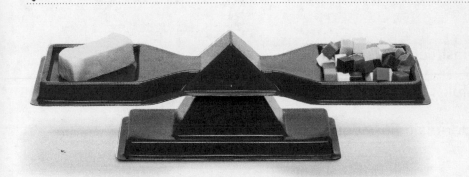

A balance like the one above can be used to measure an object's mass in grams.

Lightning Lab

Which Tool Is It?
Describe one of the tools in this lesson to a partner. Do not say what it is. Have your partner guess the tool. Then switch roles. Guess a tool your partner describes.

5. Apply Which tool would you use to study the parts of an ant?

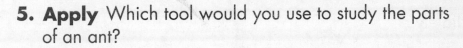

....

6. Apply Use a hand lens. Observe a tool on one of these two pages. What did you observe?

....

Microscopes use several lenses to make objects appear larger. Microscopes let you see more detail.

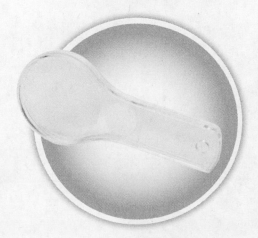

A hand lens enlarges objects too. It does not enlarge objects as much as a microscope does. It is easier to carry, though.

Safety

You need to be careful when using tools or doing other scientific activities. Some tools, such as safety goggles, help protect you. Below is a list of safety rules to remember.

- Listen to your teacher's instructions.

- Read each activity carefully.

- Never taste or smell materials unless your teacher tells you to.

- Wear safety goggles, wear gloves, and tie hair back when needed.

- Handle scissors and other equipment carefully.

- Keep your workplace neat and clean.

- Clean up spills immediately.

- Tell your teacher immediately about accidents or if you see something that looks unsafe.

- Wash your hands well after every activity.

- Return all materials to their proper places.

7. Explain Why is it important to wash your hands?

....

....

....

8. Elaborate Write a new safety tip to add to the list.

....

....

....

....

....

Investigating Safely

When scientists explore underwater, they need certain tools to stay safe. The scuba divers need tanks filled with oxygen to breathe and wet suits to protect their skin.

9. Suggest What equipment do you use to stay safe when you play outside?

....

....

....

Got it?

10. Infer Why do you think it is important to tell your teacher about accidents immediately?

....

....

11. Explain Choose one tool from this lesson and explain why it is important to scientists.

....

....

🔲 **Stop!** I need help with ....

⏸ **Wait!** I have a question about ....

▶ **Go!** Now I know ....

Inquiry

Investigate It!

How does a microscope help you make observations?

Follow a Procedure

☐ **1. Observe** a piece of yarn and a photo from a color newspaper.
Record your observations.

☐ **2.** Observe the yarn and the photo with a hand lens.
Record your observations.

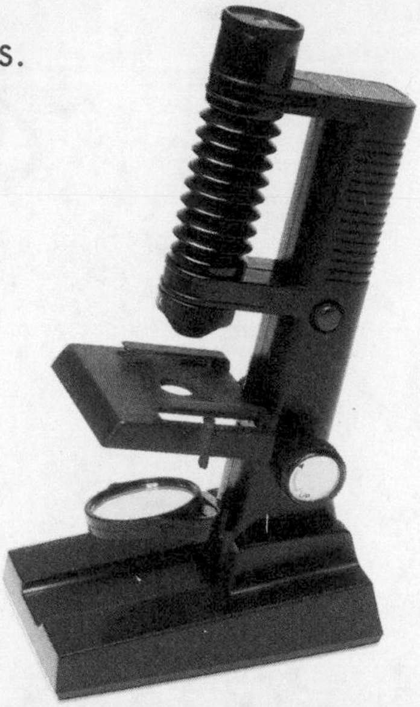

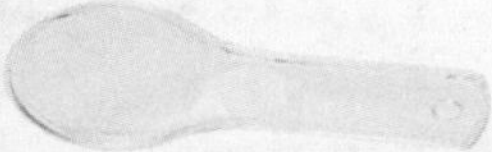

Materials

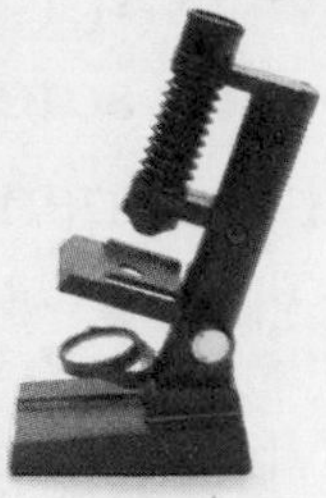

microscope

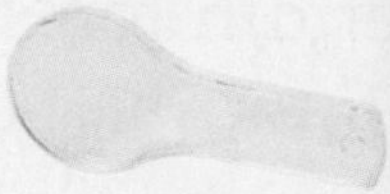

hand lens

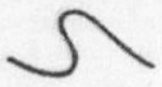

yarn

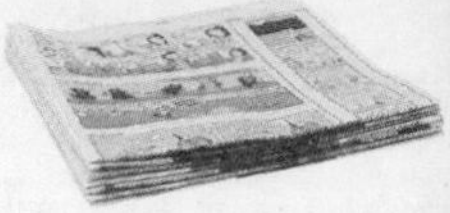

color newspaper

Inquiry Skill Scientists use tools to make **observations.**

Be careful! **Handle microscopes with care.**

Observations			
Item	**No Tool**	**Hand Lens**	**Microscope**
Yarn			
Photo			

3. Observe using a microscope. First, place the yarn on the stage of the microscope. Then, look through the eyepiece. Record your observations.

4. Repeat Step 3 with the photo.

Analyze and Conclude

5. Communicate How were your **observations** different when you used different tools?

....

....

6. Draw a Conclusion How does a microscope help you make observations?

....

....

7. Infer When might a hand lens be more useful than a microscope?

....

....

8. **UNLOCK THE BIG ?** **Investigate** List two other objects a scientist might observe with a microscope.

....

....

Observe
Insect
Behavior

You can practice observing by watching insects. Go outside with an adult and look at insects on tree trunks, on leaves, under rocks, or in cracks along sidewalks. Do not touch any insect. Bring a notebook to draw an insect. Observe it for several minutes. To keep records, write down observations about how it acts. Compare observations with the adult who is with you.

Illustrate Draw the insect.

Observe Record what you observe about how the insect acts.

....

....

Infer Use the evidence you observed to make an inference. What do you think the insect was doing?

....

....

Vocabulary Smart Cards

scientist
investigate
inquiry
infer
model
procedure
chart
bar graph
tool
unit of measure

Play a Game!

Cut out the Vocabulary Smart Cards.

Cover the words on the front of each card with sticky notes.

Use the list of words above to guess which word goes with each picture. Write the word on the sticky note.

Then remove the sticky note to see if you were correct.

infer

inferir

scientist

científico

model

modelo

investigate

investigar

procedure

Question: What material is best for keeping heat in water?

Hypothesis: If I wrap a jar in fake fur, then it will keep the water warm the longest.

Materials: 1 jar covered in fake fur, 1 jar covered in brown paper, 1 jar covered in blue paper, warm water, 3 thermometers, plastic wrap, 3 rubber bands, clock

Procedure:
1. Label the jars A, B, and C.
2. Add a thermometer to each jar.
3. Fill each jar with the same amount of warm water.
4. Quickly cover the jars with plastic wrap and rubber bands.
5. Measure the starting temperature in degrees Celsius.
6. Measure and record how many minutes it takes for the temperature to change in each jar.
7. Repeat steps 2 through 6.

procedimiento

inquiry

indagación

person who asks questions about the natural world

Write a sentence using this word.

....

....

....

persona cuyo trabajo implica hacer preguntas sobre el mundo y la naturaleza

---

to draw a conclusion

Write the noun form of this word.

....

....

....

....

sacar una conclusión

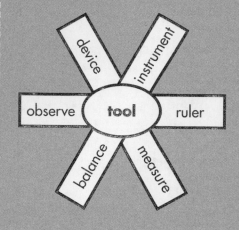

Make a Word Wheel!

Choose a vocabulary word and write it in the center of the Word Wheel graphic organizer. Write synonyms or related words on the wheel spokes.

---

to look for answers

Write the noun form of this word.

....

....

....

....

buscar respuestas

---

a copy of something

Draw an example.

copia de algo

---

the process of asking questions

Write a sentence using the verb form of this word.

....

....

....

proceso de hacer preguntas

---

a plan for testing a hypothesis

Use a dictionary. Write the verb form of the word.

....

....

....

plan que se usa para poner a prueba una hipótesis

 330

unit of measure

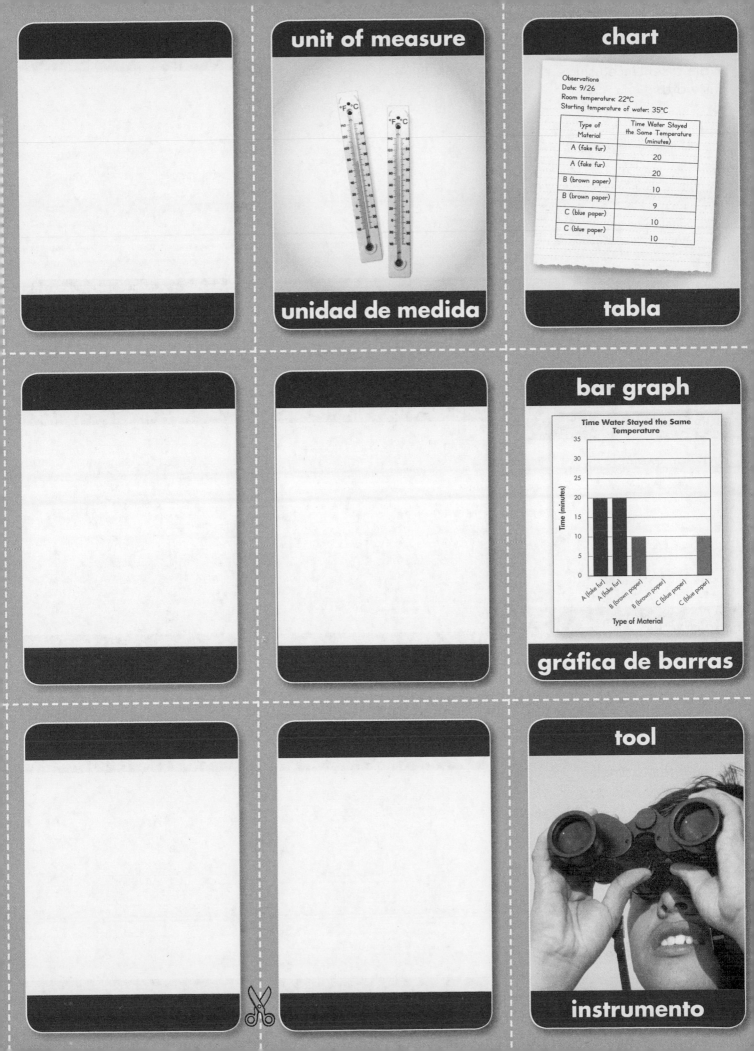

unidad de medida

chart

Observations
Date: 9/26
Room temperature: 22°C
Starting temperature of water: 35°C

Type of Material	Time Water Stayed the Same Temperature (minutes)
A (fake fur)	
A (fake fur)	20
B (brown paper)	20
B (brown paper)	10
C (blue paper)	9
C (blue paper)	10
	10

tabla

bar graph

Time Water Stayed the Same Temperature

Time (minutes)

Type of Material

A (fake fur), A (fake fur), B (brown paper), B (brown paper), C (blue paper), C (blue paper)

gráfica de barras

tool

instrumento

a kind of list

Write a sentence using this word.

....

....

....

....

tipo de lista

---

quantity you use to measure

Write three examples.

....

....

....

....

cantidad que se usa para medir

....

....

....

....

....

---

a graph that helps you compare data and see patterns

Draw an example.

gráfica que ayuda a comparar datos y ver patrones

....

....

....

....

....

....

....

....

....

....

---

object used to do work

Write three examples.

....

....

....

....

objeto que se usa para trabajar

....

....

....

....

....

....

....

....

....

....

Lesson 1

What questions do scientists ask?

- Scientists ask questions about the natural world.
- Scientists ask questions that can be answered through investigations.

Lesson 2

What skills do scientists use?

- Scientists observe by using their five senses.
- Scientists infer and predict based on observations.
- Scientists use their results to form explanations.

Lesson 3

How do scientists answer questions?

- Scientists answer questions using experiments and other kinds of investigations.
- Scientific methods are organized steps for investigations.

Lesson 4

How do scientists communicate?

- Scientists communicate to share what they learn.
- When scientists investigate, they write a procedure.
- Good records include words, charts, and graphs.

Lesson 5

How do scientists use tools and stay safe?

- Scientists use tools to observe, to measure, and to collect and record data.
- Safety is important when doing science.

Lesson 1

What questions do scientists ask?

1. **Vocabulary** Someone who asks questions about the natural world is a(n) _____.
   A. engineer
   B. model
   C. scientist
   D. teacher

2. **Apply** What is a question that cannot be answered through an investigation?

Lesson 2

What skills do scientists use?

3. **Observe** What five senses do scientists use when they make observations?

4. **Name** List three things a good investigation needs.

Lesson 3

How do scientists answer questions?

5. **Write About It** Suggest two ways a model could help you better understand the solar system.

6. **List** What are three steps that a good experiment should include?

7. **Conclude** You measure your heart rate at 70 beats per minute after resting and 100 beats per minute after exercising. Over several days you take more measurements and get similar results. What can you conclude?

Cary Fowler

Cary Fowler helped run the Global Seed Vault project.

Cary Fowler was born in Tennessee and spent his summers on a farm. Later he became a plant scientist. Fowler became worried about the plants we use as crops. Through history, people have used more than 10,000 different types of plants for food. Now there are only 150 types left. Fowler asked, "What if we lose even more?" Diseases, natural disasters, and war can all wipe out plants.

Fowler moved to Italy to help run a project called the Global Seed Vault. The Global Seed Vault is a tool used by plant scientists. It is a giant freezer buried in the ground near the North Pole in Norway. The vault is used to save different types of plant seeds from all over the world. The vault is big enough to hold more than 2 billion seeds.

The goal of the vault is to save seeds for thousands of years. Then, even if we lose a type of plant, we can use the seeds to plant more!

REVIEW THE BIG ? What did Cary Fowler infer about the crops we have left?

....

....

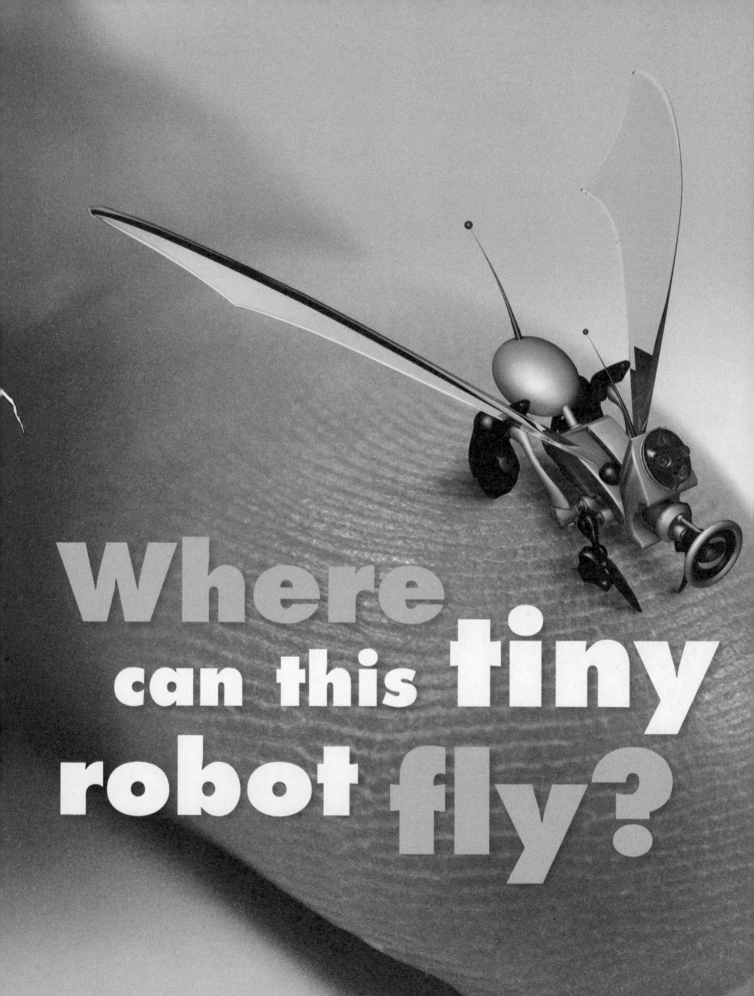

Where can this tiny robot fly?

Technology and the Design Process

This is an image of a piece of technology that is still being developed. Some scientists think that in the future, the robotic fly will be able to locate people who are trapped in a collapsed building. It can fit in tiny places where a person may not fit.

Predict Why do you think the robot was designed to look like a fly?

....

....

THE BIG ? How can technology affect our lives?

How can you design a parachute?

☑ **1. Design** a parachute that will slow the fall of a metal washer dropped from a height of 2 meters.

☑ **2. Communicate** Draw and label your design.

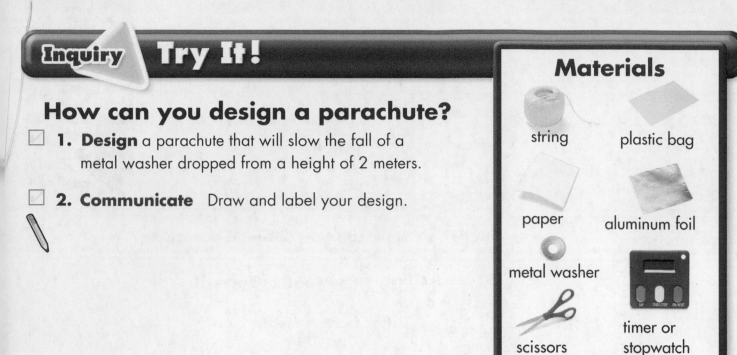

Materials

string

plastic bag

paper

aluminum foil

metal washer

timer or stopwatch

scissors

metric ruler

masking tape

☑ **3.** Build your parachute. Ask your teacher to test it 3 times. **Record.** Compare your results with others.

☑ **4.** Evaluate your design. Improve it. Repeat Step 3.

Inquiry Skill
You **infer** when you use your information to draw a conclusion.

Parachute Trials Results			
Parachute	Trial 1 (s)	Trial 2 (s)	Trial 3 (s)
1			
2			

Explain Your Results

5. **Communicate** Which parachute dropped most slowly?

....

6. Infer Why did this parachute work better than the others?

....

....

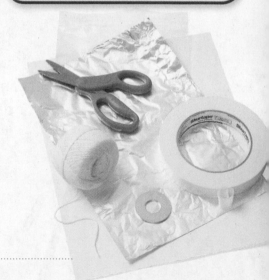

340

Main Idea and Details

Let's Read
Science!

- The **main idea** is the most important idea in a reading selection.
- Supporting **details** tell more about the main idea.

Technology and Energy

Technology has changed the way we get energy. A water-powered mill uses technology to get energy from the flowing water of a river. A solar panel can be placed on the roof of a house. It gathers energy from the sun. Energy from the wind can be captured by wind turbines. This energy helps to produce electricity. Technology allows us to recycle energy, which helps protect the environment.

Practice it!

Complete the graphic organizer below. Use it to help you list the main idea and details from the paragraph you read above.

wind turbine

Main Idea

Detail

Detail

Detail

Bird Food Is Served!

Birds eat insects and help control rodent populations. Many people also think birds are beautiful and enjoy their cheerful songs. If you would like to attract birds to your yard, you're in luck. A well-built and well-placed birdfeeder is an invitation that most birds cannot turn down.

The area birdwatchers' club has asked you to **design and build** a birdfeeder that a specific species of bird can enter.

Identify the Problem

☑ **1.** What problem will your birdfeeder address? _____

_____

_____

Do Research

Examine the chart below.

Species	Size of Base (cm)	Height (cm)	Entrance Above Base (cm)	Diameter of Entrance (cm)	Height Above Ground (m)
Bluebird	13 x 13	25	20	3.8	1.5–3.5
Chickadee	10 x 10	20–25	15–20	2.9	2.0–4.5
Nuthatch	10 x 10	20–25	15–20	3.2	4.0–6.0
House Wren	10 x 10	15–20	3–15	2.5–3.2	2.0–3.0
Tree Swallow	13 x 13	15	3–15	3.8	3.0–5.0
Purple Martin	15 x 15	15	2.5	6.4	5.0–6.0
Downy Woodpecker	10 x 10	23–30	15–20	3.2	2.0–6.0

☐ **2.** Why might different species of birds require different sized feeders?

_____

_____

☐ **3.** Why does it matter how big the entrance is and how far it is above the base?

_____

_____

☐ **4.** Why does it matter how high the feeder is above the ground?

_____

_____

☐ **5. Research** the kinds of birds in your area and **list** three that are also listed in the chart above.

1. _____

2. _____

3. _____

☐ **6. Examine** pictures of the birds you listed. **Describe** your observations.

1. _____

2. _____

3. _____

Go to the materials station(s). Look at each material. Think about how it may or may not be useful for building your feeder. Leave the materials where they are.

☐ **7.** What are your design constraints?

_____

_____

Develop Possible Solutions

☐ **8.** Decide which type of bird you will try to attract to your feeder. **Describe** two different ways that you could use the materials provided to build a bird feeder for this type of bird.

_____

_____

Choose One Solution

☐ **9.** Decide which feeder you will make. **Draw** a diagram of your feeder. **Label** all the parts, including dimensions of holes you will make or lengths of perches.

_____

_____

_____

_____

_____

☐ **10. List** the materials you will need. _____

_____

_____

☐ **11. Tell** what kinds of seed you will use to attract birds to your feeder. _____

Design and Construct a Prototype

Gather your materials plus a metric ruler. **Build** your bird feeder.

☐ **12. Record** the design details of your prototype. _____

_____

_____

Test the Prototype

Test your bird feeder. Find a place outside your classroom or home to place the feeder. Fill your feeder with the appropriate feed for the kind of bird you want to attract, supplied by your teacher. **Observe** your feeder for seven days. **Record** your observations in the chart.

Day	Observations
1	
2	
3	
4	
5	
6	
7	

Communicate Results

☐ **13.** Did your prototype work like you expected? Explain. _____

_____

☐ **14. Compare** your results with those of your classmates. How do your results compare?

_____

Evaluate and Redesign

☐ **15.** What were the flaws in your design? _____

☐ **16.** What changes could you make to your design to make it better? _____

_____

_____

What is technology?

What do you think the technology in the picture is?
How do you think it works?

my planet Diary

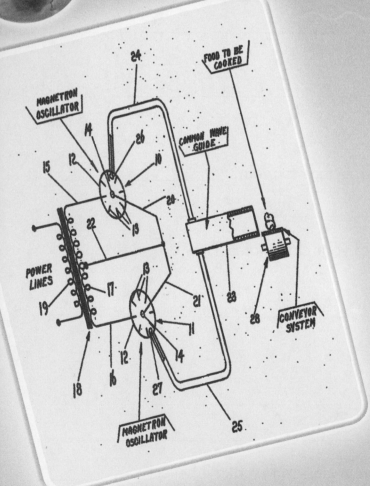

Percy Spencer's sketch
helped him build the first
microwave oven.

DISCOVERY

Sometimes technology becomes useful in unplanned ways. In 1946, Percy Spencer was working to improve radar. He was performing tests using microwave energy.

One day Spencer stood near the microwave energy. He noticed that a candy bar in his pocket melted. Curious, he put popcorn kernels near the microwave energy. They rapidly popped into fluffy pieces.

Spencer found that the microwave energy could quickly cook foods. He made a drawing that led to the first microwave oven.

Why was it important for Percy Spencer to keep asking questions after his candy bar melted?

....

....

....

UNLOCK THE BIG ?

I will know how technology solves problems and provides solutions.

Word to Know

technology

Problems and Solutions

Science helps people understand the way the world works. Technology helps people solve problems and improve their lives. **Technology** is the use of science knowledge to invent tools and new ways of doing things.

Discoveries in science are helping people solve some big problems. For example, people use energy for many things. They use energy to cook food and heat their homes. But we may be running out of some energy sources. The discovery of how to use solar energy may help solve this problem. Solar energy is energy that comes directly from the sun. Solar panels gather the sun's energy. Next, they change this energy into electricity.

Solar panels provide a new way of getting energy.

1. **Underline** the definition of technology.

2. [CHALLENGE] Solar panels work well in some places but not others. Explain why this is true.

If objects block the solar panels then they will not work.

At-Home Lab

Transportation in the Future
How might people get around in the future? Draw a picture of a tool that could help people move in the future. Write a caption for your picture.

Signals from satellites can track the exact location of a car.

Scientific Discoveries and Technology

Scientific discoveries usually are made by scientists. Engineers use this knowledge to develop technologies that change and improve the way people live. Here are some examples.

Transportation

People on ships once had to figure out where they were by looking at stars. Now sailors can use Global Positioning System (GPS) technology. This technology relies on space satellites that send signals to Earth. Each ship's GPS computer uses the signals to figure out the ship's location.

3. ◉ **Main Idea and Details** What is the main idea of the paragraph above?

   the main idea that transportation has changed over the years

Medicine

X rays were discovered more than 100 years ago. For the first time, doctors could look inside the body without touching it. Today, doctors also use digital technology to look inside people's bodies.

Scientists discovered that viruses and bacteria cause disease. This led to the development of vaccines. Vaccines are medicines that protect you from disease. Vaccines are a type of technology.

4. **Interpret** This child is receiving a vaccine, a type of technology. What is another technology that you see in this photograph?

   another technology is the needle

348

Computer Technology

A computer stores information. Computers also process and send information with great speed. Computer technology is everywhere. A digital watch tells time with a computer chip. Calculators, cameras, appliances, and cars all use these chips.

Computer chips are being made smaller and smaller. Music players, game players, and phones can process as much information as whole desktop computers once could.

5. Predict How would your life be different if computer technology did not exist?

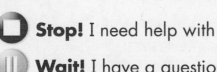

my llfe would be differnet becuuse it woid be hayrter tedo things.

Computer chips can send and receive huge numbers of electronic data signals very quickly.

Got it?

6. Give Examples Name two technologies. Tell how they have changed people's lives.

....

....

7. ◉ Draw Conclusions How can one technology lead to the development of other technologies?

....

....

⬛ **Stop!** I need help with ....

⏸ **Wait!** I have a question about ....

▶ **Go!** Now I know ....

What is a machine?

Tell how the pole helps this vaulter jump higher.

Inquiry **Explore It!**

How can a simple machine solve a problem?

Pat and Chris want to know whose clay ball is heavier. All they have is a ruler and a pencil.

☑ **1. Design** a way to solve this problem.
    Use a simple machine.

☑ **2. Communicate**   Draw your solution.

☑ **3.** Test your design. Which clay ball is heavier?

Materials

2 clay balls of different weights   unsharpened pencil

ruler

Explain Your Results

4. Name the simple machine you used.

5. Draw a Conclusion   What is another way you could use your simple machine?

UNLOCK THE BIG ?

I will know some simple machines and how they help people do work.

Words to Know

work   inclined
wheel and   plane
   axle   pulley
wedge   screw
lever

Work

Is kicking a soccer ball work? To a scientist it is. In science, **work** means the use of a force to move an object across a distance. You do work when you rake leaves, pedal a bike, or kick a soccer ball.

It may be hard to solve a math problem. But it is not work. You may push hard to move a large rock. But it is not work if the rock does not move. You only do work when you move an object. The amount of work you do depends on how much force you use and how far you move the object.

1. ◉ **Main Idea and Details** Complete the graphic organizer below. Write details about work.

Main Idea

Work is the use of a force to move an object across a distance.

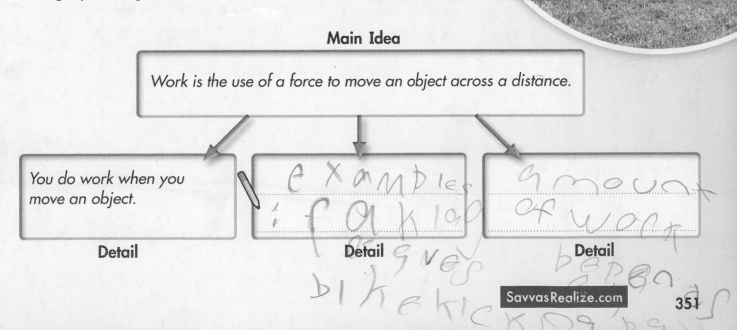

You do work when you move an object.

Detail

examples: raking, biking, kicking a ball

Detail

amount of work depends

Detail

A **wheel and axle** is a round object attached to a post called an axle. Turning the wheel causes the axle to turn. The axle turns a small distance as the wheel turns a greater distance.

Simple Machines

Do you recognize any of the objects in the pictures? They are all simple machines. Simple machines have just one or two parts. These machines do not lessen the amount of work you do, but they help make work easier. Six kinds of simple machines help you do work. They are the wheel and axle, wedge, lever, inclined plane, pulley, and screw.

A **wedge** is a simple machine made from two slanted sides that end in a sharp edge. As a wedge is pushed through material such as wood or food, it cuts or splits the material.

2. Identify You want to cut a piece of cake or pie. What is the common name for the kitchen wedge you use?

Knife

A **lever** is a stiff bar that rests on a support. A lever is used to lift and move things. When you push down on one end, the other end lifts up.

3. Apply Look at this shape ▼. Draw an ✗ on the simple machine that has this shape. How does the shape help this machine work?

....

....

4. Identify Which simple machine would you use for each task below?

A. Raise a flag on a pole. ....

B. Pry open a can of paint. ....

C. Cut an apple. ....

A **screw** is an inclined plane wrapped around a center post. Screws can be used to hold things together and to raise and lower things.

5. Apply Tell how a jar lid is a screw.

A **pulley** can make work easier in two ways. It can decrease the amount of force needed to move an object. It can also change the direction that the force is applied.

An **inclined plane,** or a ramp, is a slanted surface. It connects a lower level to a higher level. Less force is needed to move an object over a longer distance.

At-Home Lab

Complex Machines
Search your home for one complex machine. Draw and label the complex machine. Identify each simple machine in the complex machine.

Complex Machines

Simple machines are often put together to do bigger jobs. These complex machines are made up of simple machines that work together.

The can opener below is a complex machine. Find the simple machines that it is made of. These simple machines work together to grip, turn, and slice through a can lid.

The bicycle is a complex machine too. What simple machines make it up? How does each simple machine help make the bicycle work?

6. Exemplify List three complex machines that you used yesterday.

....

....

....

....

The sharp edge that cuts the top of the can is a wedge.

The winding handle is an axle that turns the gears.

The handles are made of levers.

7. Illustrate Draw a line from each simple machine to its correct part on the bicycle.

A. lever

B. pulley

C. wheel and axle

Got it?

8. Synthesize How do you know when a simple machine has done work?

....

....

9. Summarize Write a sentence that summarizes how simple machines are useful. Give examples.

....

....

....

Stop! I need help with ....

Wait! I have a question about ....

Go! Now I know ....

Lesson 3

What is the design process?

Envision It!

Tell how these two computers are different.

Inquiry Explore It!

Which design transfers sound the best?

☐ **1.** Use 2 of the cups and 3 meters of string. Thread the string through the hole in the bottom of the cup. Make a big knot.

☐ **2.** Test your model by talking into the cup. Have your partner listen. The string must be tight. **Record** how well you hear the sound.

....

☐ **3.** Change at least one of the cups in your model. Repeat Step 2.

....

Explain Your Results

4. Infer   Think about your redesign and that of others. Which material works best for transferring sound?

....

Materials

2 paper, 2 plastic, and 2 foam cups (each with a hole)

string

356

I will know how to conduct an investigation using the design process.

Words to Know

design   prototype
  process
research

Design Process

When people design something new, they follow the steps of the design process. The **design process** is a step-by-step method used to solve a problem.

People use the design process to find a solution. A solution is an answer to a problem. The design process allows engineers to produce and test possible solutions. An engineer is any person who designs new technologies.

1. Identify Why is it important for engineers to follow the steps of the design process?

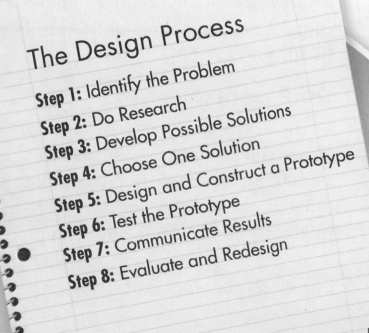

The Design Process

Step 1: Identify the Problem

Step 2: Do Research

Step 3: Develop Possible Solutions

Step 4: Choose One Solution

Step 5: Design and Construct a Prototype

Step 6: Test the Prototype

Step 7: Communicate Results

Step 8: Evaluate and Redesign

Go Green

Salvaged Solution
Save some items instead of throwing them away. Think of a simple problem. Use the items to build something to solve your problem. Test what you build to see if it works. Evaluate your solution. Share your results with someone in your class.

People may read books to research.

2. Describe How do you think Kramer researched the problem?

....

....

....

....

....

....

Identify the Problem

Engineers identify the problem during the first step of the design process. Before producing a design, engineers consider if there is a need for it. In 1979, there were only large music players that needed tapes or records to play music. British inventor Kane Kramer identified this as a problem. Kramer wanted to design a smaller music player that did not need tapes or records. His idea led to the invention of the digital audio player.

Do Research

The next step is to research the problem. **Research** means to look for facts about something. People can research problems in different ways. Some engineers research by talking to other people and reading articles. Kramer researched ways to make a digital audio player. Kramer took notes about what he learned.

Develop Possible Solutions

After doing research, engineers think of possible solutions. They consider what designs would best meet the needs of the problem. Kramer considered different materials that were available. He knew he needed to use materials that would produce a player people would use. It had to be small enough to fit in a pocket. He made different sketches of how the player could look.

Choose One Solution

People consider many things in order to choose the best solution. They think about how they will build the solution. They also think about what kinds of materials will work. Kramer chose the best solution. His player would be made of strong materials and be small in size.

Design and Construct a Prototype

After sketching the digital audio player, Kramer constructed, or built, a prototype. A **prototype** is the first working product that uses a design. Kramer made the player small and easy to use.

Test the Prototype

Engineers test a prototype to determine if it meets their expectations. They perform multiple tests to get accurate results. Kramer tested the prototype to see how well it worked.

3. **Suggest** What do you think Kramer learned from his test?

....

....

car prototype

4. **Determine** How can this car prototype help engineers?

....

....

....

....

Someone may test an inner part of a computer to see how well it works.

This is what the inside of a digital audio player looks like. Showing it to others can help them understand the design.

Communicate Results

Engineers communicate results about their tests to people working with them. Engineers may share how they designed and built the prototype. They also explain how the experiment was carried out. After testing it, Kramer sent a report of his invention to a group of people. He hoped the people would invest money in his invention. The report described the way his invention worked. It also explained how the player could change the way people listened to music.

5. Predict What would happen if engineers did not communicate their evidence with others?

....

....

Do the math!

Read a Circle Graph

Mark's digital audio player can hold 1,000 songs. Look at the circle graph below. It tells you what types of music are on Mark's player and how many songs are in each type.

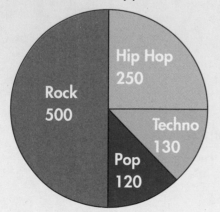

① What type of music does Mark have the most of?

....

② How many techno and hip hop songs does Mark have?

....

③ **Solve** How many more hip hop songs are there than pop songs?

....

Evaluate and Redesign

The final step is to evaluate and redesign the prototype. Evaluate means to find out how well something works. People try to make a prototype better by redesigning it. When people heard about Kramer's idea of the digital audio player, they designed their own version. The first digital audio player became available to the public in 1997. It could play about one hour of music. Newer digital audio players can hold enough music to play for more than 100 days!

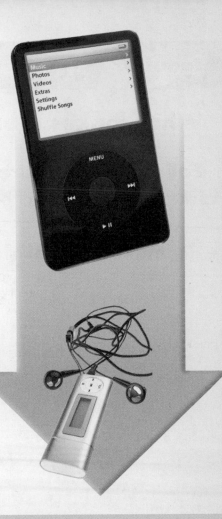

6. **Contrast** Look at the images to the right. How has the design process changed digital audio players?

....

....

Got it?

7. **Infer** How can the design process help someone invent something?

....

....

8. **Clarify** Why is it important to test a design multiple times?

....

....

⬛ **Stop!** I need help with ....

⏸ **Wait!** I have a question about ....

▶ **Go!** Now I know ....

What makes a bridge strong?

Follow a Procedure

☐ **1.** Place two stacks of books 25 centimeters apart.

☐ **2. Make a model** of a bridge between the books. Use stir sticks, tape, and a note card. Brainstorm potential solutions.

☐ **3.** Place the cup on the bridge.

Materials

ruler

4 books

10 craft sticks

10 stir sticks

note card

tape

pennies

plastic cup

Inquiry Skill   Scientists **make a model** to help them understand how something works and predict results.

4. Predict how many pennies the bridge will hold. **Record** your prediction.

5. Put pennies in the cup one at a time. Record how many pennies the bridge holds before it falls.

Which Bridge Is Stronger?		
Model	Number of Pennies	
	Prediction	Count
Stir sticks		
Craft sticks		

6. Repeat Steps 2–5. Use craft sticks this time.

Analyze and Conclude

7. UNLOCK THE BIG ? **Infer**   How did this scientific **investigation** help you determine which bridge was stronger?

....

....

....

8. How are your **models** like real bridges? How are they different?

....

....

....

....

STEM

Lawn Mowers

Engineers design and develop large and small machines. These machines are made of simple and complex machines. A simple machine can be a lever, wheel and axle, pulley, wedge, inclined plane, or screw. Simple machines are often put together to make a complex machine, such as a lawn mower. It is made of different parts. Some of these parts are simple machines, such as a wheel and axle. A wheel and axle is used in a lawn mower to help it move. A screw is another simple machine. Screws are used to hold the lawn mower pieces together.

Apply Lawn mowers have wedges. A wedge is a simple machine made of two slanted sides that end in a sharp edge. Where do you think you would find a wedge inside a lawn mower?

Vocabulary Smart Cards

technology
work
wheel and axle
wedge
lever
inclined plane
pulley
screw
design process
research
prototype

Play a Game!

Cut out the Vocabulary Smart Cards.

Cover the words on the front of each card with sticky notes.

Use the list of words above to guess which word goes with each picture. Write the word on the sticky note.

Then remove the sticky note to see if you were correct.

365

wedge

cuña

technology

tecnología

lever

palanca

work

trabajo

inclined plane

plano inclinado

wheel and axle

eje y rueda

use of science knowledge to invent tools and new ways of doing things

Draw an example.

uso del conocimiento científico para inventar instrumentos y nuevas maneras de hacer las cosas

---

two slanted sides that end in a sharp edge

Draw an example.

dos lados inclinados que terminan con un borde filoso

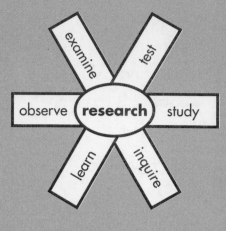

Make a Word Wheel!

Choose a vocabulary word and write it in the center of the Word Wheel graphic organizer. Write synonyms or related words on the wheel spokes.

---

the use of a force to move an object across a distance

Write a nonexample of this word.

uso de una fuerza para mover un objeto, por cierta distancia

---

a simple machine to lift and move things by using a stiff bar that rests on a support

List three examples of this word.

máquina simple que se usa para levantar y mover cosas mediante una barra rígida que tiene un punto de apoyo

---

a round object attached to a post

Draw and label a machine that has a wheel and axle.

objeto redondo unido a una barra

---

a slanting surface that connects a lower level to a higher level

Write a synonym for this word.

superficie inclinada que conecta un nivel bajo con un nivel más alto

	research	**pulley**

	hacer una investigación	**polea**

	prototype	**screw**
	prototipo	**tornillo**

		design process
		The Design Process Step 1: Identify the Problem Step 2: Do Research Step 3: Develop Possible Solutions Step 4: Choose One Solution Step 5: Design and Construct a Prototype Step 6: Test the Prototype Step 7: Communicate Results Step 8: Evaluate and Redesign
		proceso de diseño

a machine that can change the direction or amount of force needed to move an object

What is the base word in this word?

....
....

máquina que puede cambiar la dirección o la cantidad de fuerza necesaria para mover un objeto

---

to look for facts about something

Write three examples of research.

....
....
....
....
....

buscar datos sobre algo

---

an inclined plane wrapped around a center post

Write a sentence using this word.

....
....
....
....

plano inclinado enrollado alrededor de un eje central

---

the first working product that uses a design

Write a synonym for this word.

....
....
....
....

el primer producto que funciona y que sigue un diseño

---

a step-by-step method used to solve a problem

Write a sentence using this word.

....
....
....
....

método que sigue pasos y que se usa para resolver un problema

Lesson 1

What is technology?

- Scientific discoveries can lead to the development of new technology.
- Technology can help people solve problems.

Lesson 2

What is a machine?

- In science, work is done when a force moves an object.
- Simple machines, such as pulleys, make work easier.
- Complex machines are made of two or more simple machines.

Lesson 3

What is the design process?

- The design process is a step-by-step method used to solve a problem.
- People research and develop possible solutions to problems.

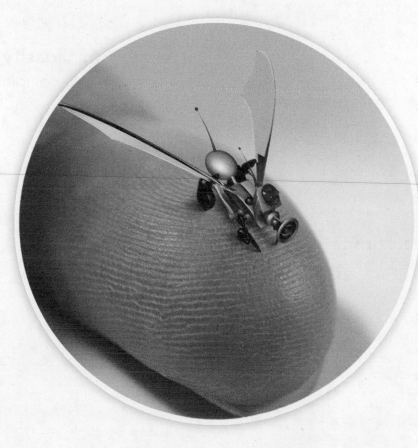

Lesson 1

What is technology?

1. **Vocabulary** The use of science knowledge to invent new ways of doing things is called _____.
   A. scientific methods
   B. evidence
   C. a tool
   D. technology

2. **Write about it** Explain how solar panels can improve our lives. Use the word technology.

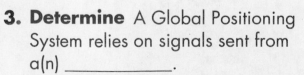

3. **Determine** A Global Positioning System relies on signals sent from a(n) _____.
   A. space satellite
   B. X ray
   C. solar panel
   D. person

Lesson 2

What is a machine?

4. **Evaluate** What kind of simple tool is a nail? What is one way you could use a nail?

5. **Vocabulary** What machine is an inclined plane wrapped around a center post?
   A. lever
   B. pulley
   C. wedge
   D. screw

6. **Classify** The nail clippers are a complex machine made up of two simple machines. Label each simple machine.

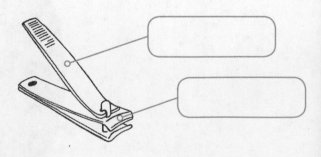

STEM

New Horizons

The *New Horizons* spacecraft can travel 60,000 kilometers per hour! That's fast! *New Horizons* is traveling on a mission to Pluto and a region of the solar system called the Kuiper Belt. *New Horizons* was launched in January 2006.

It is expected to reach Pluto in July 2015. Its purpose is to help scientists learn more about Pluto and objects in the Kuiper Belt. This information will help scientists understand how Pluto and these objects fit into our solar system.

To help scientists study these objects up close, engineers had to develop a new kind of spacecraft that is small and agile. The scientists and engineers used math to calculate the correct speed and path of the spacecraft.

Justify *New Horizons* has a student-built instrument: Student Dust Counter (SDC). Why do you think students want to know about dust in our solar system?

....

....

....

What parachute design works best?

A group of people on a small island need supplies dropped off.
You cannot land a plane on the island. The supplies are fragile and
must be dropped slowly so they do not break when they land.
The area the supplies must be dropped off at is very small.
You need to design a parachute to drop the supplies for the people
that need them.

Identify the problem.

☐ **1.** Identify the problems you need to solve with your **design.**

....

....

....

....

....

....

Possible Materials

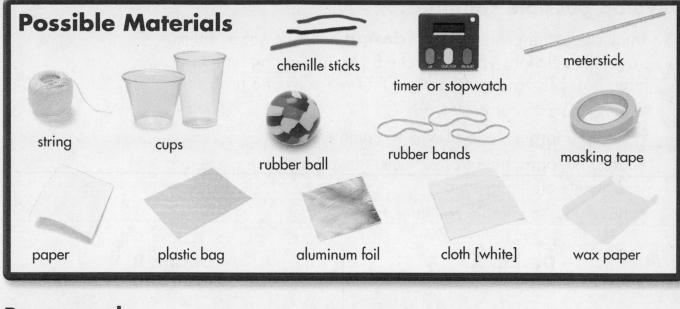

chenille sticks

timer or stopwatch

meterstick

string

cups

rubber ball

rubber bands

masking tape

paper

plastic bag

aluminum foil

cloth [white]

wax paper

Do research.

☐ **2.** Think about the problems you have identified.
Research **design** solutions others have used.
Brainstorm ideas with others.
List three solutions others have used.

Develop possible solutions.

☐ **3.** Think about the problems your **design** needs to solve. Think about the solutions you researched. Use this information to draw three possible parachute designs that will solve the problems.

When you test your prototype:

- set up a target circle 50 cm in diameter.
- drop the parachute from 2 meters away from the circle and 2 meters off the ground.
- have your teacher do all three trials.

Design A	Design B

Choose one solution.

☐ **4.** Choose one design to test. Tell which design you chose. Explain your choice.

....

....

....

....

....

Design and construct a prototype.

☐ **5.** Draw the **design** you will use to make a prototype. Label each part. Say what it is made of.

Show how your parachute design will carry the ball.

☐ **6.** List the materials you used in your prototype.

....

....

....

Test the Prototype

☐ **7.** Have your teacher test your **design** three times.

☐ **8. Record** the time it takes for your parachute to land.

☐ **9. Measure** the distance the payload landed from the center of the circle.

Prototype Testing Results		
Trial	**Time to Land** (sec)	**Distance from Center of Circle** (cm)
1		
2		
3		
Average		

Communicate Results

☐ **10.** What parts of your **design** worked in your prototype? Use the results of your trials and your **observations** to support your conclusions.

....

....

....

☐ **11.** What parts of your design could be improved? Explain.

....

....

....

....

Evaluate and Redesign

☐ **12.** Think about what did and did not work.
Use what you learned from testing to **redesign** your prototype.
Write or draw your design changes.

Master Investigator

Create a trading card for a new card game about scientific investigation. Your card will represent a scientific investigator. Describe the investigator's strengths and weaknesses. Include a question the investigator might ask to solve a problem. Compare cards to discover the best scientific investigator!

Make a Model

Use paper, glue, colored markers, and other supplies to build a model of something. You can build a rocket, a car, a bridge, or anything that interests you. Describe the parts of your model and how the parts work together.

• How does your model help explain how the real object works?

• How is your model not exactly the same as the real object?

Make a Poster

Make a poster that teaches about the different kinds of simple machines. Use magazine pictures that show simple machines, or draw your own pictures. Label each simple machine. Write how each simple machine helps people do work.

Science and Engineering Practices

1. Ask a question or define a problem.

2. Develop and use models.

3. Plan and carry out investigations.

4. Analyze and interpret data.

5. Use math and computational thinking.

6. Construct explanations or design solutions.

7. Engage in argument from evidence.

8. Obtain, evaluate, and communicate information.

Measurements

Metric and Customary Measurements

The metric system is the measurement system most commonly used in science. Metric units are sometimes called SI units. SI stands for International System. It is called that because these units are used around the world.

These prefixes are used in the metric system:

kilo- means *thousand*
1 kilometer = 1,000 meters

milli- means *one thousandth*
1,000 millimeters = 1 meter, or 1 millimeter = 0.001 meter

centi- means *one hundredth*
100 centimeters = 1 meter, or 1 centimeter = 0.01 meter

1 liter

1 cup

Volume
One liter is greater than 4 cups.

Temperature
Water freezes at 0°C, or 32°F.
Water boils at 100°C, or 212°F.

1 pound

1 kilogram

Mass
One kilogram is greater than 2 pounds.

1 meter

1 yard

Length and Distance
One meter is longer than 1 yard.

Glossary

The glossary uses letters and signs to show how words are pronounced. The mark ′ is placed after a syllable with a primary or heavy accent. The mark ′ is placed after a syllable with a secondary or lighter accent.

To hear these vocabulary words and definitions, you can log on to the digital path's Vocabulary Smart Cards.

Pronunciation Key

a in hat	ō in open	sh in she
ā in age	ȯ in all	th in thin
â in care	ô in order	ᴛʜ in then
ä in far	oi in oil	zh in measure
e in let	ou in out	ə = a in about
ē in equal	u in cup	ə = e in taken
ėr in term	ù in put	ə = i in pencil
i in it	ü in put	ə = o in lemon
ī in ice	ch in child	ə = u in circus
o in hot	ng in long	

A

absorb (ab sôrb′) to take in

absorber retener

adaptation (ad′ ap tā′ shən) a trait that helps a living thing survive in its environment

adaptación rasgo de los seres vivos que los ayuda a sobrevivir en su medio ambiente

arthropod (är′ thrə pod) an animal that has a hard covering outside its body

artrópodo animal que tiene el cuerpo envuelto por una cubierta dura

atmosphere (at′ mə sfir) the blanket of air that surrounds Earth

atmósfera capa de aire que rodea la Tierra

B

bar graph (bär graf) a graph that helps you compare data and see patterns

gráfica de barras gráfica que ayuda a comparar datos y ver patrones

C

carbon dioxide (kär′ bən dī ok′ sīd) a gas in air that is absorbed by most plants

dióxido de carbono gas en el aire que la mayoría de las plantas absorben

chart (chärt) a kind of list

tabla tipo de lista

climate (klī′ mit) the pattern of weather in a place over many years

clima patrón que sigue el tiempo atmosférico de un lugar a lo largo de muchos años

closed circuit (klōzd′ sér′ kit) a circuit with no gaps or breaks

circuito cerrado circuito que no tiene rupturas ni interrupciones

community (kə myü′ nə tē) all the populations that live in the same place

comunidad todas las poblaciones que conviven en el mismo lugar

consumer (kən sü′ mər) a living thing that eats other organisms

consumidor ser vivo que se alimenta de otros organismos

decomposer (dē′ kəm pō′ zər) a living thing that breaks down waste and dead plant and animal matter

descomponedor ser vivo que destruye residuos y materia de animales y vegetales muertos

design process (di zīn′ pros′ es) a step-by-step method used to solve a problem

proceso de diseño método que sigue pasos y que se usa para resolver un problema

ecosystem (ē′ kō sis′ təm) the living and nonliving things that interact in an environment

ecosistema todos los seres vivos y las cosas sin vida que interactúan en un área determinada

electrical energy (i lek′ trə kəl en′ ər jē) the movement of electric charges

energía eléctrica el movimiento de cargas eléctricas

energy (en′ ər jē) the ability to do work or to cause change

energía capacidad de hacer trabajo o causar cambios

extinct (ek stingkt′) no longer lives on Earth

extinto que ya no existe en la Tierra

F

flowering plant (flou′ ər ing plant) a plant with seeds that grows flowers

angiosperma planta con semillas que produce flores

food chain (füd chān) the transfer of energy from one living thing to another

cadena alimentaria transmisión de energía de un ser vivo a otro

force (fôrs) a push or a pull

fuerza empujón o jalón

fossil (fos′ əl) remains or mark of a living thing from long ago

fósil restos o marca de un ser vivo que existió hace mucho tiempo

friction (frik′ shən) a contact force that opposes the motion of an object

fricción fuerza de contacto que se opone al movimiento de un objeto

G

germinate (jėr′ mə nāt) to begin to grow

germinar empezar a crecer

gravity (grav′ ə tē) a noncontact force that pulls objects toward one another

gravedad fuerza sin contacto que hace que los objetos se atraigan entre sí

H

habitat (hab′ ə tat) the place where a living thing makes its home

hábitat el lugar donde un ser vivo establece su hogar

I

inclined plane (in klīnd′ plān) a slanting surface that connects a lower level to a higher level

plano inclinado superficie inclinada que conecta un nivel bajo con un nivel más alto

infer (in fėr′) to draw a conclusion

inferir sacar una conclusión

inherit (in her′ it) to receive from a parent

heredar recibir de un progenitor

inquiry (in kwī′ rē) the process of asking questions

indagación proceso de hacer preguntas

instinct (in′ stingkt) a behavior an animal is born able to do

instinto conducta que tiene un animal desde que nace

invertebrate (in vėr′ tə brit) an animal without a backbone

invertebrado animal que no tiene columna vertebral

investigate (in ves′ tə gāt) to look for answers

investigar buscar respuestas

kinetic energy (ki net′ ik en′ ər jē) energy of motion

energía cinética energía de movimiento

larva (lär′ və) second stage of the life cycle of some insects

larva segunda etapa del ciclo de vida de algunos insectos

lever (lev′ ər) a simple machine to lift and move things by using a stiff bar that rests on a support

palanca máquina simple que se usa para levantar y mover cosas mediante una barra rígida que tiene un punto de apoyo

life cycle (līf sī′ kəl) the stages through which a living thing passes during its life

ciclo de vida estados por los que pasa un ser vivo durante su vida

light energy (līt′ en′ ər jē) energy we can see

energía luminosa energía que podemos ver

magnetism (mag′ nə tiz′ əm) a noncontact force that pulls objects containing iron

magnetismo fuerza sin contacto que atrae objetos que contienen hierro

metamorphosis (met′ ə môr′ fə sis) a change in form during an animal's life cycle

metamorfosis cambio de la forma de un animal durante su ciclo de vida

model (mod′ əl) a copy of something

modelo copia de algo

motion (mō′ shən) a change in the position of an object

movimiento cambio en la posición de un objeto

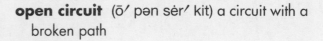

open circuit (ō′ pən sėr′ kit) a circuit with a broken path

circuito abierto circuito que tiene una ruptura en su ruta

oxygen (ok′ sə jən) a gas in the air that plants and animals need

oxígeno gas en el aire que las plantas y los animales necesitan para vivir

photosynthesis (fō′ tō sin′ thə sis) the process by which plants use air, water, and energy from sunlight to make food

fotosíntesis proceso por el cual las plantas usan el aire, el agua y la energía del sol para producir alimento

pitch (pich) how high or low a sound is

tono cuán agudo o grave es un sonido

pollinate (pol′ ə nāt) to carry pollen to

polinizar llevar polen de un lugar a otro

nutrient (nü′ trē ənt) any material needed by living things for energy, growth, and repair

nutriente cualquier sustancia que los seres vivos necesitan para obtener energía, crecer y reponerse

population (pop′ yə lā′ shən) all the living things of the same kind that live in the same place

población todos los seres vivos de la misma especie que viven en el mismo lugar

position (pə zish′ ən) the location of an object

posición ubicación de un objeto

potential energy (pə ten′ shəl en′ ər jē) stored energy

energía potencial energía almacenada

precipitation (pri sip′ ə tā′ shən) water that falls to Earth

precipitación agua que cae a la Tierra

procedure (prə sē′ jər) a plan for testing a hypothesis

procedimiento plan que se usa para poner a prueba una hipótesis

producer (prə dü′ sər) a living thing that makes, or produces, its own food

productor ser vivo que genera, o produce, su propio alimento

prototype (prō′ tə tīp) the first working product that uses a design

prototipo el primer producto que funciona y que sique un diseño

pulley (pùl′ ē) a machine that can change the direction or amount of force needed to move an object

polea máquina que puede cambiar la dirección o la cantidad de fuerza necesaria para mover un objeto

pupa (pyü′ pə) stage of an insect's life cycle between larva and adult

pupa etapa de la vida de un insecto entre larva y adulto

reflect (ri flekt′) to bounce off

reflejar hacer rebotar algo

refract (ri frakt′) to bend

refractar desviar o inclinar

reproduce (rē′ prə düs′) to make more of the same kind

reproducir hacer más de una misma cosa

research (ri sėrch′) to look for facts about something

hacer una investigación buscar datos sobre algo

scientist (sī′ ən tist) person who asks questions about the natural world

científico persona cuyo trabajo implica hacer preguntas sobre el mundo y la naturaleza

screw (skrü) an inclined plane wrapped around a center post

tornillo plano inclinado enrollado alrededor de un eje central

severe weather (sə vir′ weᴛн′ ər) dangerous conditions of the atmosphere

tiempo severo condiciones atmosféricas peligrosas

sound energy (sound en′ ər jē) energy we can hear

energía sonora energía que podemos oír

speed (spēd) the rate at which an object changes position

rapidez tasa a la cual un objeto cambia de posición

spore (spôr) a small cell that grows into a new plant

espora célula pequeña que se convierte en una planta nueva

technology (tek nol′ ə jē) use of science knowledge to invent tools and new ways of doing things

tecnología uso del conocimiento científico para inventar instrumentos y nuevas maneras de hacer las cosas

thermal energy (thėr′ məl en′ ər jē) the kinetic energy and potential energy of particles in matter

energía térmica energía cinética y energía potencial de las partículas que forman la materia

tool (tül) object used to do work

instrumento objeto que se usa para trabajar

trait (trāt) a feature passed on to a living thing from its parents

rasgo característica que pasa de padres a hijos entre los seres vivos

U

unit of measure (yü′ nit uv mezh′ ər) quantity you use to measure

unidad de medida cantidad que ser usa para medir

V

vertebrate (vėr′ tə brit) an animal with a backbone

vertebrado animal que tiene columna vertebral

volume (vol′ yəm) how loud or soft a sound is

volumen cuán fuerte o suave es un sonido

W

water cycle (wȯ′ tər sī′ kəl) the movement of water from Earth's surface into the air and back again

ciclo del agua movimiento de ida y vuelta que realiza el agua entre el aire y la superficie de la Tierra

wave (wāv) a disturbance that carries energy from one point to another point

onda perturbación que lleva energía de un punto a otro

weather (weᴛʜ′ ər) what the air is like outside

tiempo atmosférico las condiciones al aire libre

wedge (wej) two slanted sides that end in a sharp edge

cuña dos lados inclinados que terminan con un borde filoso

wheel and axle (wēl and ak′ səl) a round wheel attached to a post

eje y rueda figura circular que gira alrededor de una varilla

work (wėrk) the use of a force to move an object across a distance

trabajo uso de una fuerza para mover un objeto, por cierta distancia

Index

Gray wolves, 219
Great egrets, 207
Grocery cart, 17
Groundhogs, 218
Guitar, 75
Gulf of Mexico, 254

H

Habitat, 200
Hail, 271
Hair, 77, 163
Hair roots, 124
Hand lenses, 301, 323
Hand washing, 324
Hawks, 161
Hearing, 303
Heat
    boiling and, 41
    colors and, 69
    energy producing, 54
    light and, 68–69
    motion caused by, 82–83
    movement of, 66–67
    as transfer of energy, 48
Herbivores, 212
Hibernation, 172, 221
Honey bees, 168
Hot-air balloons, 62–63
Humans
    changes to the environment, 218
    inherited and acquired
       characteristics, 170–171
    learned behavior, 173
Humidity, 268
Hurricanes, 220, 274–275,
    302–303, 305–307
Hygrometer, 268
Hypotheses, 310
Hypothesize, 54, 55, 112, 127,
    310–311

I

Ice
    refraction in, 60
Identify, 54, 120, 149, 179, 180,
    192, 206, 212, 214, 219, 226,
    236, 237, 257, 300, 311, 316,
    352, 353, 357
Illustrate, 10, 18, 37, 73, 79, 142,
    163, 165, 186, 328, 355

Inches, 322
Inclined planes, 351–353, 365, 368
Indonesia, 134
Infer, 2, 19, 21, 35, 52, 68,
    69, 75, 76, 80, 81, 83, 116,
    122, 128, 136, 141, 149,
    151, 162, 178, 210, 212, 216,
    220, 223, 224, 258, 260, 269,
    274, 292, 302, 303, 305, 312,
    315, 325, 327, 328, 340, 356,
    361, 363
Inferences, 307
Inherit, 169–170, 172, 187, 188
Inherited behavior, 172
Inherited characteristics, 170
Inquiries. See At-Home Lab; Explore
    It!; Go Green; Investigate It!;
    Lightning Lab; STEM activities;
    Try It!
Inquiry, scientific, 299–301, 329
Inquiry Skills
    choose variables, 102
    classify, 154, 184, 185
    communicate, 22, 40, 52, 76,
       91, 102, 198, 266, 292, 314,
       317, 327, 340, 350
    design, 292, 340, 350
    draw conclusions, 14, 70, 248,
       327, 350
    infer, 2, 52, 76, 83, 116, 122,
       128, 141, 210, 216, 224, 258,
       292, 302, 327, 340, 356, 363
    interpret data, 22, 27, 176, 277
    investigate, 327, 363
    make and use models, 40, 160,
       198, 224, 270, 308, 362, 380
    measure, 26, 216, 228, 258,
       266, 267, 308, 320
    observe, 2, 22, 40, 52, 58, 70,
       76, 83, 102, 116, 122, 128,
       140, 154, 160, 176, 184, 198,
       210, 216, 228, 229, 248, 266,
       270, 276, 302, 308, 326, 327
    predict, 14, 39, 82, 83, 101,
       102, 153, 197, 248, 291,
       339, 363
    record data, 2, 14, 22, 26, 52,
       58, 70, 76, 82, 102, 154, 176,
       184, 210, 228, 258, 276, 308,
       314, 320, 326, 340, 356, 363
Insects, 60, 165, 328
    bees, 130, 168, 176
    butterflies, 128, 164, 172,
       178–179, 195
    grasshoppers, 214
Instinct, 169, 172, 187
Insulators, 80
Interaction, 206

Interactive Vocabulary
    Make a Word Frame!, 144, 188
    Make a Word Magnet!, 30, 86,
       280
    Make a Word Wheel!, 232,
       330, 366
International Space Station, 84, 151
Interpret, 318, 348
Interpret data, 22, 27, 176, 277,
    307, 311
Invertebrate, 161, 164–165, 187
Investigate, 299, 327, 329, 363
Investigate It!, 1, 26–27, 39,
    82–83, 101, 140–141, 153,
    184–185, 197, 228–229, 247,
    276–277, 291, 326–327, 339,
    362–363
Investigations, 309–313
Iris, 110, 111
Iron, 20
Ivy, 125

J

Justify, 35

K

Kalanchoe, 138
Kangaroos, 152–153
Kim, Heeyoung, 142
Kinetic energy, 37, 51, 53–55, 85, 88
Kite, 18
Kramer, Kane, 358–359

L

Label, 49, 77, 211
Lakes, 62–63, 282
Landforms, 263
Larva, 177–179, 187–190
Law of gravity, 23
Lawn mowers, 364
Learned behavior, 173
Leaves, 116–121
    classifying, 184–185
    of flowering plants, 110–112
    of mangrove trees, 122–123
    of nonflowering plants, 113

Credits

Staff Credits

The people who made up the *Interactive Science* team — representing composition services, core design digital and multimedia production services, digital product development, editorial, editorial services, manufacturing, and production — are listed below.

Geri Amani, Alisa Anderson, Jose Arrendondo, Amy Austin, David Bailis, Scott Baker, Lindsay Bellino, Jennifer Berry, Charlie Bink, Bridget Binstock, Holly Blessen, Robin Bobo, Craig Bottomley, Jim Brady, Laura Brancky, Chris Budzisz, Odette Calderon, Mary Chingwa, Caroline Chung, Kier Cline, Brandon Cole, Mitch Coulter, AnnMarie Coyne, Fran Curran, Dana Damiano, Michael Di Maria, Nancy Duffner, Susan Falcon, Amanda Ferguson, David Gall, Mark Geyer, Amy Goodwin, Gerardine Griffin, Chris Haggerty, Margaret Hall, Laura Hancko, Autumn Hickenlooper, Guy Huff, George Jacobson, Marian Jones, Abigail Jungreis, Kathi Kalina, Chris Kammer, Sheila Kanitsch, Alyse Kondrat, Mary Kramer, Thea Limpus, Dominique Mariano, Lori McGuire, Melinda Medina, Angelina Mendez, Claudi Mimo, John Moore, Kevin Mork, Chris Niemyjski, Phoebe Novak, Anthony Nuccio, Jeff Osier, Dorothy Preston, Charlene Rimsa, Rebecca Roberts, Camille Salerno, Manuel Sanchez, Carol Schmitz, Amanda Seldera, Jeannine Shelton El, Geri Shulman, Greg Sorenson, Samantha Sparkman, Mindy Spelius, Karen Stockwell, Dee Sunday, Dennis Tarwood, Jennie Teece, Lois Teesdale, Michaela Tudela, Karen Vuchichevich, Melissa Walker, Tom Wickland, James Yagelski, Tim Yetzina

Illustrations

vi-vii, 1, 33, 35, 36, 39, 89, 91–92 ©Aleksi Markku/Shutterstock; viii-x, xiv, 101, 147, 149–150, 153, 191, 193–194, 197, 235, 237–238, 244 ©Jens Stolt/Shutterstock; xi, 247, 281, 283–284 Leonello Calvetti/Getty Images; xii-xiii, 291, 333, 335–336, 339, 369, 371–372, 380 ©James Thew/Shutterstock; 103, 118–119, 134–135, 136–137, 143, 145, 147, 182, 218, 254, 261 Precision Graphics; xvii, 48–49, 85 Jeff Grunewald; 119 Sharon & Joel Harris; 124, 126, 131 Alan Barnard; 262–263, 279 Studio Liddell; 225, 233 Big Sesh Studios
All other illustrations Chandler Digital Art

Photographs

Photo locators denoted as follows: Top (T), Center (C), Bottom (B), Left (L), Right (R), Background (Bkgd)

COVER: Valerie Giles/Science Source

Front Matter

i (C) Valerie Giles/Science Source; ii (BR) Valerie Giles/Science Source; iv-v (Bkgd) Thinkstock; vi (TR) MarcelClemens/Shutterstock; vi (TR) ©Xavier Pironet/Shutterstock; vii (TR) ©Christophe Testi/Shutterstock; viii (TR) ©Jan Hopgood/Shutterstock; ix (TR) ©EcoPrint/Shutterstock; x (TR) ©Kjersti Joergensen/Shutterstock; xi (TR) ©Taylor S. Kennedy/Getty Images; xii (TR) ©Chris Johnson/Alamy Images; xiii (TR) David J. Green/Alamy Images; xiv (C) clabert/Fotolia; xv (CL) Getty Royalty Free, (TRT) Fotolia, (TRCL) ©Adisa/Shutterstock, (TRCR) ©Mytho/Shutterstock, (TRBR) ©aleks.k/Shutterstock, (TRBC) ©Daniel Aguilar/Reuters/Corbis; xvi (LTC) ©Foto011/Shutterstock, (LTR) ©Petr Jilek/Shutterstock, (L Bkgd) ©Pakhnyushcha/Shutterstock, (LC) Time & Life Pictures/Getty Images, (RTL) ©Wheatley/Shutterstock, (RTC) ©Caryn Becker/Alamy Royalty Free, (RBC) ©EcoPrint/Shutterstock; xvii (BR) Masterfile Royalty Free; xviii (TC) ©Elena Yakusheva/Shutterstock, (CR) ©Jan Hopgood/Shutterstock; xix (TR) ©Ilja Masik/Shutterstock; xxii-xxiii Pavel Losevsky/Fotolia

Chapter 1 Forces and Motion

xxiv–1 (Bkgd) ©Mark Lewis/Getty Images; 3 (Bkgd) ©Scott Hales/Shutterstock, (BL) ©Thomas M Perkins/Shutterstock; 8 (Bkgd) ©Brent Walker/Shutterstock, (CR) ©Photo Researchers/Alamy Royalty Free; 9 (CR) John Lawrence Photography/Alamy Images; 11 (Bkgd) iStock Photo/Getty Images; 12 (TL) Masterfile Royalty-Free; 13 (TR) ©Xavier Pironet/Shutterstock; 14–15 (T) ©Eric Isselée/Shutterstock; 15 (CR) Brand X Pictures/PunchStock Royalty Free; 17 (B) ©A. Ramey/PhotoEdit, Inc.; 18 (TL) Thinkstock, (B) Thinkstock/Getty Images; 19 (B) Purestock/Getty Images; 20 (L) Dvande/Fotolia; 22–23 (T) ©Joggie Botma/Shutterstock; 23 (Bkgd) ©Mike Irwin/Shutterstock; 24 (TR) ©Andraz Cerar/Shutterstock, (BL) Getty Royalty Free; 25 (T) ©Katrina Leigh/Shutterstock; 28 (Bkgd) Corbis Royalty Free, (TL) ©Bettmann/Corbis, (CL) Library of Congress, (BL) Library of Congress; 29 (TR) John Lawrence Photography/Alamy Images, (TL) Brand X Pictures/PunchStock Royalty Free, (CR) John Lawrence Photography/Alamy Images, (CL) ©A. Ramey/PhotoEdit, Inc., (BR) Masterfile Royalty-Free; 31 (TR) ©Joggie Botma/Shutterstock; 33 (CLT) ©Eric Isselée/Shutterstock, (CLB) ©Joggie Botma/Shutterstock, (B) ©Mark Lewis/Getty Images; 37 (Bkgd) ©Russell Kord/Alamy Images

Chapter 2 Energy and Its Forms

38–39 (Bkgd) ©UpperCut Images/SuperStock Royalty Free; 41 (Bkgd) DK Images; 46 (CLT) Rachel Powers, (CLB) Jennifer Taylor; 46–47 (T) Venusangel/Fotolia; 47 (CR) Design Pics/Dean Muz/Getty Royalty Free; 50 (B) Image100; 51 (TR) Image100; 52–53 (T) Sailorr/Fotolia; 53 (BR) Gary Ombler/Courtesy John Rigg, The Robot Hut/DK Images; 54 (B) ©Stone/Getty Images; 55 (TR) ©James Steidl/Shutterstock; 56 (C) ©@erics/Shutterstock; 57 (T) Tetra images RF/Getty Images; 58–59 (T) ©yuyangc/Shutterstock; 59 (Bkgd) ©Zhiltsov Alexandr/Shutterstock; 60 (TL) ©Sascha Burkard/Shutterstock, (BR) ©Tomislav Forgo/Shutterstock; 61 (Bkgd) Getty Royalty Free; 62–63 (T) ©Craig Tuttle/Corbis, (C) Getty Royalty Free, (B) Getty Royalty Free; 64 (B) ©Pierre Arsenault/Master File Corporation; 65 (TL, TC, TR) Getty Royalty Free; 66 (Bkgd) Ivan Smuk/Shutterstock; 66–67 (T) ©Joy Brown/Shutterstock; 67 (BR)

Dave King/DK Images; **68** (TR) Ruth Jenkinson/DK Images, (B) ©Johann Helgason/Shutterstock; **70–71** (T) Getty Royalty Free; **72** (BL) ©Datacraft – Hana/Alamy Royalty Free; **73** (TR) ©Christophe Testi/Shutterstock; **74** (TL) Fotolia, (BL) Getty Royalty Free; **75** (TR) ©Robert Ginn/PhotoEdit, Inc.; **76–77** (T) ©Natural Selection/Jupiter Royalty Free; **77** (BR) Roy McMahon/Getty Images; **84** (R) NASA; **85** (TR) Design Pics/Dean Muz/Getty Royalty Free, (TL) Image100, (CL) Image100, (BL) ©@erics/Shutterstock; **87** (TR) ©Zhiltsov Alexandr/Shutterstock, (TC) Getty Royalty Free, (TL) Fotolia, (CR) ©Sascha Burkard/Shutterstock, (CC) Dave King/DK Images, (BR) ©Tomislav Forgo/Shutterstock, (BC) ©Christophe Testi/Shutterstock; **89** (TLT) Venusangel/Fotolia, (TLB) Sailorr/Fotolia, (CLT) ©Sarah Curran Schaal/Shutterstock, (CLC) ©Joy Brown/Shutterstock, (CLB) Getty Royalty Free, (BL) ©Natural Selection/Jupiter Royalty Free, (B) ©UpperCut Images/SuperStock Royalty Free; **90** (TL) Image100, (C) Image100; **93** (Bkgd) ©Doug James/Shutterstock

Chapter 3 Plants
100–101 (Bkgd) ©Mark Newman/Photo Researchers, Inc.; **108** (BL) ©Andrzej Gibasiewicz/Shutterstock, (TL) ©yunus85/Shutterstock, (TR) ©Lana/Shutterstock; **109** (TC) Masterfile Royalty-Free, (BR) Getty Royalty Free; **110** (Bkgd) Thinkstock, (BR) fstockfoto/Shutterstock; **111** (TR) ©Liz Van Steenburgh/Shutterstock, (CR) Image Source/PunchStock Royalty Free, (BR) Image Source/PunchStock Royalty Free; **112** (L) ©prism68/Shutterstock, (BR) Marta Teron/Fotolia; **113** (CL) ©Matthias Spitz/Shutterstock, (CC) Tawin Mukdharakosa/Shutterstock, (CR) ©Peter Baker/Getty Royalty Free, (BRR) ©silver-john/Shutterstock, (BRL) Getty Royalty Free; **114–115** (Bkgd) Masterfile Royalty-Free; **116–117** (T) ©Elena Yakusheva/Shutterstock; **117** (CR) ©Jan Hopgood/Shutterstock; **120** (Bkgd) ©Anne Kitzman/Shutterstock; **121** (TL) ©Steve Brigman/Shutterstock; **122–123** (T) ©Shannon Matteson/Shutterstock; **123** (CR) Silver Burdett Ginn; **124** (TR) Getty Royalty Free, (B) Stockdisc/PunchStock Royalty Free; **125** (T) ©Gary Paul Lewis/Shutterstock; **126** (B) ©Petros Tsonis/Shutterstock; **127** (TR) DLeonis/Fotolia; **128–129** (T) Getty Royalty Free; **129** (BL) Brian Jackson/Fotolia; **130** (CL) Getty Royalty Free, (B) ©Varina and Jay Patel/Shutterstock; **131** (TL) ©Richard Griffin/Shutterstock; **132** (CL) Alamy Images, (BC) Fotolia, (CR) Peter Chadwick/DK Images; **133** (TR) ©Richard Griffin/Shutterstock; **134** (R) ©Paul Marcus/Shutterstock; **135** (CR) ©Kosam/Shutterstock, (BR) ©Marcel Mooij/Shutterstock; **138** (BR) ©Jupiterimages/Thinkstock; **139** (CR) ©Eye-Stock/Alamy Royalty Free; **142** (TR) Cynthia Gehrie, (R) Royal Catchfly, (Silene regia), Watercolor on paper, 16–3/4" x 11"/Published with permission by the artist Heeyoung Kim; **143** (TR) Image Source/PunchStock Royalty Free, (CR) Tawin Mukdharakosa/Shutterstock, (BL) Silver Burdett Ginn; **145** (TR) Getty Royalty Free, (CR, L) ©Varina and Jay Patel/Shutterstock, (CR, TR) Getty Royalty Free, (BR) ©Richard Griffin/Shutterstock; **147** (TLT) ©Lana/Shutterstock, (TLB) ©Elena Yakusheva/Shutterstock, (CL) ©Shannon Matteson/Shutterstock, (CLB) Getty Royalty Free, (B) ©Mark Newman/Photo Researchers, Inc.; **151** (Bkgd) JSC/NASA, (TR) NASA

Chapter 4 Living Things
152–153 (Bkgd) clabert/Fotolia; **155** (B) Getty Royalty Free; **160** (TC, TR) Getty Royalty Free; **161** (TL, TC) Getty Royalty Free, (R) ©Purestock/James Urbach/SuperStock Royalty Free; **162** (Bkgd) Masterfile Royalty-Free; **163** (TR) Getty Royalty Free, (BRT) ©Christian Musat/Shutterstock, (BRB) ©Henk Bentlage/Shutterstock; **164** (BC, BR) Getty Royalty Free; **164–165** (Bkgd) Getty Royalty Free; **165** (TR) ©Sarah Curran Schaal/Shutterstock, (TRB) ©mashe/Shutterstock, (BR) Getty Royalty Free; **166** (TR) Jane Burton/DK Images, (B) Getty Royalty Free; **167** (T) Masa Ushioda/Photoshot; **168** (TC) ©Foto011/Shutterstock, (TR) ©Petr Jilek/Shutterstock, (Bkgd) ©Pakhnyushcha/Shutterstock, (C) Time & Life Pictures/Getty Images; **169** (TL) ©Wheatley/Shutterstock, (TC) ©Caryn Becker/Alamy Royalty Free, (BC) ©EcoPrint/Shutterstock; **170** (Bkgd) Alistair Duncan/DK Images, (BL) ©Clint Farlinger/Alamy Images; **171** (Bkgd) ©Kevin Britland/Alamy Royalty Free, (TR) Masterfile Royalty-Free; **172** (Bkgd) ©Alexsander Isachenko/Shutterstock, (TR) ©Boris Bort/Shutterstock; **173** (CR) ©James Balog/Getty Images, (BL) ©Blend Images/SuperStock Royalty Free; **174** (TR) ©Eric Isselée/Shutterstock, (BL) American Society of Mammalogists, (BR) ©Rick & Nora Bowers/Alamy Images; **175** (TR) ©David Tipling/Alamy Royalty Free; **176** (TC) ©Ron Niebrugge/Alamy Images, (TR) Frank Greenaway/Courtesy of The National Birds of Prey Centre, Cloucestershire/DK Images; **177** (TL) Comstock Images/Thinkstock, (CR) ©Suzann Julien/iStock International, Inc.; **178** (TR) ©Rick & Nora Bowers/Alamy Images; **178–179** (Bkgd) ©Terry Reimink/Shutterstock; **179** (TL, CR) ©Jacob Hamblin/Shutterstock; **180** (TR) ©Splash/Shutterstock, (B) ©Malcolm Schuyl/Alamy Royalty Free; **181** (C) ©Wolfgang Staib/Shutterstock, (BL) Geoff Brightling/DK Images; **182** (BL) ©Corbis/SuperStock Royalty Free, (BR) ©Papilio/Alamy Images, (B) Dan Bannister/DK Images; **184** (BR) ©Krasowit/Shutterstock, (BL) ©Photofrenetic/Alamy Images, (CR) ©Royalty-Free/Corbis/Jupiter Images, (CL, BC) Getty Royalty Free; **186** (Bkgd, TR) ©Mark Conlin/Alamy Images; **187** (TR) ©Purestock/James Urbach/SuperStock Royalty Free, (TC) Getty Royalty Free, (CR) Masterfile Royalty-Free, (CC) ©Clint Farlinger/Alamy Images, (BR) Getty Royalty Free, (BC) ©Boris Bort/Shutterstock; **189** (TR, CR) ©Jacob Hamblin/Shutterstock, (BRT) Geoff Brightling/DK Images, (BRB) ©Malcolm Schuyl/Alamy Royalty Free; **191** (TL) Getty Royalty Free, (TLB) ©Petr Jilek/Shutterstock, (CL) ©Ron Niebrugge/Alamy Images, (B) clabert/Fotolia; **195** (Bkgd) ©Eyal Nahamias/Alamy Royalty Free

Chapter 5 Ecosystems
196–197 (Bkgd) ©tbkmedia.de/Alamy Royalty Free; **199** (B) ©Andrea Pistolesi/Getty Royalty Free; **204** (Bkgd) Warren Price/Shutterstock, (CRT, CRB) ©Windell Curole and Joe Suhayda; **204–205** (T) ©bierchen/Shutterstock; **205** (BR) ©Randy Green/Getty Royalty Free; **206** (TR) ©Kjersti Joergensen/Shutterstock; **206–207** (Bkgd) ©Nancy Carter/North Wind Picture Archives; **207** (BR) ©Lisa Dearing/Alamy Royalty Free; **208** (TL) ©Jamie Robinson/Shutterstock, (B) ©Georgette Douwma/Getty Royalty Free; **210–211** (T) ©imagebroker/Alamy Royalty Free; **211** (CR) ©sfStop/Alamy Royalty Free, (BL) ©Wouter Tolenaars/Shutterstock, (BC) ©Lynne Carpenter/Shutterstock; **212** (TR) ©Alexey Stiop/Shutterstock, (BR) ©TTphoto/Shutterstock; **212–213** (T) Serg64/Shutterstock, (B) ©TTphoto/Shutterstock; **213** (TR) Michael Lane/123RF, (BR) ©Eric Gevaert/Shutterstock; **214** (CRT) ©Clinton Moffat/Shutterstock, (CLT) ©Rusty Dodson/Shutterstock, (CTL) Michael Lane/123RF, (CTR) ©Roberta Olenick/All Canada Photos/

PhotoLibrary/Getty Images, (CBL) Fotolia, (CRB) ©Denis Pepin/ Shutterstock, (C) ©graph/Shutterstock, (BR) ©Eric Gevaert/ Shutterstock, (CLB) ©Viorel Sima/Shutterstock, (B) ©Joel Sartore/ National Geographic/Getty Royalty Free; **216–217** (T) ©Design Pics Inc./Alamy Royalty Free; **217** (BR) ©Juniors Bildarchiv/ Alamy Royalty Free; **218** (CR) ©Steve McWilliam/Shutterstock; **219** (TR) ©Cynthia Kidwell/Shutterstock; **220** (B) ©Jim Parkin/ Shutterstock; **221** (TR, TC) ©Smit/Shutterstock, (B) ©Sergey Korotkov/Alamy Royalty Free; **222** (B) ©Gary Braasch/ Corbis; **223** (TL) ©Philip James Corwin/Corbis, (C)©Phil Schermeister/National Geographic Stock; **224–225** (T) Alamy Royalty Free; **225** (CR) Colin Keates/Courtesy of the Natural History Museum London/DK Images; **226** (CL) Joy Spurr/ Photoshot; **226–227** (T) ©Andy Crawford/Courtesy of the Senckenberg Nature Museum, Frankfurt/DK Images; **227** (TC) ©mlorenzphotography/Getty Images; **230** (T) ©Joe Mamer Photography/Alamy Images, (TR) ©William Leaman/Alamy Royalty Free, (C) ©Deon Reynolds/PhotoLibrary/Getty Images, (CC) Alamy Images, (B) ©Craig Stocks Arts/Shutterstock, (BR) ©Danita Delimont/Getty Images; **231** (TR) ©Nancy Carter/ North Wind Picture Archives, (TC, BR) ©Georgette Douwma/ Getty Royalty Free, (CR) ©Jamie Robinson/Shutterstock, (CC) ©Lynne Carpenter/Shutterstock, (BC) ©sfStop/Alamy Royalty Free; **233** (TR) ©Wouter Tolenaars/Shutterstock, (TC) Alamy Royalty Free, (CR) Michael Lane/123RF, (BR) ©Sergey Korotkov/ Alamy Royalty Free; **235** (TL) ©bierchen/Shutterstock, (TLB) ©imagebroker/Alamy Royalty Free, (CLT) ©Design Pics Inc./ Alamy Royalty Free, (CLB) Alamy Royalty Free, (B) ©tbkmedia. de/Alamy Royalty Free; **239** (L) Darren Green/Fotolia, (CL) Masterfile Royalty-Free; **244** (TL) Getty Royalty Free; **245** (B) ©Eric Isselée/Shutterstock

Chapter 6 Weather Patterns

246–247 (Bkgd) ©Anton Foltin/Shutterstock; **249** (Bkgd) ©Zastol'skiy Victor Leonidovich/Shutterstock; **254** (R) ©Taylor S. Kennedy/Getty Images; **254–255** (T) ©Brand X Pictures/Jupiter Images; **255** (CR) The Earth Observatory/NASA; **256–257** (Bkgd) Fotolia; **257** (TC) ©Mytho/Shutterstock, (TR) ©Allen Stoner/Shutterstock; **258** (T) ©Armin Rose/Shutterstock; **259** (T) ©Comstock Images/Getty Images, (BR) ©aleks.k/Shutterstock; **260–261** (Bkgd) Henryk Sadura/Fotolia; **264** (TLT) ©Hisham Ibrahim/Alamy Images, (TLB) Getty Images; **266–267** (TL) ©Hill Creek Pictures/Getty Images, (TC) ©John Lund/Drew Kelly/ PhotoLibrary Group, Inc., (TR) ©MilousSK/Shutterstock; **267** (CR) ©Elena Elisseeva/Shutterstock; **268** (Bkgd) ©Serg64/ Shutterstock, (BC) ©Emil Pozar/Alamy Images, (BL) ©Tedd Foxx/Alamy Images, (BR) DK Images; **269** (C) Artur Synenko/ Shutterstock; **270–271** (T) Getty Royalty Free; **271** (CR) ©Juan Ferreras/epa/Corbis; **272–273** (Bkgd) ©Steve Bloom/Alamy Images; **274–275** (Bkgd) ©Daniel Aguilar/Reuters/Corbis; **278** (Bkgd) ©Royalty-Free/Corbis, (TL) ©Noel Hendrickson/ Masterfile Corporation, (CL) ©Ron Stroud/Masterfile Corporation; **279** (TR) Fotolia, (CL) ©adisa/Shutterstock, (CR) ©Mytho/Shutterstock, (BR) ©aleks.k/Shutterstock, (BC) ©Daniel Aguilar/Reuters/Corbis; **281** (TL) Fotolia, (TLB) ©Comstock Images/Getty Images, (CLT) ©MilousSK/Shutterstock, (CLB) Getty Royalty Free, (B) ©Anton Foltin/Shutterstock; **283** (CL) DK Images, (CC) Artur Synenko/Shutterstock; **285** (CL) ©Image Source, ©Tara Carlin/Alamy Images; **289** (TR) Fotolia, (B) ©Ted Foxx/Alamy Royalty Free

Science, Engineering, and Technology Skills Handbook

Part 1 The Nature of Science

290–291 (Bkgd) ©Kim Karpeles/Alamy Images; **298** (R) Florida Division of Forestry; **298–299** (T) ©gary corbett/ Alamy Images; **299** (CR) ©Doug Steley A/Alamy Images; **301** (TR) ©Will & Deni McIntyre/Photo Researchers, Inc.; **302–303** (T) ©Dennis Hallinan/Alamy Images; **303** (B) ©dmac/Alamy Images; **304–305** (Bkgd) ©forestpath/ Shutterstock; **305** (TR) ©matthiasengelien/Alamy Royalty Free; **307** (TR) ©Jeff Greenberg/Alamy Images; **308–309** (T) ©Science Source/Photo Researchers, Inc.; **309** (BR) ©Aaron Haupt/Photo Researchers, Inc.; **312** (TL) ©Alfred Pasieka/Photo Researchers, Inc.; **314** (T) ©Images & Stories/ Alamy Images; **315** (T) ©Chris Johnson/Alamy Images, (B) ©Images & Stories/Alamy Royalty Free; **318** (T) ©Ariel Skelley/Blend/Jupiter Royalty Free; **320** (T) ©Rob Walls/ Alamy Images; **321** (T) ©Jubal Harshaw/Shutterstock, (BR) Jupiter Royalty Free; **324** (B) ©Andy Crawford/DK Images; **325** (TR) ©imagebroker/Alamy Images; **328** (Bkgd) Tristan Denyer; **329** (TR) ©Will & Deni McIntyre/Photo Researchers, Inc., (TC) ©forestpath/Shutterstock, (CR) ©Doug Steley A/ Alamy Images; **331** (BR) Jupiter Royalty Free; **333** (TL) ©gary corbett/Alamy Images, (TLB) ©Dennis Hallinan/Alamy Images, (CL) ©Science Source/Photo Researchers, Inc., (CLB) ©Images & Stories/Alamy Images, (BL) ©Rob Walls/Alamy Images, (B) ©Kim Karpeles/Alamy Images; **337** (L) Paul Nicklen/National Geographic Image Collection/Alamy Images

Part 2 Technology and the Design Process

338–339 (Bkgd) ©Digital Art/Corbis; **341** (Bkgd) ©Martin D. Vonka/Shutterstock; **346** (CL) U.S. Patent and Trademark Office; **346–347** (T) ©Idealink Photography/Alamy Royalty Free; **347** (CR) Getty Royalty Free; **348** (CL) Thinkstock, (BL) ©Monkey Business Images/Shutterstock; **349** (TR) ©Andrey Burmakin/Shutterstock; **350–351** (T) ©Aflo Foto Agency/Alamy Royalty Free; **351** (CR) ©Photo and Co/ Getty Images; **352** (CL) Thinkstock, (BL) DK Images, (BR) ©Michelle D. Bridwell/PhotoEdit, Inc.; **353** (CR) Wuttichok Painichiwarapun/Shutterstock, (BR) ©Tetra Images/SuperStock Royalty Free, (BL) ©Bonnie Kamin/PhotoEdit, Inc.; **354** (C) Corbis Royalty Free; **354–355** (T) Philip Gatward/ DK Images; **356** (T) ©Bettmann/Corbis; **357** (T) ©axle71/ Shutterstock; **358** (T) ©lightpoet/Shutterstock; **359** (TR) ©Patrick Breig/Shutterstock, (BR) ©Mny-Jhee/Shutterstock; **360** (TL) David J. Green/Alamy Images; **361** (TR) ©D. Hurst/ Alamy Images, (CR) ©Zakharoff/Shutterstock; **364** (Bkgd) ©Jaak Nilson/Alamy Images; **365** (TR) Getty Royalty Free, (TC) DK Images, (CR) ©Photo and Co/Getty Images, (CC) ©Michelle D. Bridwell/PhotoEdit, Inc., (BR) Thinkstock, (BC) ©Bonnie Kamin/PhotoEdit, Inc.; **367** (TR) ©Tetra Images/ SuperStock Royalty Free, (TC) ©lightpoet/Shutterstock, (CR) WuttichokPainichiwarapun/Shutterstock, (CC) ©Patrick Breig/ Shutterstock; **369** (TL) ©Idealink Photography/Alamy Royalty Free, (TLB) ©Aflo Foto Agency/Alamy Royalty Free, (CL) ©Bettmann/Corbis, (B) ©Digital Art/Corbis; **373** (Bkgd) NASA; **374** ©Ilja Masik/Shutterstock; **379** (B) ©Ilja Masik/ Shutterstock; **380** (TL) Corbis/PhotoLibrary Royalty Free